W9-ACJ-105

Praise for

Nonsense

"An extremely useful primer for anyone who wants to better understand the complicated ways ambiguity affects human decision-making."

—*New York*

"Holmes is a fine writer and a clear thinker who leads us through the uses of confusion in art, business, medicine, engineering, police work, and family life. . . . If we want people to be prepared for the work of life and of living together, we should encourage lessons in the art of skepticism."

—*Washington Post*

"Uncomfortable with ambiguity? Maybe you shouldn't be. In this energetic, tale-filled, fascinating tour of a broad horizon, Jamie Holmes shows that people often prosper when and because they are uncertain. A persuasive argument, but one thing *is* clear: You'll learn a lot from this book."

—Cass R. Sunstein, professor, Harvard University, and coauthor of *Nudge*

"By clearly staking out his thesis and exploring the topic with a dash of mischief, Holmes convincingly demonstrates that stressful situations can cause us to cling more steadfastly to our beliefs and discard unwelcome information, but he also offers a primer on how to combat these natural tendencies. While life is full of nonsense, managing our response to uncertainty makes all the sense in the world."

—*Booklist*

"Jamie Holmes has written a refreshing, lively book sparkling with insights and entertaining stories that illustrate how the mind deals with ambiguity. And he makes the case well that how we manage ambiguity both as individuals and as a species is critical to our future success."

—Peter Bergen, author of *Manhunt: The Ten-Year Search for Bin Laden from 9/11 to Abbottabad*

"Holmes . . . debuts with a provocative analysis of the roots of uncertainty. . . . The author's bright anecdotes and wide-ranging research stories are certain to please many readers."

—*Kirkus Reviews*

"This isn't really about 'nonsense,' as in silliness, but about ambiguity—when it's helpful, when it's not; and how people react to it for good or ill. . . . The many fans of the work of Malcolm Gladwell . . . will enjoy this readable and thought-provoking work."

—*Library Journal* (starred)

"How do we make sense of the nonsensical? Extract meaning from endless ambiguity? In *Nonsense*, Jamie Holmes takes us on an engrossing journey into the mind's ability to process the murky world around us. From women's hemlines to Nazi spies, Henri Matisse to Anton Chekhov, Holmes is an entertaining guide into the vagaries of our comprehension of reality—and the power we can derive from nonsense, if only we give it a chance."

—Maria Konnikova, author of
Mastermind: How to Think Like Sherlock Holmes

"If you're hardwired to know and want to get more comfortable not knowing, this book will guide you down that long, dark hall."

—*Charlotte Observer*

"A book of astonishing stories and deep insights into how people deal with ambiguity, a subject that has troubled human beings forever, and never mattered more than it does now."

—Peter Beinart, associate professor, CUNY,
columnist for *The Atlantic* and *Haaretz*

Nonsense

Nonsense

THE POWER OF NOT KNOWING

Jamie Holmes

B\D\W\Y
BROADWAY BOOKS
NEW YORK

Copyright © 2015 by Jamie Holmes

All rights reserved.
Published in the United States by Broadway Books, an imprint
of the Crown Publishing Group, a division of Penguin Random House LLC,
New York.
crownpublishing.com

Broadway Books and its logo, B \ D \ W \ Y, are trademarks
of Penguin Random House LLC.

Originally published in hardcover in the United States by Crown,
an imprint of the Crown Publishing Group,
a division of Penguin Random House LLC, New York, in 2015.

Library of Congress Cataloging-in-Publication Data
Holmes, Jamie.
   Nonsense : the power of not knowing / Jamie Holmes. -- First Edition.
     pages cm
   1. Uncertainty. 2. Decision making. 3. Creative ability. I. Title.
   BF463.U5H55 2015
   153.4--dc23
   2015007205

ISBN 978-0-385-34839-3
eBook ISBN 978-0-385-34838-6

PRINTED IN THE UNITED STATES OF AMERICA

Book design by Anna Thompson
Cover design by Christopher Brand
Cover illustration by Christopher Brand

10 9 8 7 6 5 4

First Paperback Edition

To my loving parents,
Nancy Maull and Stephen Holmes

I don't trust ambiguity.

—JOHN WAYNE

Contents

IN 1996, LONDON'S City and Islington College organized a crash course in French for novices and below-average students. Paula, an earnest teenager wearing wire-rim glasses, had never spoken a word of the language before. Darminder, goateed and earringed, was not only new to French, but had also failed his Spanish General Certificate of Secondary Education (GCSE). Abdul had failed his German GCSE. Satvinder and Maria had each flunked their French GCSEs, and Emily's French teacher was so unimpressed that she advised her to give up on the language entirely. Instead of abandoning all hope, however, the students had signed up for a unique opportunity. For five full days, they'd submit to the eccentric methodology of a linguist named Michel Thomas.

Gray-haired and wearing a blue blazer, Thomas radiated poise and grace. "I'm very pleased to meet you," he told his new students, "and I'm looking forward to teaching you today, but under better physical conditions, because I don't think that where you're sitting is very comfortable. I would like you to feel comfortable, so we're going to rearrange everything." In a truck outside, Thomas had stashed some unexpected replacements for the standard classroom furniture: armchairs, pillows, coffee tables, plants, a rug, a fan, and even wicker folding screens. With a little effort, the students completely transformed the room. Plush high-backed armchairs formed a half oval, the blue curtains had been drawn, the lights dimmed, and the wicker screens enclosed the armchairs and lent the space an even cozier and more intimate feel.

There would be no desks, blackboards, paper, pens, or pencils. Thomas didn't want the students to read or write anything. He didn't want them to try to remember anything they studied either, or even review it at the end of the day. If, during class, they couldn't remember something, he advised, it wasn't *their* problem. It was his. Emily looked incredulous. Darminder and Abdul couldn't contain their impish smiles. But none of the students could hide their genuine curiosity about the old man in front of them. Was he serious? Never *try* to remember anything taught in class?

"I want you to relax."

This scene, Thomas's methods, and the results of those five days appeared in a BBC documentary titled *The Language Master*. Margaret Thompson, head of the French department at the school, was tasked with evaluating Thomas's results. At the end of the week, she watched as the students—many of whom had never uttered a word of French before—translated full sentences using advanced grammatical forms. Emily managed to interpret a phrase that would normally take years to tackle: "I would like to know if you want to go see it with me tonight." Paula praised Thomas's strong emphasis on calm and patience. The students felt, they said, as though they'd learned five years' worth of French in only five days. Rather stunned by the outcome, Thompson bashfully deferred to their self-appraisal.

Michel Thomas knew how intimidating it can be to explore a

new language. Students face new pronunciations for familiar letters, words with novel meanings, missing parts of speech, and odd grammatical structures. That's why the City and Islington students, despite the relaxed atmosphere, still exhibited the signs of confusion: nervous laughter, embarrassed smiles, muttered apologies, stutters, hesitations, and perplexed glances. Learning a foreign language requires you to journey into unfamiliar terrain. Thomas referred to a new language as the "most alien thing" one can learn. To fend off these "alien" intrusions, the mind instinctively erects barricades, and the teacher's first and often most difficult challenge is to help students pull these walls down. Thomas was able to transform the atmosphere in that City and Islington classroom from one of stressful apprehension to one of calm curiosity. He somehow instilled a greater open-mindedness in the students. Pupils who had habitually dismissed what they didn't yet grasp suddenly became more likely to venture out into the unknown.

At the time of the BBC documentary, which aired in 1997, Thomas was already legendary. He'd learned eleven languages, opened tutoring centers in Los Angeles and New York, and built something of a cult following thanks to a client list that included Grace Kelly, Bob Dylan, Alfred Hitchcock, Coca-Cola, Procter & Gamble, and American Express. Nigel Levy, who studied with Thomas before producing the BBC piece, characterized the lessons as "astonishing." Emma Thompson described her time with him as "the most extraordinary learning experience of my life." Israel's former ambassador to the United Nations called him "a miracle worker." And Herbert Morris, a former dean of humanities at UCLA, confided that he'd learned a year's worth of Spanish in just a few days with Thomas and remembered it nine months later.

"The most important thing," Thomas said, was to "eliminate all kinds of tension and anxiety" that are associated with learning.

His attention to mood was peculiar, even downright radical. He'd often begin teaching French, for example, by telling his students that French and English share thousands of words. It's only that they sound a little different. "English is French, badly pronounced," he once joked. Words ending in *-ible*, like *possible*, and *-able*, like *table*, all originate from French words, he'd explain. Recasting the unknown as familiar, Thomas provided students, from the outset, with sturdy building blocks. His pupils grafted new knowledge onto existing knowledge, bit by bit, expressing their own thoughts and never reiterating rote phrases. Thomas taught for autonomy and rarely corrected his students directly.

By 2004, Thomas's French, German, Italian, and Spanish instructional CDs and tapes—recordings of Thomas teaching each subject to two students—were the top-selling language courses in the United Kingdom. But Michel Thomas wasn't merely a linguist. He was also a war hero. That same year, he was honored at the World War II Memorial in Washington, DC, where he received the Silver Star. He died in 2005 in New York City, as an American citizen, but he was born in the industrial city of Łódź, Poland, as Moniek Kroskof. He'd survived concentration camps, led troops, and worked as a spy and interrogator for the Allies, netting more than two thousand Nazi war criminals after the war. "Michel Thomas" was his fifth false identity and nom de guerre.

Thomas's firsthand experience with totalitarian propaganda and his postwar undercover career are no mere biographical curiosities. His insights into the way our minds snap shut or unlock in the face of ambiguity—the central concern of this book—grew from his experiences in Germany. He had witnessed up close how Nazism had fostered a dismissive, even disdainful approach to uncertainty and moral complexity among its most fervent adherents. And he then spent decades developing methods to nurture a diametrically opposed attitude among language learners. Fifty years before the BBC documentary, in fact, Thomas tested his early ideas in an episode that eerily inverts his pedagogical demonstration at City and Islington.

———

IN 1946, RUDOLF Schelkmann—formerly a major in the intelligence service of Hitler's SS—was hiding in Ulm, Germany, coordinating a loose network of loyalists hell-bent on reestablishing Nazi rule. That November, Schelkmann and three other former SS officers had been baited into meeting the purported commander of a more powerful and centralized underground neo-Nazi resistance. In reality, they were about to meet Moniek Kroskof, aka Michel Thomas, a Polish-born Jew and undercover agent of the US Army's Counter Intelligence Corps (CIC).

Tasked with bringing war criminals to justice, Thomas was on a mission to identify and eventually dismantle Schelkmann's network. Another CIC agent who went by the name of Hans Meyer had been carefully building a rapport with members of the network, but Schelkmann remained reticent. The former SS man had agreed to share contacts and operational details, but only after meeting face-to-face with Meyer's commander. Thomas had to keep Schelkmann and his men from smelling a rat. Toward that end, he had meticulously arranged for the SS conspirators to be run through a tortuous routine in the hours leading up to the big meeting.

Earlier that night, the SS men had been waiting, on Meyer's orders, in a "safe house" southwest of Ulm. Without warning, motorbikes arrived to pick them up. Thomas had deliberately waited for stormy weather; as the conspirators sat on the backs of the bikes, sharp winds pressed at the men's rain-soaked clothes. Dropped off on a deserted road, the conspirators were blindfolded and hustled into two cars. In the darkness, they heard passwords exchanged as they navigated a series of staged security checks. They were pulled from the cars, marched blindly down a muddy path, and led through deep, icy puddles. They were kept waiting in an unheated corridor and were forbidden to speak. Still blindfolded, they listened to terse commands, scurrying footsteps, and doors opening and closing hurriedly. By the time Schelkmann and his men were finally led into a lodge hall and were allowed to see, it was past midnight.

Thomas—or Frundsberg to the SS men—greeted the conspirators from behind a large desk. Wearing civilian clothes except for a brown, military-style shirt, he'd been described to the Nazi loyalists as a former senior officer of the RSHA, an intelligence group once overseen by Himmler. Frundsberg's hunting lodge, as the faux headquarters of the underground "Grossorganisation" resistance, was artfully embellished with portraits of Hitler and other Nazi bigwigs and decorated with grenades, machine guns, pistols, flame throwers, and sabotage kits. Stacks of cash sat in an open safe.

Thomas nodded curtly, *sit*, and the men sat. He studied a dossier of unknown contents in silence. Then he made his position clear to Schelkmann: he would not tolerate any splinter resistance groups. Military actions taken outside his command were acts of treason, plain and simple. With seemingly offhand gestures, Thomas belittled Schelkmann and his small group, taking frequent phone calls to emphasize his indifference to them. Subordinates came and went with apparently urgent communiqués. Flustered, the Nazi major now offered some of the details that Thomas was after: his background, the backgrounds of the other SS men in the room, the name of his network, its charter, methods, and structure, and how its members were recruited.

The CIC's operation that night wasn't flawless. Thomas's elaborate fiction required roughly thirty people acting in concert, each

with assigned scripts. Small mistakes and inconsistencies in the theatrical performance were inevitable. Counterintelligence operations
turn on such minutiae—on whether the strange hesitation, bizarre
response, or involuntary twitch is interpreted as sinister or benign.
That's why a certain Soviet spy, as the anthropologist Margaret
Mead once noted, smoked a pipe. It immobilized his facial expres-
sions. Buttons whose holes were sewn in a crisscross rather than a
parallel pattern could reveal an agent's nationality and destroy an
otherwise perfect operation. In Egypt, a foreign agent was once discovered because of his giveaway stance at a public urinal. No detail
is insignificant to the intelligence operative, as Thomas knew, and
Schelkmann's background in intelligence was formidable.

Schelkmann had two chances to unmask that night's hoax. His
first came when he asked to be appointed Thomas's head of intelligence. "I had not anticipated this," Thomas later told his biogra-
pher, Christopher Robbins. "I could hardly grant the man's request
without bringing him into the organization, which was obviously
impossible. I pointed out the weakness in his operation, which in
reality I was forced to admire." Thomas not only had to feign the
workings of a fake espionage conspiracy, but also had to disparage a
well-managed spy network on cue. Schelkmann didn't catch on and
didn't protest. The second make-or-break moment of the night—the
most dangerous one, according to Thomas—was when Schelkmann
unexpectedly asked for orders.

"Und was befehlen Sie uns jetzt zu tun?"

And what would you command us to do now? Thomas feared, as Robbins recounted it, that "his mask had momentarily slipped and that
he had stepped out of character." Yet again, the SS men didn't notice.
Thomas recovered, ordering the Germans to hold off on any pend-
ing operations and to prepare for an inspection. His performance
was vulnerable twice. But Schelkmann had missed it both times.

Here was the payoff of the gauntlet of blindfolds, switched vehicles, muddy marching, rain-soaked clothing, and humiliating treatment that the conspirators had been forced to endure: clues ignored, tells overlooked. The success of that night's scheme didn't depend on its perfect execution. On the contrary, Thomas knew there would inevitably be slip-ups that might reveal the charade and force him to arrest the Nazis immediately. His talent was to manipulate their mood and undermine their sense of control so that they would be less likely to notice such momentary stumbles.

Some months later, when Thomas left his work with the CIC in Germany for America, a new agent took over the task of roping in the diehard Nazi underground. Posing as Frundsberg's deputy, this replacement arranged a meeting with Schelkmann and his men at a local beer hall. Wives and girlfriends were allowed. This time, when a tense moment came and the undercover agent seemed flustered, the German conspirators sensed that something was off. They questioned him aggressively. The panicking CIC agent pulled a gun, and the other CIC undercover officers tucked elsewhere at the bar—his backup—had no choice but to move in and arrest the men, netting far fewer of the group's contacts than they'd hoped.

Schelkmann himself would serve twelve years in prison. When they were initially charged, he and his men vehemently denied the prosecution's seemingly incomprehensible claim that Frundsberg, too, had been working for the Americans. Just as Thomas's students opened their minds, the SS men had closed theirs.

———

THIS BOOK LOOKS at how we make sense of the world. It's about what happens when we're confused and the path forward isn't obvious. Of course, most of the challenges of daily life are perfectly straightforward. When it's snowing, we know to put on a jacket before venturing out. When the phone rings, we pick it up. A red stoplight means we should brake. At the other end of the spectrum, vast stores of knowledge completely confound most of us. Stare at Babylonian cuneiform or listen to particle physicists debate, and if you're like me, your mind will draw a blank. We *can't* be confused without some foothold in knowledge. Instead of feeling uneasy because we half understand, we're as calmly certain in our ignorance as we are assured in our everyday rituals. This book examines the hazy middle ground between these two extremes, when the information we need to make sense of an experience seems to be missing, too complex, or contradictory. It's in these partially meaningful situations that ambiguity resides.

The mind state caused by ambiguity is called uncertainty, and it's an emotional amplifier. It makes anxiety more agonizing, and pleasure especially enjoyable. The delight of crossword puzzles, for example, comes from pondering and resolving ambiguous clues. Detective stories, among the most successful literary genres of all time, concoct their suspense by sustaining uncertainty about hints and culprits. Mind-bending modern art, the multiplicities of poetry, Lewis Carroll's riddles, Márquez's magical realism, Kafka's existential satire—ambiguity saturates our art forms and masterpieces, suggesting its deeply emotional nature. Goethe once said that "what we agree with leaves us inactive, but contradiction makes us productive." So it is with ambiguity.

Tourism, science museums, and brainteasers testify to the extraordinary potential of ambiguity and mystery to captivate the imagination. But they also suggest just how tentative our relationship to perceived disorder can be. We like our uncertainty to be as carefully curated as a modern art exhibit. Most contexts in which we enjoy ambiguity are unthreatening, as when music flirts with dissonance or horror films toy with madness. When we face unclear experiences beyond these realms, we rarely feel so safe. Real-life uncertainties take the form of inexplicable events, indistinct intentions, or inconclusive financial or medical news. Maybe your spouse doesn't get a job that he or she seemed exceptionally qualified for. Or perhaps you're not feeling well, but the doctor's diagnosis doesn't explain all of your symptoms. Maybe you're negotiating a business deal with someone you don't quite trust. Or maybe you're trying to work out a business plan in a rapidly shifting, highly competitive market. The key decision points in our lives—from choosing a college to deciding on a place to live—have always involved handling ambiguous information in high-stakes circumstances. Today, though, the world feels more overwhelming and chaotic than ever.

The paradox of modern life is that while technological acceleration—in transportation, communication, and production—should provide *more* free time, those same inventions increase our options at an exponential rate. Email was far faster than snail mail, but the Internet also brought Twitter, YouTube, and so on. As the German sociologist Hartmut Rosa described it, "no matter how much we increase the 'pace of life,' " we cannot keep up with the deluge of information and options. The result is that "our share of the world" feels continually squeezed, even as we gain more efficient access to it. Estimates are that 90 percent of the world's data has been created in the last five years. We're all drowning in information, a reality that makes even the simplest decisions—where to eat, which health plan to sign up for, which coffee maker to buy—more fraught.

Meanwhile, we face the social anxieties of increasing inequality and an uncertain economic future as machines appear set to replace humans in many industries. Managing uncertainty is fast becoming an essential skill. The economist Noreena Hertz recently argued that one of today's fundamental challenges is "disorder—a combination of the breakdown of old, established orders and the extremely unpredictable nature of our age."

Automation and outsourcing will require tomorrow's workers to be more innovative and creative. Success or failure, as Harvard economist Lawrence Katz recently put it, will hinge on one question: "How well do you deal with unstructured problems, and how well do you deal with new situations?" Jobs that can be "turned into an algorithm," in his words, won't be coming back. "What will be rewarded," Katz told me, "are the abilities to pick up new skills [and] remain attuned to your environment and the capacity to discover creative solutions that move beyond the standard way of doing things."

Just as workers today must learn to adapt to the unknown, tomorrow's workforce has to prepare for it. Miguel Escotet, a social scientist and education professor, has framed the argument well. Schools should "educate for uncertainty," he said, simply because for many students, "it is almost impossible to know what will happen by the time they will join the job market." For Escotet, educating for uncertainty involves helping students be flexible, self-critical, curious, and risk-embracing—the very capacities that tend to disappear when anxiety gets the better of us. Similarly, entrepreneurs cannot innovate without the ability to dwell calmly among multiple unknowns. Being able to handle ambiguity and uncertainty isn't a function of intelligence. In fact, as we'll see, this ability has no relationship whatsoever to IQ. It is, however, an emotional challenge—a question of mind-set—and one we would all do well to master. Today's puzzle is to figure out what to do—in our jobs, relationships, and everyday lives—when we have no idea what to do.

Scientific interest in ambiguity has exploded over the last decade. Much of that attention has focused on exploring a concept called the *need for closure*. Developed by a brilliant psychologist named Arie Kruglanski, a person's need for closure measures a particular "desire for a definite answer on some topic, *any* answer as opposed to confusion and ambiguity." Like Michel Thomas's unorthodox teaching methods, Kruglanski's concept—and indeed the modern psychological study of ambiguity—can be traced to an attempt to understand Nazism.

In 1938, a Nazi psychologist named Erich Jaensch published *Der Gegentypus* (The antitype), an odious text in which he described certainty as a sign of mental health. To Jaensch, the very tolerance of doubt was evidence of psychological illness. After the war, Else Frenkel-Brunswik, a psychologist at the University of California, introduced the concept of *ambiguity intolerance*. In one experiment, she showed subjects a progression of images, starting with a sketch of a dog. The images gradually morphed slide by slide into the image of a cat. Subjects intolerant of ambiguity—people who tended to see the world in rigid categories—would insist stubbornly that the image was still a dog. Neatly reversing Jaensch, Frenkel-Brunswik suggested that the intolerance of unclear information was what characterized the unhealthy mind.

Kruglanski would offer a more modest and somehow more disturbing proposal than Frenkel-Brunswik's. He understood that humans have a need to resolve uncertainty and make sense of nonsense. It wouldn't be very adaptive, he reasoned, if we had no mechanism pushing us to settle discrepancies and make decisions. Without some type of urge for resolution, we'd never get anything done. That's the need for closure. But Kruglanski also suspected that our aversion to uncertainty isn't static. What if, he wondered, extremism results when our thirst for clear answers goes into hyperdrive? What if Nazism was partly fueled by the dangerous pairing of a hateful ideology with its adherents' inflated aversion to doubt?

That, in fact, is what Kruglanski and other researchers discovered. Our need to conquer the unresolved, as we'll see, is essential to our ability to function in the world. But like any mental trait, this need can be exaggerated in some people and heightened in certain circumstances. As Kruglanski told me, "the situation you're in, your culture, your social environment—change any of these factors, and you're going to change someone's need for closure." Aversion to uncertainty can be contagious, picked up subconsciously from those around us. In stressful situations, we trust people in our social groups more and trust outsiders less. Fatigue heightens our appetite for order. So does time pressure. When our need for closure is high, we tend to revert to stereotypes, jump to conclusions, and deny contradictions. We may stubbornly insist, like Rudolf Schelkmann, that the dog is still a dog and not a cat.

Michel Thomas came to grips with the power of context to open or close the mind. He learned how to manipulate the situational levers controlling our discomfort with ambiguity. Think of how perfectly the CIC's setup in Ulm inverted Thomas's lessons at City and Islington. Wanting the SS men to feel time-pressured, he answered telephone calls during the meeting and made sure his "aides" interrupted him. He wanted to intimidate the conspirators, so he stocked the hunting lodge with weapons and bundles of cash. To put the SS men on the defensive, he lodged them at an unfamiliar safe house. To tire them out and make them uncomfortable, he had them ride through the rain, wait in the cold, and march through icy puddles. In London, by contrast, Thomas encouraged his students to have patience. To ensure that they were relaxed, he told them it wasn't their responsibility to remember anything. He even had them cart away the classroom desks and replace them with living room furniture and wicker screens. His students arranged their own learning space. To further help them take control, he assured them that they were already familiar with thousands of French words.

Thomas turned the Nazis' own doubt-repressing tools against

them and later employed their logical opposites to help students learn. Intimidation, discomfort, time pressure—all allies of Thomas the CIC officer—were his enemies as a teacher. He knew how to raise the likelihood that Schelkmann and his men would blot out potential contradictions, just as the spy-turned-teacher later learned how to lower the chances that his students would disengage from a peculiar new language. He understood that our need for closure isn't always tied to the particular ambiguity we're dealing with. Comfy chairs have nothing to do with French pronouns, just as cold puddles have no direct bearing on whether to trust someone. Our response to uncertainty, he saw, is extraordinarily sensitive even to unrelated stress.

As Kruglanski pointed out, we typically aren't aware of how a situation raises or lowers our need for closure or how drastically this affects our reactions to ambiguity. That's what makes Thomas's methods so striking. We don't normally think about closed- and open-mindedness as being so strongly influenced by our circumstances. While we may acknowledge that some people are more or less comfortable with uncertainty, we tend to see this trait as hardwired. But we're not as beholden to our genes as we once thought.

This book argues that we often manage ambiguity poorly and that we can do better. Over the last several years, new discoveries from social psychology and cognitive science have extended our understanding of how people respond to ambiguity in ways that researchers couldn't have fathomed in the 1950s. The researchers' breakthroughs suggest new and smarter approaches to handling uncertainty at work and at home. Their insights point to ways that ambiguity can help us learn something new, solve a hard problem, or see the world from another perspective.

Part 1 will lay the groundwork. We'll explore the trade-offs inherent in our mental machinery and meet a young psychologist in the

Netherlands who is leading a vanguard movement toward a new, uni-fied theory of how we make sense of the world. Part 2 focuses on the hazards of denying ambiguity. We'll look at the differences between wise and hasty reactions to destabilizing events, watch a master FBI negotiator deal with an ambivalent cult leader, and see how a cancer patient's comfort with uncertainty is helping change the way that we make medical decisions. We'll also learn how one business readies for the future by acknowledging the futility of predicting it. Part 3 highlights the benefits of ambiguity in settings where we're more challenged than threatened: innovation, learning, and art. What are the uses of uncertainty? How can teachers better prepare students for unpredictable challenges? Can embracing uncertainty help us in-vent, look for answers in new places, and even deepen our empathy? We'll see how a Grand Prix motorcycle manufacturer responded to a surprisingly dismal season, and we'll get to know a Massachusetts in-ventor who pushes beyond the hidden limitations of language. We'll look at the advantages of bilingualism and meet a daring filmmaker in Jerusalem.

Along the way, I'll hope to convince you of a simple claim: in an increasingly complex, unpredictable world, what matters most isn't IQ, willpower, or confidence in what we know. It's how we deal with what we don't understand.

PART ONE

Making Sense

ONE

The Resolving Mind

HOW SENSE MAKING WORKS

GÖRAN LUNDQVIST ARRIVED home from work and asked his wife a rhetorical question. "Today," he said to her, "we made a deal with Damien Hirst and another with John Irving. Guess which business I'm in?" In a past life, Lundqvist had been a professional athlete. He had competed in the Olympics as a diver twice, in 1960 and 1964. He was also an actor, appearing in four Ingmar Bergman films, including the Golden Globe–winning *Wild Strawberries*. But in the late 1990s, he was the president of a company.

At that time, the company was in the midst of one of the most productive advertising campaigns in the history of marketing. The campaign, which was launched in November 1980, was not only immensely effective, but also exceedingly long-running. In 1992, the company was inducted into the American Marketing Association's Marketing Hall of Fame, in a class with only two others, Coca-Cola and Nike. It achieved that honor, uniquely, without the help of television ads.

In its heyday, the company ran ads developed by Andy Warhol,

Kurt Vonnegut, the *New Yorker*'s cartoonists, Marc Jacobs, T. C. Boyle, Helmut Lang, Jean Paul Gaultier, and Versace. Ads featured Salman Rushdie, Chuck Close, David Bowie, and Gus Van Sant. The company hired painters, sculptors, writers, musicians, interior and fashion designers, and folk artists. In 2002, *Forbes* ranked them as the world's top "luxury brand," ahead of Gucci, Tiffany, and BMW.

The company's product was vodka. Its name was Absolut.

In 1979, Absolut sold five thousand cases of vodka in the United States. Ten years later, it was shipping 2.5 million cases and had passed its rival Stolichnaya, completing a move from last to first in US imported vodka sales. As sales of spirits were dropping overall, Absolut was seeing annual growth of over 30 percent. In 1979, it had a 1 percent share of imported vodka sales. By 1989, it had a 60 percent share. "Absolut is in a category of its own," one prominent industry consultant gushed.

Carried out primarily in a single medium—glossy print magazines— Absolut's campaign was so compelling that it grew addictive. People who didn't even drink liquor would cut out the ads from magazines: collect, sell, and trade them. The Absolut Collectors Society was founded in 1995. It had a monthly newsletter and, at its peak, 2,500 members. High school and college librarians had to start streaking the ads with black markers so that students wouldn't remove them.

Absolut's success is especially noteworthy considering the long odds it faced. For one, vodka is hard to market. It doesn't have much of a taste or smell. It's not like whiskies, wines, or lagers. Vodka-tasting courses and vodka connoisseurs are rare. People don't usually order vodka flights at bars. There are also restrictions on how you can advertise liquor. You can't pass out samples door-to-door like detergent. Perhaps most dauntingly, Absolut is from Sweden. This drew a blank for many Americans, who often confused the country with Switzerland. At most, Americans thought of Volvo, blond women, or snow. They didn't think of vodka. Russians drink vodka. Stolichnaya had the right heritage. Even Smirnoff, one of the top-selling American vodkas, had a Slavic name. It was a lot to overcome.

The company decided that for starters, it needed a unique bottle. In advertising, there's an adage: if you can't sell the product, sell the package. Nothing distinctive about vodka? Create a distinctive bottle. Absolut would mimic the perfume industry and transform the bottle into a work of craftsmanship or a fashion accessory. High-end perfume bottles are sculptures. Made of frosted or colored glass, the most exotic seem to have emerged from the sea or space or some foreign civilization.

Absolut took its inspiration from old Swedish medicine bottles. While most liquor bottles had long necks and square shoulders, Absolut's would have round shoulders and a short neck. Instead of a paper label, as other liquor bottles had, its label would be printed directly onto the glass. As final touches, the designers added decorative text and a seal of the Swedish distiller Lars Olsson Smith.

The advertising outfit TBWA (now TBWA Worldwide) was hired to promote Absolut. In his book *Adland*, Mark Tungate described the consumer feedback the ad company got when it tested the product. "We were given three pieces of advice," Claude Bonnange, the *B* in TBWA, explained. "First, change the name, because Absolut sounds arrogant. Second, change the bottle, because it looks like it's designed for urine samples. And third, change the logo, because the blue lettering is printed directly onto the glass, which means you can't see it on the shelf." But Michel Roux, head of Absolut's US distributor, liked the bottle's uniqueness. It would stay as it was.

Now TBWA just needed a memorable way to market the product. Traditionally, liquor ads were bottle-and-glass ads, which you can probably picture, or lifestyle ads, with photos of smiling models at fashionable parties. One of TBWA's first ideas was to poke fun at

Sweden's climate. A mock-up pictured a man ice bathing. THERE'S NOTHING THE SWEDES ENJOY MORE WHEN IT'S COLD, it read. An image of the Absolut bottle sat in one corner. TBWA's Geoff Hayes and Graham Turner knew it wasn't good enough, and it was Hayes who made the first breakthrough. He was lounging around one night in a Spartan apartment Turner described as consisting of "a bed and a mug." Sketching Absolut bottles, Hayes drew a halo over one of them. "Absolut," he wrote. "It's the perfect vodka." Turner simplified the catchphrase the next day to "Absolut Perfection."

The slogan set the template for hundreds of ads to come: a two-word headline, with Absolut as the first word. In the campaign's early years, the bottles in the ads were presented realistically and often embodied a person or a thing. In "Absolut Perfection," the bottle was an angel (or a haloed rascal). In "Absolut Elegance," the bottle was sporting a bow tie. "Absolut Profile" showed the bottle turned ninety degrees to one side.

One virtue of the ads was their touch of humor. Many of them flirted with self-parody. When Hayes created the "Absolut Perfection" ad, he knew that he was toying with comic-strip elements by presenting vodka as an angel as mischievous as Calvin of *Calvin and Hobbes.* "Absolut Dream" was also cartoonish. It portrayed a thought bubble with the bottle's innermost fantasy: filling up a pair of martini glasses.

Richard Lewis, who was in charge of Absolut at TBWA and authored two books on its advertising story, emphasized that the ads also took a moment to digest. "Any piece of learning should take a second or two," Lewis told me. "We always believed that one of the cardinal aspects of the campaign was to treat the audience as smart. You create a little puzzle, or game, to bring them in, and then they feel better about themselves and better about us." Lewis knew that the ads challenged and "even befuddled" readers. The clues couldn't be too obvious. The haloed bottle didn't read "Absolut Angel." "Absolut Elegance" didn't read "Absolut Black Tie." The ads hollowed out tiny spaces for readers to fill in with their imagination, like little brainteasers whose solutions were flavored with comedy. It's worth pausing to reflect on how outlandishly fruitful this simple approach became, and what Absolut's triumph tells us about the mind's attitude toward ambiguity.

———

IN 1949, TWO Harvard psychologists published a landmark experiment on reactions to incongruity that offers a complementary perspective to Absolut's case study. Jerome Bruner and Leo Postman believed that human perception, and more broadly how we make sense of the world, wasn't an altogether passive process. At that time, theorists had begun to conceptualize the mind as a computer, as if our brains simply respond by rote formula to different inputs, a view that stubbornly persists today across swaths of psychological science. Bruner and Postman instead thought that sense making was more active than reactive, and they engineered a way to test their suspicions: a peculiar set of playing cards where some of the black and red colors were reversed.

Bruner had first tried to get an American playing card company to produce the reverse-colored cards, taking care to use Harvard stationery to avoid looking like a card shark running a scam. But despite his best efforts and intentions, the company was reluctant to help out. "They were being a pain in the ass," he later recalled. Eventually he went to an art store accompanied by T. S. Eliot's sister-in-law, with whom he'd taken drawing lessons, to purchase the paints to create the trick cards.

Reverse-colored cards, observed for an instant, are ambiguous.

A red spade can look like a black spade or a red heart. A black heart could be a red heart or a black spade, and so on. Bruner and Postman guessed that the trick cards, glimpsed briefly, would trigger competing interpretations. For their experiment, they asked subjects to identify playing cards flashed before their eyes and describe what they saw. Mixed in with normal cards were those that shouldn't exist: red spades, red clubs, black hearts, and black diamonds. Each card was shown for a hundredth of a second and then for longer durations up to a full second, or until people correctly identified the card.

A remarkable 96 percent of participants, at first, described the trick cards as normal cards. People saw what they expected to see, denying any possible anomalies. One subject identified the black three of hearts as a red three of hearts sixteen times. Another described the same card as the three of spades twenty-four times. Yet another did the same thing forty-four times. Normal cards, the psychologists found, were identified after an average of twenty-eight milliseconds. People could name the number and suit of the normal cards almost instantaneously. Trick cards took four times longer, and even at a full second of exposure, subjects failed to identify the trick cards 10 percent of the time.

When some cards were flashed for longer durations, Bruner and Postman discovered, the subjects seemed torn between two different ideas of what the cards were. Here's how some people described the colors of red spades and red clubs:

Brown
Black and red mixed
Black with red edges
Black in red light
Purple
Black but redness somewhere

Rusty color
Rusty black
Black on reddish card
Olive drab
Grayish red
Looks reddish, then blackens
Blackish brown
Blurred reddish
Near black but not quite
Black in yellow light

Fifty percent of subjects were suspended in this cognitive limbo at some point. Even when they partially grasped that the trick cards were different, the subjects' perception still wasn't working like a camera. Reality was being skewed, dynamically constructed to align with drilled-in expectations. And when the subjects were stuck and yet still *had* to describe what they saw, many of them experienced the ambiguity of the trick cards as strikingly unpleasant. One subject, after seeing a red spade card, said this: "I can't make out the suit, whatever it is. It didn't even look like a card that time. I don't know what color it is now or whether it's a spade or heart. I'm not even sure now what a spade looks like! My God!"

Another subject was just as upset. "I'll be damned if I know now whether it's red or what!" Fifty-seven percent of participants shared this reaction.

Bruner and Postman unmasked the mind's natural tendency to paper over anomalies. They also revealed our distaste for ambiguity when we're under pressure—in this case, brought on by the experimenter's request to describe the cards. The stress of the experiment made the mental conflicts caused by the trick cards unpleasant. (Absolut ads aren't unpleasant, partly because readers aren't being observed or evaluated.) More generally, Bruner and Postman vividly illustrated how mechanically our minds fill in gaps and dissolve discrepancies, and how preconceptions actively distort our experiences.

Our preconceptions are vital for making sense of things, planning, and taking action. Every day, automatically, we rely on small conjectures about the world to function. Think of them as the cause-and-effect associations—between objects, actions, events, people, and ideas—that guide our actions. For example, when driving a car, we expect that a red light means stop. We expect that when we turn on the kitchen faucet, beer won't pour out, but water will. We assume that working overtime will eventually lead to a raise. And we trust that spades will be black, not red. The stronger these assumed relationships are, the more automatically and actively our minds foist them upon whatever we encounter. That's why the subjects in Bruner and Postman's study saw red spades as black spades or red hearts. Playing cards' prototypes are ingrained so deeply that the subjects recognized them without truly looking.

Maybe the wildest example of expectations warping perception is the so-called McGurk effect, first reported in 1976. Imagine watching a silent video where a pair of lips utters the syllable "va." If you sync that video to an audio clip of the syllable "ba," what you see will dominate what you should hear. If you're looking at the lips, you'll actually hear "va." Close your eyes, and the correct "ba" sound will return. Our expectation that the syllables we hear and the way lips move will match is so strong that it changes the perception of sound. Check it out on YouTube—you'll be astonished.*

---

* Harry McGurk and John MacDonald first discovered the effect accidentally. They had been studying something else, and when MacDonald first watched the video, he thought that the technicians had misaligned the syllables and moving lips. The audio technicians hadn't noticed it, MacDonald told me, because as the audio was playing they had been looking down at their dubbing instrumentation. Search "BBC McGurk" on YouTube, and you'll find a nice demonstration of the effect.

Here's another illustration. In this example, we're consciously aware of the problem even as we unconsciously resolve it:

> Aoccdrnig to rseearch at Cmabrigde Uinervtisy, it deosn't mttaer in waht oerdr the ltteers in a wrod are, the olny iprmoatnt tihng is taht the frist and lsat ltteer be in the rghit pclae. The rset can be a taotl mses and you can sitll raed it wouthit porbelm.

Amzanig, huh? What academic publications now call the "Cambridge University effect" actually began as a hoax. The scrambled words were circulated online in 2003, and there was never any study at Cambridge. But the hoaxer had made his or her point.

We should be thankful that the brain works in this way. It has to. We encounter so much information every day, we can't possibly absorb it all in fine-grained detail. We have to overgeneralize. The "fundamental problem of life," as the psychologist Jordan Peterson described it, "is the overwhelming complexity of being." To make our way, we have to be constantly stemming the deluge and, in his words, "eradicating vast swathes of information" irrelevant to our goals. Peterson praises this capacity of the mind as "the miracle of simplification." The only way we can manage the flood of perception is by creating and automatically deferring to working theories of what we're going to encounter—beliefs about the world, in the broadest sense.

"Belief," Flannery O'Connor once wrote, "is the engine that makes perception operate." Our expectations and assumptions—whether generous or hopeful, pitiless or woebegone—constantly bend and even warp the world we see. That's how we cope with what William James called life's "great blooming, buzzing confusion." We're endlessly reducing ambiguity to certainty, and in general, the system works well. Absolut's marketing triumph showed that the mind's resolution urge is so powerful and innate that simply by baiting our habituated associations, by hinting at connections left out, advertisers could transform liquor ads into captivating little puzzles.

———

IN 1953, A writer named Leonard Stern was working on a script for the television show *The Honeymooners*. Stern was in his New York City apartment overlooking Central Park, sitting at his typewriter, and he was at a loss. He was trying to figure out how to describe the nose of one particular character, Ralph Kramden's boss, and for half an hour, as he later remembered it, he found himself "wallowing in clichés."

Stern's best friend, Roger Price, dropped by the apartment. They were writing a comedic book together: *What Not to Name the Baby*. Stern assured Price that he'd be with him in just a minute and they'd get to work on it.

"No, we won't," Price retorted. "You're in your idiosyncratic-pursuit-of-a-word mode. I could be standing here for hours. Do you want help?"

"I need an adjective that—"

"Clumsy and naked."

Stern laughed. Ralph Kramden's boss now had either a clumsy nose or a naked nose. "Clumsy and naked," Stern recounted, "were appropriately inappropriate adjectives that had led us to an incorrect but intriguing, slightly bizarre juxtaposing of words." Price thought it was funny, too.

Instead of cataloging regrettable baby names, the pair spent the day writing stories with key words removed from them. At a party that night, they tested their new invention: they'd ask people for a part of speech to replace the removed words and then read back the completed story. Another five years would pass before the pair came up with a suitable name for the game. It wasn't until 1958, at Sardi's restaurant in New York, that they overheard a conversation between an agent and an actor. The actor had decided to ad-lib an interview, which the agent told him was a mad idea.

It was the birth of Mad Libs. The children's game is absurdly simple. You may remember that the blanks ask for nouns, adjectives, adverbs, body parts, exclamations, silly words, or animals. Here's a Mad Libs snippet that will prove a useful reference as we go: "A good wine, served _____ (adverb), can make any meal a truly _____ (adjective) occasion. The red wines have a/an _____ (adjective) flavor that blends with boiled _____ (plural noun) or smoked _____ (noun)." You end up with sentences like: "A good wine, served happily, can make any meal a truly fast occasion. The red wines have a purple flavor that blends with boiled pants or smoked road."

How could this game possibly be successful? Why is it funny? These aren't glib questions. Mad Libs is such a cultural phenomenon that it now seems obvious that having readers fill in "appropriately inappropriate" words to construct little stories would make for a runaway hit product. But is it really so obvious?

It wasn't at the time. Stern and Price's publisher didn't think it would work as a book, and suggested they take the idea to a game manufacturer. So they took it to a game manufacturer, and were told that it wouldn't really work as a game, but that a book publisher might be interested. In the end, Stern and Price had to publish it themselves. To help promote their new product, Stern asked Steve Allen, whose top-rated Sunday night television show he wrote for, to try using the idea in his introductions. Allen employed the winning format to bring out Bob Hope, allowing the audience to fill in the missing words in the bio line: "And here's the scintillating Bob Hope, whose theme song is 'Thanks for the Communist.'"

Mad Libs became a bestseller, with over 150 million copies sold.

To put that in perspective, one of the top-selling novels of all time, Charles Dickens's *A Tale of Two Cities*, has sold over 200 million copies. *The Lord of the Rings* has sold over 150 million. Taken together, then, the Mad Libs series ranks among a select group of the top-selling titles in the history of book publishing. That's a bit strange, don't you think? What treasure, precisely, had Stern and Price stumbled upon? Why does the human mind enjoy filling in words and laughing at their appropriate inappropriateness?

———

IN 1970, THE Swedish psychologist Göran Nerhardt was developing a thesis about the nature of humor. His hypothesis, expressed in stiff academic vernacular, was that "the inclination to laugh is a function of the divergence of a perceived state of affairs from the expected state"—in other words, the kinds of weird juxtapositions in Mad Libs stories. We expect wine might have a fruity flavor and so "purple flavor" is funny.

To test his sweeping theory, Nerhardt devised an experiment. His subjects were not informed of the true purpose of the study. They were merely told to close their eyes and hold out their hands as an experimenter passed them a series of weights, one by one, and asked them to judge whether the weight was light or heavy. Depending on the reply, experimenters also asked if the weight was very light, quite light, or between light and heavy, or alternatively, very heavy, quite heavy, or between heavy and light. The weights varied from 20 to 2,700 grams.

Nerhardt's experimenters first habituated people to a limited range of weights. Then, once subjects had formed a rough idea of what to expect, they were handed an oddly out-of-place weight. So, for example, a subject might get a series of weights of 740, 890, 1,070,

1,570, and 2,700 grams, and then they'd be handed a 70-gram weight. When people picked up the odd weight, Nerhardt found, something unusual happened. They laughed. Not only that, but the greater the difference between the weights they'd been holding and the suddenly odd weight, the more people giggled. Michael Godkewitsch, another humor psychologist, reported a similar effect. His subjects found adjective-noun word pairs funnier the odder they were, so that "hot poet" was funnier than "wise egg," which was funnier than "happy child."

Nerhardt and Godkewitsch seemed to be onto the very thing that made Mad Libs enjoyable. But Nerhardt might have been aware that he didn't have the full story. After all, humor can't be that simple, can it? In testing his odd-weights experiment outside of the laboratory, in fact, Nerhardt experienced an interesting failure. He attempted a version of the study in Stockholm subway stations, telling people that he was conducting a consumer survey and having them pick up suitcases of various weights. When they picked up a much lighter or much heavier suitcase than expected . . . nothing happened. Nobody thought it was funny. No one laughed. Psychologist Rod Martin, who published a history of the psychology of humor, thinks that the critical difference was that commuters at a train station had different expectations for the experiment.

"At the train station," Martin explained, "passengers were either getting off or about to get on a train. Maybe they were going to work. They were in a serious mode of thinking. But subjects in a lab setting know it's a psychology experiment. They're more likely to think, 'Why would an experimenter give me a weight that is so obviously different and ask what it weighs? Something strange is going on.'" People were ready to partake in a serious scientific experiment, and it turned out to be a silly game. That's what was funny. Subjects were laughing at the *idea* of the experiment. In Nerhardt's lab, the odd weight was unexpected *and* it allowed people to make bizarre sense of the situation. At the train station, there was no puzzle that people could solve. An oddly weighted suitcase was unexpected, but not in any meaningful way.

Surprise, to be sure, is critical to the humor in Mad Libs. But for the bizarre word combinations to be truly funny, the surprises have to mean something. Certainly, "purple flavor" and "served happily" and "fast occasion" are slightly odd. But they do make sense by some strange logic. Kids might say grape juice has a purple flavor. A drunk serves wine happily. Drunkenness can speed an evening along. You can imagine a universe not so far from our own where an eccentric sommelier reported catching a whiff of "boiled pants" or "smoked road" in a Barbaresco.

Many jokes follow similar rules. Think, for example, about the elements that constitute this joke:

> There are only three kinds of people in the world: those who can count, and those who can't.

First, we expect to hear about three types of people. (If we know it's a joke, we guess that the punch line will involve the third type.) Second, we're a little surprised when there's no description for the third kind of person. Finally, we discover an alternative rule that makes sense of the surprise: the joke teller can't count. Try to consider each element as you read through these English phrases that tourists found abroad:

> *On a Swiss menu*: Our wines leave you nothing to hope for.
> *In a hotel lobby in Bucharest*: The lift is being fixed for the next day. During that time we regret that you will be unbearable.
> *In a cocktail lounge in Norway*: Ladies are requested not to have children in the bar.

In an airline ticket office in Copenhagen: We take your bags and send them in all directions.

In a French hotel elevator: Please leave your values at the front desk.

In an Athens hotel: Visitors are expected to complain at the office between the hours of 9 and 11 a.m. daily.

In a Swiss mountain inn: Special today—no ice cream.

In a tailor shop in Rhodes: Order your summers suit. Because is big rush we will execute customers in strict rotation.

From a hotel air conditioner instruction booklet in Japan: Cooles and Heates: If you want just condition of warm in your room, please control yourself.

We imagine what the texts should say. Our wines won't disappoint you, you won't be able to take the elevator because it's broken, please don't bring your children to the bar, and so on. Second, there's an odd juxtaposition between what's expected and what is. Third, we *are* able to make appropriately inappropriate sense of them. We picture the cartooned worlds they animate: despairing wine drinkers, cranky hotel guests, and women impolitely giving birth in cocktail lounges. The humor here hinges on ambiguous meanings. "Nothing to hope for" could mean either "not wanting" or "hopeless." "Unbearable" could be "untransportable" or "intolerable." "Have children" could mean either "give birth" or "bring children." We get the joke when we grasp how the alternative meanings are actually somehow sensible.

Here's another example where the humor clearly depends on uncovering an ambiguity (a pun) that we first overlook:

1) Call me a cab.
   You're a cab.

There's an expectation. You'd expect someone to reply "no problem" or "right away." The actual reply doesn't fit, and then we go back and get the joke by noticing that the first line is ambiguous. It could mean "please refer to me as a taxi." Now take a look at two altered versions of the same joke:

2) Call a cab for me.
   You're a cab.
3) Call me a cab.
   Yes, ma'am.

Number two removes the ambiguity from the first line. So it's still weird, but like Nerhardt's train-station experiment, it's not funny. There's no way to make sense of it. In number three, the double meaning in "Call me a cab" is back, but it doesn't register because the ambiguity is never exposed. Humor experts at McGill University tested the preceding example and similar variations on kids in grades one, three, five, and seven. The youngest kids, the researchers found, were equally satisfied with versions one and two of the joke. Children in grades three and up, by contrast, enjoyed the first version the most. Older kids preferred to discover the hidden meaning.

Laughter, psychologists Howard Pollio and Rodney Mers once wrote, "is a partial exclamation of achievement rather than an expression of surprise over incongruity." For puns and jokes, laughter is a testament to the voracious power of our sense-making minds, as all three of the processes involved—expectation, surprise, and the discovery of a rule that resolves the puzzle—happen almost instantaneously. Not all humor, of course, derives its alchemistic power this way, and the solution doesn't always lie in a hidden pun. Stand-up, parody and caricature, everyday humor, and slapstick often play by different rules. But chuckling also springs from our exploration of hidden meanings and our delighting in clever, unexpected connections that we normally disregard.

One of the fascinating things about humor is the way it acknowledges how our minds fill in gaps, resolve discrepancies, and reduce the hypercomplexity of everyday life. It exposes our lightning-fast assumptions by toying with them.

———

IN 1998, BILL Cosby was hosting a television show on CBS. The idea for *Kids Say the Darndest Things* was that Cosby would conduct on-stage interviews with small children. To coax the funniest moments out of his tiny interviewees, Cosby had developed a number of shrewd strategies. One was to ask the kids about concepts that would stump them. Here's a chat, for example, that he had with five-year-old Kemett Hayes:

Cosby: I have a cut [he shows the boy his finger]. See it?
    What do you do for that?
Kemett [without hesitation]: You've got to put a little
    Neosporin on it. And then put a bandage over it. Then
    it'll go away.
Cosby: Where does it go?
Kemett: It go, um, it go . . . down here [he points to his
    finger] . . . in your blood.
Cosby: And where does it go?
Kemett: Then it'll go in another country.

The audience laughed. Cosby let the crowd enjoy the idea. Then he made good use of it. ("What country do you think mine is going to go to?" "Uh, China." Kemett, aware of the joke now, smiles.) Think about how similar the comedy here is to the humor in Mad Libs. Kemett fills in an answer almost automatically, it doesn't fit, and then the crowd laughs, without malice, at his mistake and the alternative world it animates. What truly made the show was the fascinating logic that kids—and all of us, by extension—employ to explain the world. And to be fair, Kemett's first explanation for where a cut goes when it heals, "in your blood," is actually pretty good. Compare his logic with that of another five-year-old:

> Interviewer: What makes the wind?
> Julia: The trees.
> Interviewer: How do you know?
> Julia: I saw them waving their arms.
> Interviewer: How does that make the wind?
> Julia [waving her hand in front of his face]: Like this. Only
> they are bigger. And there are lots of trees.

The interviewer here is Jean Piaget, the renowned Swiss philosopher and psychologist. His investigative techniques included interviews with small children, and many of the interviews were amusingly similar to Cosby's. As Seymour Papert of the Massachusetts Institute of Technology once put it, Piaget "was the first to take children's thinking seriously."

Piaget found that when children try to understand a mysterious phenomenon, they often just extend a concept they already have about how the world works. Where can things go when they go away? They can go to another country. How is wind made? It's made in the same way I create a breeze with my hand. Piaget called this kind of reasoning *assimilation*. Children assume that things that move must be alive, for example. In their model of the world, which is built up from observing animals, there is an assumed link between movement and life. If it seems to move by itself, it's alive. They assimilate other moving things into this conception. The sun, moon, and wind move, and so, like animals, must be alive. The sun and moon even follow us when we're out walking, just like a pet dog. It's the same kind of analogical thinking that has trees waving their arms and cuts migrating to parts unknown. As one child phrased it, the wind feels "Because it blows" and water feels "Because it flows." A six-year-old, asked what it means to be alive, replied very clearly: "To be able to move all alone." Piaget showed that all of us have mental models of the world—he called them *schème*—and that we apply them to new situations or things we don't understand. That's often appropriate. *This* hotel-room faucet probably works like *that* faucet at home.

But sophisticated thinking requires more flexibility, and when children were challenged by an inconsistency, they also sometimes adjusted the way they saw the world. Piaget called this reaction *accommodation*. Kids accommodate their thinking when they allow new information to change their minds, a process that often begins with isolating a contradiction, as when one child retorted, after being told that dead leaves were certainly not alive, "but they move with the wind!" Leaves move, things that move spontaneously are alive, and now the boy has learned that fluttering leaves are dead. He's facing a direct challenge to his assumption that movement equals life. He can engage in denial, or he can decide that not all things that move "on their own" are alive, as one of Piaget's ten-year-olds did when he admitted, at last, that the moon wasn't really following him around or running after him, as he once imagined.* Alternatively, the child may remain stuck between assimilation and accommodation, believing that the sun follows him yet remaining slightly aware that this

---

* To be fair to the seven-year-old, the illusion that the sun and the moon follow us is real and is based on the comparatively rapid movement of other landscape features. As Piaget noted, the illusion is more convincing with the moon. Remember the book *Goodnight Moon*?

can't be true. This child, Piaget writes, "tries to avoid the contradiction so far as he can," reasoning that maybe "the sun does not move but its rays follow us, or the sun remains in the same place but turns so it can always watch us." He's motivated to resolve uncertainty.

Our propensity for avoiding or shutting down what could otherwise be a process of endless deliberation was probably a product of natural selection. It's what allows us to stop thinking and move on with our daily lives. There comes a point when we just have to decide. Our need to simplify means that we all have an innate ability to form impressions based on limited information. We *must* have the capacity to see people in stereotypes and envision objects and ideas prototypically. Our urge for resolution is vital both for managing complexity and, as Piaget understood, for learning. Clarifying ambiguity helps us to act and to build knowledge. Our appetite for consistency is a means to an end.

Mad Libs flourished partly because children enjoy the shocking and silly. But this doesn't entirely explain the pleasure of Mad Libs. We're also laughing at the discovery of colorful new meanings, just as Leonard Stern chuckled when he realized that a clumsy nose was meaningful in a way he'd never considered. Absolut ads succeeded, too, not only by portraying the bottle in strange ways, but also because they achieved some new kind of logic, expanding the ways we normally think of things. *Kids Say the Darndest Things* was based on exposing the naive assumptions and imagined worlds that children (really, all of us) project onto the mysterious world.

"I use the analogy of a Swiss Army knife," Rod Martin, the humor psychologist, said. "Our brain is the knife. It has all these tools for processing information and making sense of the world, and what we do in humor is play with them. We turn them upside down, and use them in ways they're not normally used." We're amused by fiddling with our own brains' remarkably proactive, ambiguity-eliminating tendencies. Puzzles and humor illustrate our relationship with the particular ways our minds cope with the incoherent. Evolution has endowed us with a powerful magnet by which to haul the messy world toward clarity. Sometimes, we seek out little brainteasers to exercise this mental machinery. Sometimes, admirably, we laugh at its follies.

—

IN THE 1980S, Absolut's competitor, Stolichnaya, had some image problems. In 1983, the Soviets accidentally shot down a Korean Air Lines flight that had ventured into Soviet airspace. Over 250 people on the flight—including a US congressman—were killed, and in 1984 the USSR boycotted the Olympic games in Los Angeles, citing "anti-Soviet hysteria." Absolut took advantage of its rival's misfortunes, and during the latter half of the 1980s, the Swedish company expanded its famous ad campaign, having made a vital conceptual leap by removing the realistic bottle from some of the ads.

Instead of the actual bottle always taking center stage, ads in the late 1980s and 1990s conveyed the iconic bottle's shape either plainly or slightly disguised. In an "Absolut Boston" ad, the "bottle" was formed by dozens of Absolut boxes floating in a nighttime harbor. In "Absolut Philadelphia," Benjamin Franklin's old-fashioned spectacles were subtly redesigned as two bottles touching at the bridge of his nose. Most of the ads retained the dash of humor, verging on parody, that had always endeared them to fans. Some were visual puns that baited expected connections, and still others created *I Spy*–type puzzles, where the reader hunts for the bottle shape.

Even early on in the campaign, the Absolut bottle had become so iconic that readers recognized it automatically, mentally filling it in at a glance like Bruner and Postman's subjects staring confidently at red spades and calling them black. In the "Absolut Rarity" ad, that assumed familiarity resulted in a comic outcome. In the ad, the blue letters on the bottle read "Asbolut Vodka." The rarity was the typo. But readers didn't notice it. The misspelling didn't register, and the ad had to be pulled.

Two

The Hidden A's

THE SECRETS OF SENSE MAKING

TILBURG, IN THE Netherlands, is the kind of European town where well-behaved citizens stroll around politely on brick sidewalks. As a boy, Van Gogh took his first serious drawing lessons here. Trappist monks produce a delicious beer, La Trappe, on the eastern outskirts of the city. When I traveled there in the fall of 2012, the De Pont contemporary art museum, formerly a wool spinning mill, was exhibiting the sculptor Anish Kapoor. Visitors circled a pale, tubular mass with red lacquered lips; a gigantic funhouse mirror flipped the exhibition hall upside down; and a bloodied cannon sat aimed at a corner clotted with red, tumorous lumps like some sad war's spent organic ammo. At the town's central train station, long rows of bicycles hung from hooks on the wall and lined the racks like plates stacked neatly in a dishwasher.

The Netherlands is a hotbed of psychological research, competing in cited papers with the United States, Great Britain, and Germany. Travis Proulx, a social psychologist at Tilburg University and a rising star in his field, was the reason for my trip. With animated blue eyes and sporting a reddish stubble, Proulx conveys a slightly frenzied energy. If his friends described him, he half-joked, they'd call him a "neurotic extrovert." He spent his twenties studying at the University of British Columbia in Vancouver and working at an independent video store. "In many ways, I'm a reformed hipster," he said, grinning. He is surprisingly direct, in person and in his research and writing.

Over the last few years, Proulx and another psychologist, Steven Heine, have conducted a series of extraordinary experiments. Their goal has been to build a deeper understanding of how people react to confusing and ambiguous events. In one 2009 study, they had subjects read a version of one of the most disorienting short stories of the twentieth century, Franz Kafka's "A Country Doctor." In the surreal original, a doctor gets a call to help a boy ten miles away. There's heavy snow, and the doctor doesn't have a horse. A stranger appears with horses and bites the doctor's servant girl on the cheek. Reaching the patient, the doctor sees that the boy isn't ill at all, but then, no, he realizes, the child has a wound filled with worms; he's going to die. Villagers strip the doctor naked and ask impossible things of him. The story dissolves.

"A Country Doctor" describes a nightmare world. Literary critic Henry Sussman wrote that the tale actually "never becomes what might be properly called a story. The results are so inconclusive, the characters so blurred as to deny any pretense to narrative cohesion." Yet for all its twists and turns, Sussman adds, "There is no lack of structure here." The story employs the musical logic of consonance and dissonance. Albert Camus, as Proulx and Heine noted, pointed to "the fundamental ambiguity" of Kafka's talent: "These perpetual oscillations between the natural and the extraordinary, the individual and the universal, the tragic and the everyday, the absurd and the logical, are found throughout his work and give it both its resonance and its meaning."

For their experiment, Proulx and Heine created an altered version of Kafka's story, removing all references to death so that the subjects wouldn't be distracted by thoughts of mortality—a powerful psychological factor, as other studies have shown. A control group read another, coherent version of the story that followed a standard narrative arc.

After reading the story, the subjects were shown a series of forty-five letter strings and asked to copy them down. Each string was between six and nine letters long and was made up of the letters *M, R, T, V,* and *X.* What the participants didn't yet know was that the strings contained patterns. Precise rules governed this artificial grammar, or Grammar A. Next, subjects received a sheet of paper with sixty new letter strings. Half of these novel letter strings followed the Grammar A rules, and half of them followed rules of a different artificial grammar. The participants were then told for the first time about the patterns in the strings they'd previously copied, and were asked to place a check mark beside the new strings that they thought matched.

The results reflected the subtle power of incoherence. Those who had read the surreal Kafka story checked off 33 percent more letter strings than the control group. The Kafka subjects saw more patterns and showed improvements in identifying which of the patterns were in fact Grammar A. These increases, critically, were the result of unconscious processes. Subjects weren't looking for particular letter sequences when they copied down the Grammar A strings. Yet even without knowing it, people who had read a disorienting story were more alert to the patterns.

In another experiment, Proulx and Heine had people argue against their "self-unity." The researchers asked participants to remember a situation in which they had been bold and one in which they'd been shy. Some people were then asked to argue that these two memories showed that they had "two different selves," while others were asked to argue that despite these conflicting memories, they were a "uni-fied self." Subjects then performed the Grammar A letter-strings task. The results echoed the Kafka experiment. Those who argued against their self-unity—a potentially confused position—identified more patterns in the letter strings. In yet another experiment led by Daniel Randles, subjects were subliminally presented with nonsense word pairs that might have pleased Mad Libs fans. Having phrases like "turn-frog," "quickly-blueberry," "juicy-sewing," and "belly-slowly" flashed before their eyes again made people more pattern hungry. In yet another study, subjects shown the René Magritte painting *The Son of Man*, which depicts a man in an overcoat and a bowler hat, his face obscured by an apple, reported feeling a greater need for order in their lives than those who looked at a more conventional landscape painting.

What was going on here?

Jean Piaget's assimilation and accommodation, it turns out, aren't our only reactions to confusing experiences. Scientists have uncovered other, hidden *A*'s.

———

PROULX AND I marched across the Tilburg University campus to the nondescript psychology building. His office looked out to birch trees on a flat landscape. There was a single plant on the windowsill beside a Dutch translation of Kafka's short stories and some classical music CDs. Scattered elsewhere were a DVD of Woody Allen's *Crimes and Misdemeanors*, Freud's *Civilization, Society, and Religion*, a stray bottle cap, a loose roll of tape, mountainous stacks of psychology papers, an unopened bottle of Château Beaulieu Côtes de Bourg, 2009, and a book on Søren Kierkegaard.

Proulx sat me down at his desk and opened a computer program. He'd agreed to let me try out a recent experiment that he and University of California, Santa Barbara, psychologist Brenda Major had adapted from Bruner and Postman's trick-card study. After subjects fill in some background information, Proulx explained, they're assigned to either the reverse-colored cards or the control condition, where only normal cards appear on the screen. One by one, the subjects see a particular card and are asked to designate its value as odd or even. Jacks are odd, queens even, and kings odd, Proulx added. Then he stepped out into the hallway to grab coffee.

The red queen of spades appeared on the screen. Three seconds passed, and I clicked the "even" option. Next were a black two of spades, a red seven of hearts, and a king of clubs, whose red suit I didn't notice at first. I began to grasp that as I was calculating whether a card was odd or even, I'd miss its suit. That's apparently the point. The experiment is designed so that people look at the anomalous cards without consciously noticing their atypical color. Reporting whether the card is odd or even is merely meant to be distracting. The funny thing is, I soon knew perfectly well that some of the cards were trick cards, and I still didn't catch them all. The same thing actually happened to Proulx. He'd received some scans of the reverse-colored cards from a colleague who had employed them for a different experiment. "I'm thinking," he said, "this idiot didn't send me any anomalous cards. These are all normal cards! So I'm starting to type out this email, and my colleague says, 'Travis, look at the screen. The four of hearts is black.'"

Proulx and Major put Bruner and Postman's cards to a completely new use. They asked their subjects (via a questionnaire) whether differences in how hard people work justified social inequality. Then, some subjects were subliminally exposed to the reverse-colored cards as they were busy calculating the cards' values. Finally, Proulx and Major measured people's support for affirmative action. Those who believed that inequality was unjust—and who'd seen the trick cards—expressed *greater* support for affirmative action. Somehow, seeing anomalous cards made people more committed to their existing beliefs. Again, the increased commitment was the result of exposure to anomalies that didn't reach conscious awareness. Anyone who later reported consciously noticing the trick cards was excused from the experiment. People didn't register the reverse-colored cards, yet the incoherence of what they'd encountered stayed active in their unconscious minds, leading them to ardently affirm unrelated beliefs.

Proulx has spent his career studying how disorder—be it in the form of a surreal story, the idea of a contradictory self, a nonsense word pair, or reverse-colored cards—can stimulate behaviors that seem completely unrelated. Working toward nothing less than a comprehensive theory of how people deal with inconsistency, he describes through his research a sort of homeostasis that people seek to maintain between sense and nonsense, uncertainty and clarity. Along the way, he has helped spark a movement of psychologists and other researchers who are now collaborating on a general model of how people react to contradictions and threats. Together, they have detailed the precise relationship between Proulx's two major research threads: how confusion motivates the search for new patterns; and how it leads to the avid affirmation of ideals. A hunger for new connections in the face of uncertainty may seem opposed to a heightened commitment to existing beliefs. Yet these two reactions are actually sequential, integral parts of coevolved and functionally intertwined cognitive systems.

Proulx's work builds on Piaget's, as well as on that of another giant of twentieth-century psychology, Leon Festinger. It was Festinger who, in the 1950s, pioneered a new understanding of mental conflicts.

ON DECEMBER 16, 1954, the *Chicago Daily Tribune* ran an exceptional headline: HE QUITS JOB TO WAIT END OF WORLD DEC. 21. The "he" in question was a forty-four-year-old physician named Charles Laughead who had been working for the Michigan State College hospital. Laughead (pronounced "laughed") had apparently predicted that the world would end only five days later, on a Tuesday.

John Hannah, president of the college, explained that Laughead seemed quite certain that before the world ended, flying saucers from Mars would scoop up a few select people from a Vermont mountaintop. Hannah asked Laughead to resign for holding "sect" meetings at his home and upsetting some of the students. One pupil even made a down payment on a Cadillac because, Hannah said, "he figured he wouldn't have to make the rest of the payments and wanted to enjoy it while he could."

Hannah described Laughead as happy to resign, saying that the physician "only seemed concerned about getting his way . . . for the balance of the month"—until doomsday hit. Laughead had gone off to Chicago to meet up with other believers.

The day after the *Chicago Daily Tribune* article, the *Los Angeles Times* ran a longer, more detailed accounting, along with two photos: one of Laughead looking respectable in a tie and jacket, and another of a fifty-four-year-old dark-haired woman with a bony frame. The caption read: "Mrs. Dorothy Martin of Oak Park, Ill., describes communications from outer space she gave Dr. Charles Laughead." Martin, it seemed, was one of Laughead's direct connections to the aliens.

There were more details. Laughead had not actually predicted the world's end, but rather a cataclysmic event that would affect Chicago and both seaboards. He foretold that the underwater continents of Atlantis and Mu would rise again. A new sea would cover central North America. Martin had received a number of communications via automatic writing: "My arm feels warm. It's hard to explain, but I just put a pencil to paper and write." She asked that alien spacecraft not be referred to by the vulgar name of "flying saucers," but instead as "disks."

Additional particulars emerged, also on the seventeenth, from a *Tribune* follow-up. "There will be much loss of life, practically all of it, in 1955," Laughead said. "There will be a tidal wave, a volcanic action, and a rise in the ground extending from Hudson's bay to the Gulf of Mexico which will seriously affect the center of the United States.

"It is an actual fact that the world is a mess," he added. "But the Supreme Being is going to clean house by sinking all of the land masses as we know them now and raising the land masses now under the sea. . . . There will be a washing of the world with water. Some will be saved by being taken off the earth in space craft." Laughead wasn't the only devotee to visit Dorothy Martin's Oak Park home. Fifteen believers, eight of whom were deeply convinced of the upcoming flood, would congregate there between the middle of November and December 20. Some would take drastic steps, quitting school, their jobs, or throwing away their belongings.

Martin informed the group that the spacemen, fulfilling their promise to save the believers, would pick them up in her backyard on the seventeenth. When it didn't happen, the group concluded that this "false alarm" had been a training session. Eager reporters fishing for additional kooky details were now regularly ringing Martin's phone. The story had gone national, and all sorts of visitors began to show up in person. Martin started to receive prank calls, including one, the *Washington Post* relayed, inviting her to a party at a Chicago bar that would last until the end of the world. "That is typical of the moronic calls I've been getting," Martin said. "We have to expect that." The *Post* further noted that "Chicago newsmen, armed with ball-point pens that write under water," were prepared for the impending flood.

On the night of the twentieth, Laughead and the other believers again waited expectantly at Martin's house, where pickup was set for midnight—and not, it seemed, on a Vermont mountaintop. They were to be carried off just hours before the onset of the flood. By this time, among the eclectic group of believers now crowded into Martin's home was a cast of characters later identified only by pseudonyms. Mark Post had flunked out of a technical institute and was still dependent on his mother. Bob Eastman, a student of educational administration, spent three years in the army and liked to swear and drink. Arthur Bergen was a pale, thin, deferential boy of around fifteen. Bertha Blatsky was a former beautician from the northwest side of town.

At about 11:15 p.m., Dorothy Martin received another message from the aliens: prepare for pickup. The mood among the believers was anxious and excited. They'd packaged up Martin's "secret books" filled with the aliens' messages to take with them on their journey. Because wearing metal in a flying disk is apparently dangerous, they had taken care to remove their zippers, metal clasps, belt buckles, and bobby pins. Arthur Bergen peeled the tinfoil from every last stick of gum in his pocket. They were ready.

———

IT WAS NEARING midnight in Martin's home. But unbeknownst to the believers, they were not alone. A group of psychologists from the University of Minnesota had secretly infiltrated the group. Led by Leon Festinger, Henry Riecken, and Stanley Schachter and posing as believers, the researchers had set out to document how the group would react when the world wasn't destroyed. The result was a riveting minute-by-minute account.

There were two clocks in the room that night, one of which ran nine minutes faster than the other. When the first reached

12:05 a.m., one of the infiltrators pointed out that midnight had passed. No no, everyone said, the slower clock was correct. Four minutes remained. The second passing of midnight brought hushed silence:

> There was no talking, no sound. People sat stock still, their faces seemingly frozen and expressionless. Mark Post was the only person who even moved. He lay down on the sofa and closed his eyes, but did not sleep. Later, when spoken to, he answered monosyllabically, but otherwise lay immobile. The others showed nothing on the surface, although it became clear later that they had been hit hard.

The believers' initial reaction was to not react at all. They couldn't even move, stuck between their beliefs and a cold reality. Hours passed. Poor Dorothy Martin "broke down and cried bitterly." The rest of the group didn't fare too well, either. "They were all, now, visibly shaken and many were close to tears," the psychologists reported.

Five a.m. had nearly arrived before Martin received another message from the aliens. The cataclysm had been called off. The believers' own good spirits had saved the earth from the tidal wave and earned Chicago a reprieve. There *had* been some seismic activity, actually, in Italy and in Eureka, California. As part of a string of interviews, Martin told reporters that these quakes "might have been" part of the "advance information" of the disaster. "It all ties in," she said. "The California earthquake is bearing this out." Even though a higher power had intervened, disaster would still eventually come, and she predicted it would strike "like a thief in the night."

Over the following days, Martin and Laughead fought to keep the group together. But as time went on, Martin couldn't help but keep relaying intergalactic messages that were consistently disproven. When yet another prediction of a pickup on Christmas Eve proved faulty, Laughead was put in the awkward position of having to explain himself to a reporter. The aliens had instructed them to sing Christmas carols on the sidewalk until pickup, but once again the "space brothers" had pulled a no-show:

> Newsman: Didn't you say you were going to be picked up by the spacemen?
>
> Laughead: No.
>
> Newsman: Well, what were you waiting out in the street for singing carols?
>
> Laughead: Well, we went out to sing Christmas carols.
>
> Newsman: Oh, you just went out to sing Christmas carols?
>
> Laughead: Well, and if anything happened, well, that's all right, you know. We live from one minute to another. Some very strange things have happened to us and—
>
> Newsman: But didn't you hope to be picked up by the spacemen? As I understand it—
>
> Laughead: We were willing.
>
> Newsman: You were willing to be picked up by the spacemen. But didn't you expect them to pick you up? As I understand it, you said that you expected them to come but they might change their minds, that they're unpredictable. Is that correct?
>
> Laughead: Well, ahh, I didn't see the paper, what was actually printed in the paper.
>
> Newsman: Well, no, but isn't that what you said?

This conversation, a "mélange of incompatible and halfhearted denial, excuse, and reaffirmation," as the psychologists put it, was "typical of the untidy fashion" in which the believers tried to explain away the failed pickup that Christmas Eve.

Believers were spending most of their time in between Piaget's two reactions of assimilation and accommodation, in that uncomfortable middle ground. They couldn't possibly feel assured that their beliefs had been entirely correct, but they also weren't willing to simply replace their false beliefs about the cataclysm. Like the child who knows that the sun doesn't follow him or her but still insists that its rays do, Martin's followers felt that they had to adjust to reality and yet were reluctant to alter their views.

Festinger and his colleagues were interested in the side effects of this mental limbo. After the no-show cataclysm, in particular, he and his coauthors described two fascinating and noteworthy reactions— responses that would later be confirmed beyond the realm of fanatical doomsday prophets and their followers.

First, the psychologists noted an increase in the number of visitors to Martin's home that she and the other believers suspected might be spacemen. Disconfirming events, in fact, had led them to scrutinize visitors more intently and made them more generally suspicious:

Following the major disconfirmation, [Dorothy Martin] made additional predictions. . . . [T]here was a growing tendency on the part of the group to identify their visitors as spacemen. . . . Though one or two visitors had been identified as spacemen in the months before the [first] disconfirmation of December 17th, after [that] disconfirmation not a day passed without two or three telephoners or visitors being nominated for the position. . . . Floundering, increasingly disoriented as prediction after prediction failed, they cast about for clues, watching television for orders, recording phone calls the better to search for coded messages, [and] pleading with spacemen to do their duty.

Martin's disciples could neither deny the series of failed prophecies nor shed their belief that she was in touch with aliens. Imprisoned by a chronic uncertainty, they grew pattern hungry in their search for confirmation.

Second, especially in the long term, Festinger and his colleagues noticed that the believers turned to one another for social support. In the weeks following those December events, for example, the former beautician Bertha Blatsky found comfort in the network of group members. When she tried to cope alone with what hadn't happened, Bertha's "life had been a misery." But after getting together with some of the group on January 7, her spirits lifted. She described it as an answer to a prayer. "The funny thing about it is that previously, I am the one that others leaned on—and now all of a sudden I am the one to need the help." Instead of bolstering her beliefs by discovering new information, she found confirmation by surrounding herself with fellow believers.

Some of the believers, of course, came to acknowledge that Martin wasn't in touch with aliens after all. Pale Arthur Bergen followed this route, modifying his views slightly, as he reported in February: "Arthur indicated that he no longer had faith in Mrs. Martin. He still believed in flying saucers, still believed in the possibility of contact with outer space, but he had given up on [Martin] and her beliefs." Bergen had left Martin's home at 2:30 a.m. on the morning of the twenty-first, just a few hours after the failed pickup and before the onset of the "flood." He never returned.

———

FESTINGER, RIECKEN, AND Schachter's 1956 narrative report on the doomsday group, *When Prophecy Fails*, painted a comprehensive picture of the believers' responses. At a basic level, each of their reactions served the same end: stabilizing a belief system that had been shaken by devastating counterevidence.

Festinger used the case study to further develop his theory of *cognitive dissonance*, a now-classic term that refers to the disturbing feeling of experiencing two conflicting cognitions—opinions, ideas, desires, or beliefs about the world, oneself, or one's behavior. We experience cognitive dissonance, for example, when we feel an urge to smoke despite a desire to be healthy, or when we flirt even when we expect to be rejected, or when we're fired from a job we thought we were good at. Festinger was focused on conflicts between beliefs and behaviors—for instance, how people react when they know a task is boring but have to publicly defend it later. He found that subjects try to dispel the unpleasant anxiety these inconsistencies cause, often by changing their opinions to align with past actions. Over a thousand published studies have made cognitive dissonance one of the most thoroughly confirmed theories of attitude change in all of psychology.

For Festinger, the unpleasant feeling of uncertainty was the signal that a discrepancy needed resolving. In 1974, psychologists Mark Zanna and Joel Cooper reported critical support for this idea in a study titled "Dissonance and the Pill." They told their subjects that they were interested in the effects of drug "M.C. 5771" on memory. Then they gave participants a placebo pill—just powdered milk— and told one group of subjects that it might make them tense, and another group that the pill would have no effect. Afterward, the participants were asked to support an opinion unrelated to the experiment and that ran counter to their beliefs. In this case, some subjects were gently requested to write an essay in support of banning inflammatory speakers from campus. Others were more forcefully instructed. Finally, all of the subjects completed a questionnaire assessing their views on excluding radical orators.

Participants who had been asked (but not instructed) to write anti–free speech essays were more likely to tell researchers that they supported such measures. This result reflects Festinger's classic finding: if we feel responsible for doing something that we believe to be wrong, we sometimes change our beliefs so that they align with our past actions. We resolve the dissonance by changing our minds.

Here's where things get interesting. When Zanna and Cooper's subjects were told that the placebo pill might make them feel tense, this readjustment effect disappeared. Subjects who had been asked nicely to support a ban on inflammatory speakers didn't revise their opinions in the questionnaire. If their discomfort was explainable, they weren't compelled to revisit their beliefs. When people had a plausible reason for their physical anxiety—even when the pill was powdered milk—they ignored having contradicted themselves. Zanna and Cooper's finding, known as the *misattribution of arousal*, implied that the physical discomfort of mental conflicts motivates attitude change. Any reasonable explanation for anxiety, it turned out, shut down the mind's drive for consistency: the heat or ventilation in the room, or even the lights.

Since Zanna and Cooper's study, the theory of cognitive dissonance has been subject to an intense tug-of-war. Some researchers questioned whether Festinger was correct at all. One camp argued that the true motivation underlying cognitive-dissonance effects was the need to maintain a positive self-image. Another camp claimed that Festinger's studies were actually concerned with "ego defense." Yet another group emphasized that the consistency urge was about avoiding negative outcomes. Part of the problem, especially in the 1980s, was that the measures used to detect dissonance—like changes in skin moisture—were unreliable. In the 1990s, however, researchers developed more-subtle measures and designed cleaner experiments to control for the role of self-interest. In the last fifteen years, accumulating research and advances in neuroscience have empowered a remarkable resurgence of Festinger's theory. Today's researchers have moved far beyond Festinger's early focus on attitude change toward a broader exploration of any conflict between opinions, beliefs, behaviors, desires, and ideas.

In 2014, nine researchers (including Proulx) across seven universities published an in-depth treatise laying out the growing evidence that a subtle physical anxiety is in fact the engine motivating us to reestablish order after encountering disorder. But the psychologists had in mind something even more ambitious than resurrecting elements of Festinger's original thesis.

———

THE STUDY OF human psychology, as Travis Proulx and others have mournfully detailed, is fragmented. Far too frequently, researchers fail to collaborate on general theories. Instead, they design micro-theories around provocative experimental effects. Gaps between related theories, consequently, are too rarely explored and identical psychological phenomena are too often reframed and presented as new.

We've seen the unhealthy outcomes of scientific competition in other times, in other fields. One illustrative case concerned the fossil hunters and rivals Edward Cope and Othniel Marsh. In the 1870s, Cope and Marsh were unearthing huge horned mammals and colossal Jurassic dinosaurs in the American West, revealing, to the world's amazement, a slew of gigantic creatures never before imagined, including *Stegosaurus* and *Triceratops*. But the men hated each other. They were in a fierce struggle to be the first to name new species in what became known as the Bone Wars. Fossils from Wyoming, Colorado, Montana, and Kansas were quickly classified and published as new discoveries. A third fossil hunter, Joseph Leidy, was also in the mix. The problem was that the three men were separately "revealing" and classifying the same species under different names.* Between Cope and Marsh alone, one species was "discovered" no less than twenty-two times. The paleontologists *were* making great discoveries, but were making overlapping discoveries.

Now imagine a field of inquiry in which the "bones"—that is, human reactions classified by psychologists—are far more difficult to parse. Researchers are enticed not merely to discover new evidence but to generate new explanations, a problem compounded by the bedeviling issue of language: there are many ways to say essentially the same thing. As psychologists (and husband and wife) Eddie and Cindy Harmon-Jones wrote in 2012, too often "social psychologists try to make their mark by coming up with a new name for an old phenomenon. . . . [T]his tendency has been rewarded by a field that prizes innovation." Proulx, in a 2012 article with the University of Toronto's Michael Inzlicht, was more bruising, arguing that fragmentation has resulted in a "scientific field that runs somewhat in reverse, generating an increasing number of labels for an increasing number of descriptions of increasing numbers of analogous effects." As Proulx, Inzlicht, and Eddie Harmon-Jones put it, it's as if "Newton had replaced his theory of gravity with a separate theory for every object that falls."

---

* Keith Thomson, in *The Legacy of the Mastodon*, writes: "It turns out that the suspicions first voiced out in Wyoming in July 1872 were correct: these rivals did all have the same materials. Marsh's *Dinoceras* and *Tinoceras* were really Leidy's *Uintatherium*. Leidy's *Uintamastrix* was his own *Uintatherium*. Cope's *Loxolophodon* was also the same as Leidy's *Uintatherium*. These uintatheres form the basis of Marsh's Dinocerata. Cope's *Eobasileus* was really Leidy's *Titanotherium* and therefore belonged with Leidy's *Palaeosyops* in the different group of giant, hornless mammals called titanotheres. Cope's *Megaceratops* was really the animal that Leidy in 1871 had described as *Megacerops* and it, too, was a titanothere."

Proulx and his colleagues proposed that swaths of current theories are simply different parts of the same skeleton. When assembled—using the broadest conception of cognitive dissonance as the spine—these pieces reveal that humans have a central meaning-making system that responds to incoherence in a predictable sequence.

First, some situation, event, or message disturbs our sense of order and consistency. There's a mismatch, an "error" between what is and what should be. Rain is falling but the ground is not wet. You try to push open a door, but the door doesn't open that way. Whenever our assumptions about the world are violated, we experience a spike in brain activity, an error message that may or may not reach consciousness, and a jolt of adrenaline. Different brain regions have been implicated in error detection, but the anterior cingulate cortex, or ACC, appears to play a special role.

This human alarm system, as it has been described, goes off even if the violation ends up being *good* news. In a 2010 experiment out of the University of California, Santa Barbara, and Harvard University, Latinas, who expected to—but *did not*—encounter prejudice in a social setting, exhibited cardiovascular stress responses. In another study led by Wendy Mendes, subjects encountering an "error" as mild as an Asian American person speaking with a Southern accent reacted as if they were experiencing a threat. In a 2013 experiment, subjects with low self-esteem displayed lower changes in blood pressure when they received negative rather than positive feedback.

During the second phase of our response to incoherence, we enter a state of anxious vigilance. Here, we're more alert, motivated to seek out new information. In light of the pattern retrieval characterizing the phase, Proulx and Inzlicht have dubbed this response *abstraction*. It's when we're galvanized to collect clues from our environment. Abstraction probably evolved, Proulx and his colleagues suggest, as a tool for overcoming obstacles to our goals. Think, for example, of a mouse that's looking for food and smells a cat nearby. The mouse becomes more hesitant and anxious. It continues to look for food but does so more alertly now, scanning the environment for the cat, rearing its head and sniffing. The neural network responsible for error detection and abstraction is called the *behavioral inhibition system*, and mice with lesions to this system are unable to solve problems by altering their course of action. Abstraction happens in a hyperattentive, anxious, and impulsive state of mind.

After some period, a second neural network, known as the *behavioral approach system*, takes over. This system coevolved with the behavioral inhibition system to deal with the anxiety of mental conflicts. It soothes our angst by pushing us *toward* commitment to an idea or a course of action. The approach system satisfies the need for closure, and Piaget's two *A*'s—assimilation and accommodation—likewise enter the picture here. Let's say, for example, you see a white crow. At first you're a little surprised. You peer at the bird with heightened attention, and then eventually you switch into the more domineering mind state that making decisions requires. You can assimilate the experience and decide that the bird is a dove. Or you can accommodate it and recognize that albino crows exist. The rub, as Proulx's collaborator Steven Heine told me, is that "assimilation is so often incomplete." We act as if we're sure the bird is a dove, but the feeling that it's not is still there in the unconscious, leaving us trapped in a similar middle ground as the doomsday believers were, stuck between assuming we've understood and sensing we haven't. One way we respond to these lingering anxieties is by finding comfort in our social groups and passionately emphasizing our ideals.

Proulx and Inzlicht called this reaction *affirmation*. Affirmation is the intensification of beliefs, whatever those beliefs might be, in response to a perceived threat. In Proulx's research, it's when subjects grew strident about affirmative action after seeing anomalous playing cards (without realizing it). After being reminded of death, authoritarian-leaning participants in a recent study evaluated an immigrant more critically than like-minded subjects who hadn't received such a reminder. The same effect held true for liberal participants' positive evaluation of the immigrant: their views grew more favorable. In another study, subjects who felt a lack of control expressed greater faith in God *or* Darwin's theory of evolution, as long as Darwin's theory was presented as predictable. Through affirmation, we turn to our existing sources of meaning for stability. We swim back to friendly shores.

Researchers have been selecting different parts of this puzzle— error detection, vigilant abstraction, and affirmation—and describing their effects under different banners. Proulx and his colleagues have argued that the theory of willpower depletion, for example, derives its evidence from cognitive dissonance: most famously, by forcing you to resist the chocolate that you want to eat. The so-called depletion occurs because anxious vigilance makes people impulsive.

Similarly, different theories describe various forms of affirmation. One of the theories under Proulx's scrutiny suggests that when we feel that we're losing control over an experience, we emphatically assert control elsewhere. Another theory suggests that when our personal goals are threatened, we affirm our personal values. After being reminded of death, another model suggests, we affirm our beliefs. All of these theories share the same pattern, and Proulx's most novel claim is that the beliefs we affirm can be completely distinct from the fact or beliefs that were violated. He calls it *fluid compensation*. In one of the strangest studies showing just how content-free our counter-adjustments to feelings of uncertainty can be, participants who ate an unexpectedly bitter chocolate later described their lives as more meaningful.

Our search for patterns (abstraction) and our fervent expression of beliefs (affirmation) are sequential. That's why researchers studying affirmation effects observe them most easily after a delay: in experimental settings, it's roughly five minutes after a subject encounters a jolt to his or her sense of normalcy. In fact, Proulx found that reading an ambiguous Kafka tale not only led people to identify more patterns, but in another experiment, the reading also pushed subjects, after a delay, to express their nationalism more fervently. The same held for nonsense word pairs. People grew pattern hungry, but after a delay in a different experiment, they ardently affirmed their beliefs. Festinger seemed to make the same observation of the doomsday believers. In the near term, they anxiously scanned their environment for new evidence, but later on, they reverted to their social support systems. Just holding a loved one's hand, a 2006 study found, mutes the activity of the brain's error center, the ACC.

"What's amazing," Proulx said, "is how much of human behavior bottlenecks at this very basic system." He speculates that dissonance reduction—broadly understood as our various efforts to restore order after sensing disorder—may explain as much as 60 percent of our day-to-day behavior.

As we'll see next, the effect of unrelated contradictions on our general relationship to uncertainty has wide implications. In Part 2, we'll explore how to handle ambiguity in daily life, especially in stressful situations. When we're under pressure, our urgent search for patterns and our dogmatic avowal of ideals can play out with dramatic consequences. Guarding against the pitfalls of the most powerful feelings of uncertainty in our lives means coming to grips with how our minds wrestle with ambiguity under hardship. Instability doesn't have to derail us. Understanding how and when we're vulnerable to mistakes, even in the face of shocking tragedies like natural disasters, makes uncertainty easier to master.

PART TWO

Handling Ambiguity

THREE

Shocks and Tremors

THE PROBLEM WITH URGENCY

IN THE DAYS after the April 18, 1906, San Francisco earthquake—one of the worst natural disasters in US history—a number of unusual events occurred. Rumors spread of a newly formed Matrimonial Bureau, a cooperative of single women who were now homeless after the quake and looking for husbands. Hearing the news, a man named William Perkins hurried over to Harbor Hospital, where he believed the bureau was located, and immediately proposed to the young matron on duty.

"Don't judge me by my clothes," he pleaded. "I am a brakeman and did not have time to dress up. I saw in *The Call* where a man from Fresno and another from Seattle had put in applications and I said to myself, 'We need all our pretty girls at home,' and as soon as I could get away I hurried over. Are you the only one left?"

Rebuffed, Perkins continued his frantic search for a refugee with a "reasonable love of pleasure" who could "make a cherry pie in a minute." Ideally, the woman would be "rather small and blond," but not "too small and not too blond." His mother would vet applications. Another suitor, J. M. Meyers of San Diego, wrote a letter to the mayor of Oakland requesting a respectable woman with a dark complexion and who was willing to live on a farm. Yet another gentleman, J. Loganbiel, spread word that he was seeking "a brunette, plump and not afraid to work," preferably of German ancestry. He could also offer her work: $8 a month and, if he earned a raise, $16 a month.

Initially, the city coroner William Walsh reported only 428 "deaths from shock from earthquake and fire." That figure was misleading. Government officials and business interests were afraid of scaring away investors and slowing down efforts to rebuild the city. In reality, the disaster would claim over 3,000 victims. The massive rupture of the San Andreas Fault, at a magnitude of 7.9, shook the ground all the way up to Coquille, Oregon, down to Anaheim and as far east as central Nevada. Beds of sand and silt liquefied under the pressure, shifting swaths of earth along the Pajaro and Salinas Rivers and bubbling to the surface through cracks like miniature volcanoes. Hundreds of thousands of people were left homeless, and Golden Gate Park and the Presidio were blanketed with makeshift tents. The refugees arrived in a sad parade, "some of them carrying nothing but a birdcage," by one reckoning. In all, roughly 80 percent of the city was destroyed by the quake and the resulting fires. Over three days, more than four square miles of San Francisco burned to the ground.

Eyewitness descriptions of the quake portrayed it "as a violent to-and-fro interspersed with sudden jolts and terrifying circular swings." During the forty-five or so seconds of the main quake, one former reporter wrote, there were no human sounds to be heard, no screams. "It was as if every man, woman, and child was stunned into silence." Roads split open, streetcar tracks were bent upward "into hideous shapes . . . revealing gaping chasms beneath. Loosened cobblestones danced about like popcorn in a pan. Power cables snapped and fell to the ground, 'writhing and hissing like reptiles,' in the words of one eyewitness." At an animal exhibit on Haight Street, lions trembled like kittens. Monkeys huddled in a corner.

Then it was over, in less than a minute.

William James, lying awake in a flat at Stanford University, "felt the bed begin to waggle," got up, and took a train into the city. "It was indeed a strange sight," he observed, "to see an entire population in the streets, busy as ants in an uncovered ant-hill scurrying to save their eggs and larvae."

As deliberately as the newly homeless recovered their keepsakes, suitors wandered amid the rubble. In the days following the disaster, more couples were married than in any similar period in San Francisco's history up to that time. From April 18 to May 18, according to the county clerk's office, 418 couples married, breaking (by 18) the high-water mark for any calendar month on record. San Francisco's marriage clerk, Grant "Cupid" Munson, estimated that if you included couples married without a license by ministers in public parks, the true figure was over 700. (Munson, it was noted, had been "besieged by several ministers who officiated at these weddings for requisite papers.") April 28, ten days after the quake, marked the single busiest day in the history of Alameda County's marriage bureau. In those ten days in San Francisco and Alameda, 180 couples married, over four times the normal rate. The *Louisville Courier-Journal* remarked on the strange phenomenon of couples "earthquaked into marriage."

The *Oakland Tribune* recounted the "amusing sights at the ruined City Hall in San Francisco," where "young couples [were] scrambling about among the ruins trying to find where marriage licenses were issued. As they usually refused to tell anyone what they were looking for they were considerably hampered in their search." Some couples had moved up long-planned weddings. Others who had previously split were reuniting. Some met for the first time in refugee camps, having lost everything.

One couple met on a train fleeing the city, fell in love, and were engaged before they had disembarked in Seattle. Another pair rushed into marriage so quickly that the groom, Murty Sullivan, hadn't even asked the bride's first name. Three weeks after the quake, this minor detail came to light in a conversation with a county clerk.

"What's the lady's name?" asked the clerk.

"It's on the paper," replied Sullivan.

"But her first name?" persisted the clerk.

"It's on the paper," Sullivan said. "That's all I know."

"What did you call her when you proposed?" the clerk insisted.

"That's my business," Sullivan snapped. The clerk relented, issuing the marriage license to Murty Sullivan and "Mrs. Waler."

These were not normal times.

———

ROUGHLY 15 PERCENT of Americans will experience a natural or human-made disaster in their lifetimes. If you include personal traumas like the untimely death of a loved one or a serious car crash, the figure rises to over two-thirds. After a sudden catastrophe, people experience what psychologist Ronnie Janoff-Bulman called a "double dose of anxiety." The first dose reflects longer-term fear for our well-being: suddenly, the world doesn't feel as safe. The second dose of uncertainty comes from the challenge to our working models of the world, from the threat to our "conceptual system, which is in a state of upheaval." The world feels less safe, but the assumptions that provided us with a sense of coherence are also often challenged.

After a trauma, many people have to face the reality that, in Janoff-Bulman's words, "the known, comforting old assumptive world is gone, and a new one must be constructed." As we saw with the doomsday believers—who battled over days and weeks to explain a series of unfulfilled prophesies—that's no straightforward task. We don't say to ourselves, "It's time to reconstruct my worldview." Janoff-Bulman compared this struggle to cope with posttraumatic instability to the frustrations and anxieties that scientists face when confronting ambiguous new evidence that doesn't fit their theories. We somehow have to manage this "powerful data." The psychology of how we resolve these discrepancies—particularly when they're accompanied by feelings of physical vulnerability—helps explain what happened in San Francisco over a hundred years ago.

Feeling threatened is often all it takes to raise our desire for certainty. A 2010 study showed that simply reminding Americans of 9/11 increased their need for closure. Getting experimental subjects to focus on mortality, in fact, is one of the most common and reliable methods in experimental psychology for studying people's increased commitment to their worldviews after threats. But our craving for certainty doesn't have to be triggered by anything so dire. An event doesn't have to be dangerous to increase our need for closure. It merely has to challenge how we see the world.

Seeing the earth from space, for example, seems to raise our desire for certainty. Indeed, the recollections of astronauts and others who have ventured into space reveal the same psychological reactions that we explored in the last chapter. Being in space led some to search for new explanations, while others with existing religious beliefs grew more confident in them. In both cases, they rejected uncertainty and moved toward firmer and clearer views. Journalist Frank White dedicated an entire book, *The Overview Effect*, to experiences of space, interviewing over twenty astronauts and other "space flyers" with a focus on the "shifts in consciousness that can occur."

White detailed similar reactions to space from people like Russell Schweickart, an Apollo 9 astronaut; Michael Collins, who accompanied Buzz Aldrin and Neil Armstrong to the moon; Eugene Cernan, the last man to walk on the moon; and Bill Nelson, now a senator from Florida. These men weren't merely astonished by what they saw. Each of them described an enlightening realization. Many spoke in rapturous language of the same moral revelation: that seen from space, the earth has no borders, tribalism looks petty, and violent boundary disputes seem absurd. Not all astronauts reacted the same way to being in space, of course. Some felt that the experience reflected a self-fulfilling prophecy. Space travel was supposed to be powerful and life-changing, so it was. Others said that the view above earth eventually felt commonplace. But for many of those who were affected spiritually, it upended their lives.

In 2014, psychologists Piercarlo Valdesolo and Jesse Graham showed that mere simulations of experiences of wonder can increase our desire for certainty. First, they showed some of their subjects awe-inspiring clips from BBC's *Planet Earth*, including picturesque shots of space, mountains, plains, and canyons. Then they showed participants a series of twelve-digit number strings and asked them to determine which had been created intentionally (by people) and which had been produced by a computer. In reality, all the number strings had been randomly computer generated. Yet subjects who had watched the awe-inspiring clip, as opposed to control videos, identified more numbers as intentionally patterned.

Even something as harmless as watching videos of space can heighten our need for closure. The threat to physical safety that natural disasters can bring is piled on top of the awe and wonder that they convey, raising the stakes further and making ambiguity even harder to deal with. After a disaster, "sure things" soon become essential.

ON SEPTEMBER 10, 1989, a tropical depression developed off the coast of Africa south of the Cape Verde Islands, where it became Hurricane Hugo. It traveled west over Guadeloupe and Saint Croix, passing Saint Thomas before skirting the tip of Puerto Rico. On the twenty-second, it reached the United States at Charleston, South Carolina.

Winds in Bulls Bay north of town reached 135 miles per hour. Electricity went out as uprooted trees and debris severed power lines. Roofs peeled off as easily as yogurt tops. Tides of twenty feet flooded the coast up to Myrtle Beach, and McClellanville was entombed under five feet of water and mud. Timely warnings kept the death toll low. But they didn't stop Hugo from causing $9 billion in economic losses, mostly in the United States, making it then the costliest hurricane in American history. Twenty-four counties in South Carolina were declared disaster areas.

Hugo, like San Francisco's quake, permanently altered the life course of many families. In 2002, Pennsylvania State University's Catherine Cohan and UCLA's Steve Cole investigated the effects of Hugo on couples. They examined aggregate data on marriages, divorces, and births before and after the storm. It turned out that the average number of marriages had been consistently declining in South Carolina, but that in 1990, the trend reversed. Remarkably, Cohan and Cole found increases not only in marriages but also in divorces and birth rates. And these changes were significantly more pronounced in the areas hardest hit by the hurricane. Roughly 800 more marriages and 570 more divorces took place than predicted. Some 780 more babies were born than expected. Hugo literally brought new life into the world.

Not all natural disasters produce these strange effects, in part because different catastrophes can feel so different psychologically. An earthquake in 2006 isn't as unexplainable as one in 1906, just as a tornado that causes no casualties in a town is radically unlike one that leaves forty families homeless. But recent natural disasters seem to tell a similar story. Following the 2011 tsunami in Japan, there were accounts of a spike in marriages, and according to Reuters, divorce ceremonies tripled in the months afterward. After Hurricane Katrina, there were reports of impulsive romancing. "People were doing crazy things, like they do in wartime," one New Orleans resident, Janelle Simmons, told the *Daily Beast*. "People were having a lot of sex with people they didn't know. It was just such a crazy time." Simmons herself filed for divorce two weeks after Katrina and went "gallivanting around the country" with a new beau.

Cohan, for her part, has come to see natural disasters as events that cause reappraisal. "Whoever is standing next to you," she told me, "you reevaluate that person." A natural disaster can apparently make existing feelings of uncertainty more unpleasant and compel us toward clearer judgments. Under a high need for closure, couples who felt confused but slightly pessimistic about their relationships presumably grew more pessimistic, prompting divorces. Other partners who felt unclear but fairly optimistic would have resolved their misgivings, too, and gotten married. Hugo probably took existing feelings of romantic uncertainty and amplified them. Decades earlier, couples who met as strangers after the San Francisco earthquake seemed to have been carried along by the same impulse toward certainty. Uncertainty from a traumatic event (a natural disaster) made ambiguity in other areas less tolerable. Clarity in general grew more valuable.

Natural disasters and space travel are extreme cases. But they help illustrate one key difference between psychological experiments in the lab and events in the real world. As Travis Proulx demonstrated, a single ambiguity can push us to affirm unrelated judgments and beliefs or pick out new patterns. His playing-card study, for example, tested a single cause of uncertainty: trick cards. But most day-to-day experiences involve more variables than Proulx examined in his studies. That's because lab experiments aim to carefully tease out cause and effect, whereas real life is messy and involves many kinds of ambiguity at once. Feelings of uncertainty often come from multiple sources. An earthquake can be a physical threat, an existential crisis, and an economic disaster. Space can feel both unexplainable and a little scary.

As uncertainties add up, they ultimately accelerate our drive toward certainty. This tendency has vast repercussions. It affects whom we love or befriend or hire or fire. It influences whether we admit to mistakes or stereotype someone (a particularly damaging but cognitively cheap form of certainty). It changes the way we evaluate an idea or consider an explanation, and it makes us less creative and more confident about a course of action even when we are wrong. We've already seen that cognitive closure is a bit like shutting the windows of our open minds. When various pressures pile up, these windows don't merely close. They slam shut, and then they lock.

———

IN THE 1980S and 1990s, Arie Kruglanski and his colleagues began to examine how minor, additional pressures affected people's comfort with ambiguity. Could even small amounts of extra stress affect our willingness to dwell in uncertainty? In one study, the researchers explained to participants that they were conducting a simulation of how juries work. Then they handed participants a judge's instructions and a case summary: after a plane crash and fire, a lumber company was suing an airliner. Half of the participants were left without a strong opinion in favor of either the plaintiff or the defendant. The other half read an expert legal analysis that laid out clear evidence one way or another. Subjects reported their views and then were asked to reach a shared verdict with another "juror"—actually a confederate who was working for the researchers and who had been prepped to disagree with them. The critical twist was that for some subjects, a rickety printer was working noisily in the background while they argued.

For participants who received no expert advice, the irritating printer made them more likely to change their relatively uncertain minds and agree with the confederate. It also significantly *sped up* that process. When the participants who didn't read the legal analysis were arguing in a quiet room, the average time it took for the pairs to agree was 5 minutes and 40 seconds. With the printer going, the time fell to about 3 minutes 50 seconds. Subjects resolved ambiguity faster.

For subjects who did read the expert analysis, the noisy printer made them less likely to change their original views. Unlike their waffling counterparts, people were less inclined to agree with the confederate, and those who did took longer to do so. These subjects were just as eager to escape uncertainty as the first group—but they found their exits through dogmatism rather than deference.

Both of these outcomes reflect what are called the *urgency* and *permanence* tendencies. As Kruglanski and Donna Webster put it, the urgency tendency "represents an individual's inclination to attain closure as soon as possible," whereas permanence is "an individual's inclination to maintain [closure] for as long as possible." Additional pressures lead people to grab on to certainty faster and more firmly.

Urgency, in short, makes for inflexible minds.

Substitute a screaming toddler or an angry boss for the rickety printer, and you can see how this tendency toward inflexibility might play out in the real world. Urgency can cause serious headaches, for example, when conducting job interviews. Imagine that you're part of a panel evaluating a candidate for president of your firm. Let's call her Jane. Jane's answers impress you during the first half of the interview. She comes across as an effective leader; productive, sensitive, and courteous toward customers; and caring about her employees. During the second half of the interview, however, Jane's performance dives a bit. It comes to light that she failed to lure an important client to her previous company, that she was inattentive to employee problems, and that she can occasionally be disorganized. The interview ends, and you have to rate how likely you'd be to hire her. Now imagine the same interview but with one crucial difference: in this version, Jane performs poorly initially but ends the interview commandingly.

Across a range of experiments simulating hypotheticals like this, participants under time pressure—another tool that Kruglanski and his colleagues employ to raise subjects' need for closure—seized on early information and ignored later cues. In one study, subjects were asked to rate how effective a job candidate would be on a scale from 1 to 10. When people had time to think about their appraisals, they rated candidates at about a five, regardless of whether the flattering facts emerged earlier or later. But when subjects had to make a decision quickly, job applicants with strong first impressions were rated at a 7 on average, while candidates with faults conveyed early on were rated at a 3. (This is a little surprising, given the usual emphasis on finishing strong.) In both cases, it wasn't merely that subjects formed their impressions faster, but they also *ignored* the later, contradictory information about the candidates. Other studies showed that under similar pressures, people fit early impressions into stereotypes—about women in the workforce, for instance, or ethnic groups. Since fatigue also raises people's need for closure, any additional stress can lead to urgency.

The same inflexibility under pressure shows up in recent experiments on the psychology of trust. Faith in others, it turns out, is one of the primary ways we manage uncertainty. That's because social interactions always involve calculating unknowns. Think of trust as the oil greasing the wheels of social life, a shortcut freeing us from otherwise agonizing Machiavellian calculations.

In 2014, researchers at BI Norwegian Business School in Oslo published a series of remarkable experiments on trust and our malleable need for closure. In one study, the researchers had participants play a variation on a classic investment game. The original version of the game requires two players, whom we'll call the investor and the broker. The investor is given a sum of money to start and told that he or she can transfer any amount of it to an unknown counterpart, the broker. Any money the investor sends would triple by the time it reaches the counterpart. After that, the broker can send any, all, or no money back to the investor. Nothing happens to the money the broker sends back ($20 sent is $20 received), and both sides learn the rules up front. The more the investor transfers, the greater the risk of losing that money, but the more the investor might be rewarded for the gamble, too. In the Norwegian study, all subjects played the role of the investor, and for some participants, the broker was anonymous (as in the original experiment). For another group, the subjects were told that the broker was "a good friend who was particularly close to them." The researchers manipulated people's need for closure via time pressure, and all subjects also rated the brokers' trustworthiness.

On average, subjects risked 63 percent of their endowment. For participants not under pressure, whether or not they knew the broker didn't change how much they decided to transfer. When the broker was a good friend, the subjects sent a little more money on average (but not significantly more). Subjects whose need for closure had been artificially heightened, however, sent 80 percent of their money to the good friend and 51 percent to the stranger. Participants' trust evaluations reflected the same effect: without time to think, they expressed greater trust in the close friend than they would have ordinarily and less trust in the anonymous stranger than normal. Just as Hurricane Hugo seems to have led to more marriages *and* more divorces, trust judgments were polarized, leading both to undeserved trust and undeserved distrust.

Some years ago, investigators observed a similar rigidity at play in romantic relationships. The higher someone's baseline "uncertainty intolerance" was, the more extreme their judgments of trust in their partners were. Men and women who in general didn't like uncertainty found trusting their partners a moderate amount more unpleasant than trusting them a lot or a little (as both trust and distrust, perhaps counterintuitively, are comforting insofar as they provide certainty). As you'd guess, they also tended to shoehorn any conflicting or ambiguous information about their partners into preexisting views. They were more mentally locked in.

Unfortunately, what's called for during uncertain times is greater flexibility.

———

GROUP DECISIONS UNDER a high need for closure mirror individual ones. Struggling to cope with today's shifting economic and cultural realities, then, some groups only naturally grab for farfetched conspiracies, whereas others fall back on their groups' core beliefs. The present age seems likely—through both acute events like 9/11 and chronic cultural and economic instability—to continue to intensify people's appetite for absolutes. And the explanations that we hold on to can do permanent harm, compounding the problem. "We're going to exhibit these tendencies," Dan Ariely said in 2008, "at the times when they're most dangerous for us."

Under time pressure, one study showed, group members who

voiced opposition to a given consensus were more quickly marginal-
ized and ignored. Another study found that when a stressful noise was
present, group members were again less tolerant of any information
that conflicted with their beliefs. A 2003 experiment revealed that
groups under a high need for closure adopt more dictatorial decision-
making styles, favoring autocratic leaders who tend to dominate the
discussion.

For better or for worse—although often for the worse—what
human nature craves in the face of psychologically acute threats like
the 2008 economic meltdown, ISIS, or Ebola is decisiveness. That's
partly why the approval of George W. Bush, who famously bragged,
"I don't do nuance," jumped more than 30 percentage points after
9/11. Americans found closure in expressing increased trust in a self-
convinced government. Bush's popularity tracked up and down with
the Department of Homeland Security's color-coded threat warning. Inflated DHS threat levels even boosted Americans' approval
of Bush's handling of the economy. Among the more immediate impacts, 9/11 left Americans with less room for unrelated doubts.

In 2012, Kruglanski and Edward Orehek pointed out that a
heightened need for closure has been linked to "support for militancy,
torture, the use of secret prisons in foreign countries, and the notion
that national security is more important than individual rights." In a
climate where indecision is chronically unpleasant, opinions on both
sides of controversial issues can become amplified as people flee the
uncertain ground in between. When the world is less predictable,
people are more likely to jump to conclusions or entrench their existing views. That's the problem with striving for certainty or making rashly informed judgments of trust to escape from ambiguity.
Urgently fixating on certainty is our defense mechanism against the
unknown and unstable. However, what we need in turbulent times is
adaptability and calculated reevaluation.

There's a reason why, one 2009 study found, over 50 percent of *Fortune* 500 companies were founded in a recession or bear market. It's the same reason that led economist Frank Knight to note famously that "profit arises out of the inherent, absolute unpredictability of things." While uncertain times can be painful, they are also by definition eras of change. They're destabilizing because they're a threat to the status quo, which is also precisely why they represent an opportunity for innovation and cultural rebirth.

In 1929, John Dewey published *The Quest for Certainty*, a book concerned with the natural human urge to move beyond subjective beliefs to the firmer ground of knowledge. Experimental psychologists have now shown that the quest for certainty that shapes our actions isn't calm and static but is rather an ever-changing tide—rising and ebbing after shocking events and during periods of disorder.

An awareness of these psychological insights isn't sufficient. It's not enough simply to know that when making hiring decisions, coping with organizational change, forming a political opinion, or making other decisions, we should take our time. Dwelling calmly among feelings of uncertainty, to be clear, *will* help you make a more rational decision. Accepting uncertainty for longer periods will improve your odds of making rational decisions, even when you're nearly positive that you're correct. It's good advice to string decisions that involve ambiguity over a period of days and revisit them in different moods. But reading that advice here, or even embracing it, will only go so far.

Across a range of experiments, psychologists have successfully counteracted the problem of urgency by cautioning people to make deliberate judgments *before* the judgments are about to be made. Subjects are usually told that they'll have to justify their evaluations in front of a group afterward, that their judgments will be compared with the actual performance of candidates later on, or that their evaluations will be contrasted to expert ones. In a study where soldiers evaluated military recruits, for example, the participants were informed that their decisions would affect soldiers' actual placement and that misjudgments could harm recruits' military careers. In a study on medical decisions, researchers counteracted urgency by emphasizing the harmful consequences of poor choices beforehand. These subjects presumably knew not to make rushed decisions. But for people to actually change their minds in light of late information, they needed reminders at the start of the experiment.

To defeat the ill effects of urgency, then, we need two types of tools: those fostering a greater awareness of our situational need for closure at a particular juncture, and those that keep the consequences of decisions salient at the right moments. As we'll see in the next chapter, our need for closure can be scientifically measured in as few as fifteen questions. Adding these kinds of questions to periodic polls might provide a useful tracking tool and point of reference. Measuring our shifting attitudes toward uncertainty—even in large groups—can help us avoid its pitfalls by highlighting periods of danger in collective decision making.

Finding ways to bear in mind our personal shifting attitudes toward ambiguity is a little easier. When making a decision, make a habit of consciously considering your stress level at that time. Are you feeling rushed? Are you tired? Are you having personal problems? Formalize reminders of how different kinds of anxiety affect your decisions and the consequences of those judgments. In hiring, you can deliberately set up policies to create accountability. Hires are investment decisions, and making the wrong judgment is extremely costly in terms of time, efficiency, and company morale. Yet few firms have in place formal systems that reward or punish managers for employees' later performance. Incentives like these would work to slow unduly fast closure and to expand the time frame in which ambiguity is tolerated and even embraced.

Taken across their range of manifestations, stressful or otherwise order-disrupting events alter how we deal with uncertainty. They can turn a deliberate decision into a rushed one or an undecided voter into a staunch partisan. In the wake of calamity, the psychology of urgency means that we need to be wary of the disproportionate power of early explanations. We have to find ways to remind ourselves that dogmatism comes in subtle shades. When trying to make sense of a confounding event, like San Franciscans in 1906, we need tools that help us remain aware of our wild search for answers in places where they may or may not exist. And above all, we need to be reminded of the stakes. Dashing into war can be a total catastrophe, while rushing into marriage may or may not be a personal disaster. Ultimately, urgency can sometimes be a good thing: while it can lead to stereotyping (as we'll see), a high need for closure also makes us more prone to commit to ideas, beliefs, and courses of action. Surrounded by the right people, we may stumble on the right course of action—or even the right person.

—

ON APRIL 18, 1969, Joseph Alioto, the mayor of San Francisco, held an "anti-earthquake party" in memory of those who had lost their lives in 1906 and in honor of those who survived. The crowd gathered in front of City Hall before 5 a.m. to commemorate the precise moment that the quake struck. Five thousand people showed.

The 1930s classic film *San Francisco* played on an outdoor screen. Clark Gable, Jeanette MacDonald, and Spencer Tracy strode determinedly through the rubble. The crowd observed a moment of silence. The bard known as Brother Antoninus read a poem called "The City Does Not Die." The band played, and the crowd sang the song "San Francisco" in unison. They munched on free doughnuts, drank free coffee, and sipped minestrone soup. It was, the *Boston Globe* reported, a "frolicsome festival."

Mayor Alioto had staged his bold antiquake bash in response to predictions from amateur prophets that the San Andreas Fault would soon split open and dump San Francisco into the sea. "I want to make it plain," he said from the balcony, "that nobody is here to tempt the gods or anger them. We are here to demonstrate that, though we know we live in earthquake country, nobody has to get hysterical."

Alioto had a personal connection to the quake. His father, Giuseppe Alioto, was a fish dealer and, on the morning of the disaster, was down by Fisherman's Wharf. Not far from Giuseppe were the Lazios, a Sicilian family, also in the fish trade, that had come to San Francisco in 1892. In the midst of the quake, rushing from their home on Filbert Street, the Lazios had gathered on one of their boats for safety. When Mr. Lazio saw Giuseppe running by, he called out to the stranger: "*Salta, giovanotto! Salta!* Jump, young man! Jump!"

Giuseppe jumped aboard the boat, and in that moment, a strange feeling overtook him. He couldn't help but notice how beautiful Lazio's oldest daughter was. She was too young for marriage, but Giuseppe knew then that she was the one.

She must have made a permanent impression, because eight years later, he did marry Domenica Lazio. She was Mayor Alioto's mother.

FOUR

Fifty Days in Texas

WHY INTENTIONS ARE MISREAD

THE 1993 STANDOFF outside of Waco, Texas, ended on April 19, after a tense and protracted siege. The Branch Davidians, a religious sect, had holed up at a ranch they called the Mount Carmel Center, or more fondly, the "anthill." Their leader was thirty-three-year-old David Koresh, born Vernon Howell. He was suspected of converting semiautomatic weapons to fully automatic ones in violation of federal law. Months earlier, a UPS driver had spotted the outlines of grenade casings in a package addressed to Mount Carmel. The Bureau of Alcohol, Tobacco and Firearms (ATF) found additional evidence in shipping and sales records and ultimately planned a raid on the compound. In the background hovered allegations of child and sexual abuse against Koresh.

ATF agents set February 28 as the date of the raid. Surprise was essential, but they did a poor job of hiding their plans. Some 150 hotel rooms had been reserved for the night of the twenty-eighth. The agents had notified area hospitals to stay at the ready and had contacted an ambulance service. That morning, ten reporters and camera people were already circling Mount Carmel in six vehicles. One of these media members was Jim Peeler. Driving a white Chevy Blazer, he got lost and asked directions from a rural mailman. The mail carrier turned out to be David Koresh's brother-in-law, David Jones, who promptly drove to the compound and told the Branch Davidians that something was afoot. An undercover source inside the compound warned the ATF honchos that Koresh now knew about the raid, but they decided to proceed as planned regardless.

A little before 10 a.m., ATF tactical units stormed Mount Carmel with warrants to search the premises and arrest Koresh. Three National Guard helicopters were employed. The agents were decked out in bulletproof vests and helmets. The team assigned to breach the front door carried a battering ram and fire extinguishers to ward off the dogs. It was meant to be a public relations triumph. Instead, the raid quickly devolved. A firefight broke out. Scaling walls and breaking windows, ATF troopers threw flash-bang grenades. Forty minutes passed with few lulls in the shooting.

Five Branch Davidians were killed along with four ATF agents. Sixteen more agents were wounded. In *The Ashes of Waco*, Dick Reavis describes how videotape "showed the federal raiders in a rout, loading their dead onto the hoods of civilian vehicles. Wounded, bloodied agents hobbled away gasping, arms across the shoulders of retreating comrades." Somehow the Davidians, he wrote, these "Texas—Child Molester—Gun Cult—Crazies," as the government painted them, had engaged in a military-style confrontation with US law enforcement, and won.

The FBI was called in. For fifty days, negotiators worked to resolve the siege with as little loss of life as possible. On the fifty-first day, at about 6 a.m., combat engineering vehicles equipped with hydraulic booms began punching holes in the compound and filling it with tear gas. Bradley armored vehicles shot in football-size tear-gas canisters or ferret rounds. Inside, the Davidians had gas masks, but the FBI knew that the masks could only function for a few hours. Loudspeakers delivered a message:

> This is not an assault. Do not fire. If you fire, your fire will be returned. We are introducing non-lethal tear gas. Exit the compound now and follow instructions. No one will be injured. Submit to proper authorities.

By ten in the morning, the FBI had been gassing the Mount Carmel compound for four hours. There were still no signs of surrender— high winds may have been diluting the effects of the gas. Then, around noon, the FBI saw smoke coming from the southwest corner of the compound. A man was spotted crawling across the roof. A fire broke out. Helicopters circling the scene spotted flames in three locations. Snipers peeking through telescopic sights reported seeing Branch Davidians spreading what might be flammable liquids. Apparently, munitions stockpiled inside the compound exploded. By half past noon, the fire had completely engulfed Mount Carmel.

Waco was a national embarrassment. Over seventy Davidians died, including twenty-five children. Conspiracy theorists claimed that the US government was responsible for the catastrophe and that agents set the blaze intentionally, though audiotapes revealed that the Davidians themselves set the fires. Whatever mistakes were made by the US government, Koresh was ultimately to blame for the tragedy. Here was a man who used his charismatic power to mesmerize adults and children and ultimately send many to their deaths. Americans' eyes were opened to the dark influence of cults. But there were other lessons to be learned from Waco.

OUR DESIRE FOR certainty, as we've seen, isn't stagnant. For all of us, it surges in high-pressure situations and dwindles in controlled, comfortable ones. But people also have different individual baseline degrees of discomfort with ambiguity and disorder. These propensities can make the difference between a prudent decision and a reckless one.

Donna Webster and Arie Kruglanski's 1994 need-for-closure scale was designed to measure these individual differences in our baseline craving for clarity. Of course, a strong natural longing for structure isn't always bad, just as a low need for closure isn't always good. Nor do high scores on the scale necessarily suggest adherence to one side or the other of the political spectrum. Conservatives and liberals can be equally dogmatic and defensive. The scale has less to do with *what* you believe than how anxious you become when those beliefs are challenged. One caveat is that conservative beliefs, by definition, tend to be more structured, more black-and-white, and more authoritarian in content than liberal beliefs. Say that you had a deep-rooted need for closure and could choose allegiances: if you lived in a neighborhood with an equal number of liberals and conservatives, you'd be more likely to gravitate toward the conservative ideology.

Originally, the need-for-closure scale was composed of forty-two questions, revised down to forty-one in 2007. But given how widely the scale is now used—and that researchers were selecting groups of questions from it arbitrarily—psychologists Arne Roets and Alain Van Hiel published a shorter version of the scale in 2010. Their fifteen-item adaptation pulls three questions from each of the original five subdomains identified by Webster and Kruglanski: the desire for order and structure, discomfort with ambiguity, decisiveness, desire for predictability, and closed-mindedness. When tested with a sample of over 1,500 people, Roets and Van Hiel's version showed no significant differences in measurements from the complete scale. To score yourself on it, mark each statement between a 1 (completely disagree) and a 6 (completely agree):

1. I don't like situations that are uncertain.
2. I dislike questions that could be answered in many different ways.
3. I find that a well-ordered life with regular hours suits my temperament.
4. I feel uncomfortable when I don't understand the reason why an event occurred in my life.
5. I feel irritated when one person disagrees with what everyone else in the group believes.
6. I don't like to go into a situation without knowing what I can expect from it.
7. When I have made a decision, I feel relieved.
8. When I am confronted with a problem, I'm dying to reach a solution very quickly.
9. I would quickly become impatient and irritated if I could not find a solution to a problem immediately.
10. I don't like to be with people who are capable of unexpected actions.
11. I dislike it when a person's statement could mean many different things.
12. I find that establishing a consistent routine enables me to enjoy life more.
13. I enjoy having a clear and structured mode of life.
14. I do not usually consult many different opinions before forming my own views.
15. I dislike unpredictable situations.

Now simply add up the total. Your need for closure (right now) is above average if you scored 57 or above. Note that this scale can be used either to measure individual differences in the need for closure or to measure situational differences. Depending on your mood, your score may go up or down, but different people will still end up having a range of average scores. A greater need for closure simply implies that the mind's natural aggressiveness in papering over anomalies, resolving discrepancies, and achieving the "miracle of simplification" is set a bit higher.

Developing research led by Northwestern University's Bobby Cheon has produced some of the first evidence that the need for closure also has a genetic component. Subjects with at least one short allele (a gene variant) of a gene associated with greater emotional response to threat—called 5-HTTLPR—reported greater discomfort with ambiguity and unpredictable situations. People with at least one short allele of 5-HTTLPR appear less able to control their moods because of an inefficient regulation of serotonin levels in the brain. In 2013, Cheon and his colleagues published evidence on 5-HTTLPR's link to another outcome consistently associated with having a high need for closure—prejudice—and in 2015, they confirmed that subjects with at least one short allele of 5-HTTLPR showed higher levels of need for closure.

In 2015, psychologists in Poland also enriched the picture by looking directly at how someone's need for closure might affect neurocognitive processes. When people with a high need for closure faced a complex task, it turned out they exhibited greater brain activity in the early stages of cognitive processing. How would this lead to errors? The researchers suggested that a higher need for closure leads to heightened attention early on, which paradoxically makes people less able to resist their first impulses and leaves them less aware of their own mistakes. In a low-stakes environment, that might be okay. But in stressful circumstances, missing key information can be disastrous.

—

ONE OF THE best examples of the effects of varying needs for closure comes from a careful case study that the University of Haifa's Uri Bar-Joseph coauthored with Kruglanski. Their detailed review of Israel's Yom Kippur War also sheds light on what went so disastrously wrong in Waco.

The Yom Kippur War began on October 6, 1973, when Egypt and Syria launched a surprise attack on Israel. The conflict lasted a long twenty days before Israel prevailed. While the Soviet Union provided support to its Cold War allies Egypt and Syria, the United States rushed supplies to Israel. The intensifying melee threatened to draw the two superpowers into direct conflict. One reason the war lasted as long as it did was that Israel was taken by surprise. Egyptian forces crossed the Suez Canal with startling efficiency, penetrating the Sinai Peninsula. Syria, meanwhile, opened up a successful attack on the Golan Heights. It took several days for Israeli forces to regroup.

Israel shouldn't have been unprepared for the initial attack. Its intelligence services had collected sufficient evidence that Egyptian forces were preparing for war and not simply engaged in a training exercise. On October 2, the Israeli Directorate of Military Intelligence (AMAN) disseminated an updated version of the Syrian plan to go to war. Since early 1972, AMAN had known about Egypt's intention to cross the Suez Canal. By 1973, there had been hundreds of warnings about an imminent attack. The Agranat Commission, which investigated the Yom Kippur War, concluded that military intelligence "had plenty of warning indicators" in the days before the surprise offensive. The head of Mossad, Zvi Zamir, estimated in April 1973 that Egypt had built up its military and was more capable than ever of launching an attack on Israel.

So why was Israel caught off guard? Bar-Joseph and Kruglanski pin a large part of the blame on two key military figures, Major-General Eli Zeira and Lieutenant-Colonel Yona Bandman. Zeira was the director of AMAN. Bandman was the head of Branch 6 of AMAN, responsible for analyzing intelligence streaming out of Egypt and North Africa. Both men were very bright. But they shared a fatal penchant for overconfidence and absolutism. As Bar-Joseph and Kruglanski write:

> Both exhibited a highly authoritative and decisive managerial style. Both lacked the patience for long and open discussions, and regarded them as "bullshit." Zeira used to humiliate officers who, in his opinion, came unprepared for meetings. At least once he was heard to say that those officers who estimated in spring 1973 that a war was likely should not expect promotion. Bandman, although less influential in AMAN than Zeira . . . [was] known for his total rejection of any attempt to change a single word, even a comma, in a document he wrote.

For both Zeira and Bandman, their personalities seem to have led them to freeze on the idea that neither Egypt nor Syria had the capacity or ambition to attack Israel. They shared that assessment since at least 1972, and despite subsequent mounting evidence to the contrary, they wouldn't reconsider it. In September 1973, a month before the attack, they confidently asserted that Egypt would be unlikely to try to occupy part of the Sinai desert in the next five years. Zeira and Bandman were so self-assured that they deliberately excluded, when reporting to policymakers, contradictory assessments within AMAN regarding Egyptian and Syrian military intentions.

Twenty-four hours before the war began, Bandman remained persuaded that Israel was safe. He described massive Egyptian movements of tanks and other heavy weaponry as "routine activity." Zeira, meanwhile, was meeting with Prime Minister Golda Meir to explain why the Soviets were conducting an emergency evacuation from Syria and Egypt. He offered three confused explanations. The Soviets, he suggested, might have suspected that Israel was going to attack Egypt and Syria. Or perhaps they imagined that Egypt and Syria were intending to attack Israel. Last, there may have been a crisis in Soviet-Egyptian and Soviet-Syrian relations. Zeira then simply reverted to his old assessment. Even if the Soviets did think that Egypt and Syria planned to attack, he told Meir, it was only because "they don't know the Arabs well enough." His confidence had led to a botched analysis. The Russians had somehow been given a heads-up.

Zeira's need for certainty was even more apparent in a statement he made to some Knesset (Parliament) members a few months earlier. Zeira, as the director of military intelligence (DMI), was, remarkably, describing his *own* role here:

> The Chief of Staff [of the Israel Defense Forces] has to make decisions and his decisions should be clear. The best support that the DMI can provide him with—if this is objectively possible—is to provide him with an estimate as clear and as sharp as possible. It is true that the clearer and sharper the estimate is, then if it is a mistake, it is a clear and sharp mistake—but this is the risk of the DMI.

Zeira apparently felt that the role of an intelligence analyst was to winnow out all doubts before briefing a higher-up. Sure, he admitted, that meant that the analyst was either completely right or completely wrong, but at least there was "precision." Zeira's predecessor, by contrast, was known for considering alternative opinions. When reporting to superiors, he'd present his own analysis alongside con-tradictory viewpoints. For the Yom Kippur War, Zeira and Band-man's frozen analyses proved costly. Israel lost over two thousand soldiers, many in the early days of the war.

War isn't the only situation in which a high need for closure can be detrimental. In business negotiations, parties at the table often have to manage missing or conflicting information. If negotiators read too much into any one fact, if they stretch for answers, they typically make mistakes. A wide range of studies shows that negotiating a good deal requires someone who can handle confusing and contradictory messages without getting emotional, assuming too much, or fixating on one tidbit or another. At the same time, feeling pressured or threat-ened makes uncertainty feel more unpleasant. Negotiating requires handling ambiguity; crisis situations heighten the need for closure. Imagine, then, the challenges of negotiating in the midst of a crisis.

—

"WHEN MOST PEOPLE hear a gunshot," Gary Noesner told me when we first spoke, in 2012, "they assume someone is being killed." I'd asked Noesner, a former FBI hostage negotiator, about his first major standoff, in October 1982.

The trouble began on October 7, at 10:40 p.m., to be precise, when a man listed on an Amtrak passenger manifest as "W. Rod-riguez" boarded a New York–bound Silver Star in Jacksonville, Florida. He'd reserved a first-class sleeping car for himself, his sister Maria, her nearly four-year-old daughter, Julie, and her nine-month-old son, Juan. Rodriguez's real name was Mario Villabona. He was a twenty-nine-year-old Colombian drug trafficker.

On Friday, October 8, passengers in the next berth woke up to the sound of Mario and Maria arguing loudly in Spanish. Then they heard gunshots. The conductor called in the incident to the police, who were waiting as the train pulled into Raleigh, North Carolina. The officers evacuated the other passengers, detached the car that held Mario, Maria, and her children, and moved it onto a side track. Using a loudspeaker to talk to Mario, the police received no response. An officer stealthily attached a microphone and speaker to the train car to communicate with the gunman. At a little past noon, officers heard four more gunshots. There was another at 8 p.m., and two more at 11:37 a.m. the next day.

Noesner had gotten the call from his negotiation instructor at Quantico. Local law enforcement needed a negotiator who spoke Spanish. Noesner's first thought was Ray Arras, a recent graduate of the FBI hostage-negotiations training course. So Noesner and Arras flew down to Raleigh together from Virginia, arriving at the station at around 6 p.m. on Saturday, just as Villabona fired two shots through the compartment door. From the listening device, the local police chief guessed that Maria was dead. Mario, they had learned, had been incarcerated in three US prisons before being paroled on the condition that he return to Colombia. His file noted that he had a vicious temper.

Should the officers do nothing? Should they raid the car? Should they simply wait? Was Villabona shooting his captives? They just didn't have enough information. "This is Ray," Arras said in Spanish through the speaker system. "I'm here to help you. How are the children?" No reply. As the sun rose the next morning, a wafting stench would confirm that Villabona's sister was in fact dead inside the compartment.

The information available to those trying to resolve the crisis was about as ambiguous as it could be. There was no clear motive— Villabona had probably shot his sister in anger. What he would do next was unpredictable. From the rapid-fire bursts, law enforcement knew he had a machine gun. With a child and baby inside the car, an assault was too risky. The Amtrak car was built with heavy-gauge steel, and the glass windows were effectively bulletproof. Their best chance was to patiently lure Villabona out, yet the threat of the children dying from dehydration was rising. Arras emphasized the need to end the standoff safely and the importance of the kids getting food and water.

Slowly, Villabona began to open up to Ray Arras. He told Arras that the infant had died overnight: "I woke up today and he was blue and stiff." In the background, Arras and Noesner could hear the girl complaining that her stomach hurt.

"Will you meet me at the window and give me Julie?" Arras asked. "I will come unarmed." Before Noesner could think to stop him, Arras walked to the train car and took Villabona's hand in a show of good faith, and Villabona handed the girl to him. In all likelihood, Arras saved the girl's life. He'd been negotiating for over thirty hours. The next day, with the help of his onetime attorney, Villabona peacefully surrendered.

"Different police departments have different perspectives," Noesner told me. "But when I was very actively involved in this business, there would be some tactical people who would draw automatic conclusions from a gunshot. The gun went off, therefore we have to go in to stop the killing. . . . And then you stop for a minute and say, wait a minute, maybe that was an accidental discharge, or firing into the ceiling out of frustration. Maybe it was a warning shot. We don't know what it was. We don't have enough information to take an action that could end up being even more dangerous." Noesner recounted the Mario Villabona ordeal and Arras's heroism in his 2010 memoir, *Stalling for Time*. He described it as one of the bravest things he'd ever seen an FBI agent do.

Noesner retired from the FBI in 2003 after thirty years, including twenty-three as a hostage negotiator. During his last decade on the job, he was the FBI's chief negotiator. Throughout his career, he was involved in more than one hundred international kidnapping cases involving US citizens. He interrogated terrorists, negotiated with airplane hijackers, ended a prison-riot-turned-hostage-standoff, talked down right-wing separatists, and even helped solve international diplomatic crises. Along the way, he reformed how FBI negotiators are trained, encouraging the bureau to incorporate active-listening techniques used by therapists. He knows how to talk to despicable and desperate people to save lives.

Noesner is not an indecisive or squeamish man. The very first episode he recounts in his memoir has him successfully coaxing a hostage taker into an open field so that a sniper can get a clean shot at him. When a situation is beyond hope, Noesner has no qualms about acting swiftly and conclusively. What he does believe in, under more ambiguous circumstances, is delaying for however long it takes to make his case and deliberately weigh the risks. Successful negotiations often require marathon-level patience, the kind that he and Arras displayed with Villabona.

Effective negotiators, he told me, have at least one thing in common: "They're all people who can dwell fairly effectively in the areas of gray, in the uncertainties and ambiguities of life."

Not everyone who gets embroiled in hostage situations responds with such restraint. Consider the July 1993 case of Joel Souza. The man was holding his two kids at gunpoint in Antioch, California, where he had retreated to an upstairs bedroom of the home he had once shared with his estranged wife. A trained hostage negotiator, Officer Michael Schneider, spoke with Souza over several hours. Schneider even managed to get Souza to lower four rifles out of the window. The officer told him to take his shirt off when he surrendered, so that the SWAT team outside would know that he wasn't armed. About five hours into the standoff, a police captain arrived on the scene. He suggested to Schneider that they set a time limit. Schneider talked him out of it, and the captain allowed his subordinate four more hours before finally insisting on a deadline.

"I'm tired of this shit," the captain said. "Give him ten minutes—then we're coming in." Nine minutes later, Souza killed his two children and himself. He was found shirtless. As Noesner detailed in *Stalling for Time*, of the case:

> Oddly enough, though, the captain and Joel Souza may have had more in common than the captain imagined. The psychological makeup of traditional law enforcement officers tends to include a fair amount of classic controlling behavior, though they may not be self-aware enough to realize it.

Crisis negotiators, Noesner said, sometimes have to conduct two negotiations at once. They have to talk to the hostage taker, of course. But sometimes, he told me, they also have to convince their fellow law enforcement officers to have more patience and more faith in the negotiations:

> The very first slide in the negotiation course that I taught for many years at the academy was on self-control. If you cannot control your own emotions, how can you expect to try to control someone else's? Self-control not only applies to you as a negotiator, but it also affects commanders and SWAT team leaders and everybody else. If they allow their emotional response to events to dictate their actions, chances are they won't be making the best decisions they can. I'm not saying negotiators don't get emotional. But we try to make decisions according to the outcomes we want instead of how we feel about something.

Noesner's ability to keep a cool head in a crisis set him apart. It was also a capacity that was sorely tested when he arrived in Texas, on the last day of February 1993, and picked up the phone to speak to David Koresh.

"Hi, David. This is Gary. I just got down here, and I want to make sure that you and your family get out of this situation safe and sound."

"Yeah," Koresh told him. "We're not ready to come out."

—

ON THE DAY the ATF had its initial lethal firefight with the Davidians, Noesner got a page as he was leaving his local hardware store in Virginia. His boss told him to go to the airport. Two FBI planes waited on the tarmac. The smaller, slower propeller plane was for him. The larger plane, an executive jet, was for other FBI and ATF brass, including Dick Rogers, the head of the FBI's elite Hostage Rescue Team (HRT).

Rogers's nickname was "Sergeant Severe." His red hair, tense jaw, and adamantine posture fit the moniker. Just months earlier, Rogers had called the shots at the deadly standoff on Ruby Ridge, in north Idaho. A man named Randy Weaver, a former factory worker planning to escape a corrupt world, had moved his family to a remote patch of land. Weaver had attended an Aryan Nations meeting and, in 1989, sold two sawed-off shotguns to an ATF informant. Indicted, he never showed up for the trial. By the end of the summer of 1992, the US Marshals Service had decided to try to arrest Weaver near his Ruby Ridge cabin, and six marshals set out into the wilderness with M16 rifles. An exchange of fire broke out, and Weaver's fourteen-year-old son and a deputy marshal were shot and killed.

When Rogers arrived, Weaver had taken refuge in his cabin. Rogers sent HRT snipers to find a vantage point on him. The Justice Department, looking into the incident afterward, reported that Rogers had essentially "instructed the snipers that before a surrender announcement was made they could and should shoot all armed adult males appearing outside the cabin." Those rules of engagement were later criticized as unconstitutional. At the sound of an FBI helicopter, Weaver stepped outside and a sniper fired, wounding Weaver and killing his wife as she held their ten-month-old daughter.

Heading to Texas, Noesner's smaller plane couldn't make it in one hop and had to refuel in Little Rock. Someone up top apparently felt that Rogers, the head of the HRT, had to reach the scene immediately, but that Noesner, the head of the negotiation team, did not. At around 10 p.m., Noesner arrived at a former air force base outside Waco; the base would function as the group's command post. Hustling past a group of technicians setting up computers and phone lines, Noesner met with Jeff Jamar, the special agent in charge of the FBI office in San Antonio and the FBI on-scene commander. About six feet four, Jamar had the look, Noesner wrote, of "a pro football player on game day."

One important consideration was how the negotiation team would coordinate with Rogers and the tactical unit. When Noesner asked about it, Jamar said that he, Jamar, would be the relay with Rogers. Contrary to standard protocol, communications with the tactical command would go through Jamar. Normally, the tactical and negotiations units conferred more directly.

Noesner and Jamar were set up about eight miles from Mount Carmel. Rogers waited with some of his tactical team just outside the compound at the forward command post. When Noesner arrived at the base, the ATF was still nominally in charge as the FBI awaited the formal transfer of power from Washington. Led to what looked like a former World War II–era military barracks, Noesner found about a dozen ATF agents and others looking haggard, along with Jim Cavanaugh, the ATF supervisor who had been on the phone with Koresh in the hours after the shootout.

One of the most pressing problems Noesner encountered was that the two phone lines inside Mount Carmel hadn't been secured to prevent unwanted calls. Koresh and others inside could still reach anyone they wanted. News organizations, including *A Current Affair* and CNN, were conducting interviews, interrupting the negotiation process. Koresh called his mother to tell her good-bye, something Noesner would have liked to prevent. But it wasn't all bad news. After negotiators arranged for a radio station to recite a verse of scripture, Koresh allowed four children to leave.

Cavanaugh phoned Koresh, introduced Noesner, and handed over the line. Koresh was wounded from the firefight and sounded exhausted. Throughout that first night, Noesner and Koresh spoke by phone every few hours. Noesner emphasized that there was no need for further bloodshed and that the important thing was the safety of the children. The FBI transcripts show Noesner fishing for information:

> Noesner: How many kids are there, David?
> Koresh: You'll find out when you get them all.
> Noesner: Okay.
> Koresh: There's a lot, okay?
> Noesner: Oh, there is? Do we need any special—I mean, are they all old enough to walk or—
> Koresh: No, some of them are like, newborns.
> Noesner: Newborns, yeah, okay.

Noesner also spoke, in those early hours of the standoff, with Steve Schneider, a Branch Davidian who would act as a spokesman and intermediary for Koresh throughout the siege. Schneider told Noesner that people inside Mount Carmel had seen an "army tank" or an "armored carrier vehicle of some sort" and were worried about an escalation. "I mean, what is this going to be, World War III or what?" he asked.

"Don't, don't misinterpret what that stuff means," Noesner told him. "The, the way the federal government responds to these things—"

Schneider brought up Ruby Ridge. "Well, I do remember reading about that Weaver story and a number of other stories—"

"Yeah, yeah."

"In the past—"

"That's right."

"—in the past and, you know, it definitely unsettles a person," Schneider said.

"Yeah."

"I know a lot of the people involved are just people doing their job and don't understand and—"

"But, but you have to know . . . in the, in the Weaver case," Noesner said, "from the moment negotiations started, there wasn't a single shot fired and there wasn't a single person hurt after that point in time . . . [O]nce we started talking up there it, it worked out in the best way that it could, which was no further loss of life."

The irony of this exchange speaks volumes about what would eventually happen at Mount Carmel. By the morning of March 1, negotiations had secured the release of eight children. The negotiators had begun to gain Koresh's trust, and yet the tactical team seemed to be working at cross purposes with the negotiation team. Schneider couldn't, of course, have known that Rogers, the same man who had botched Ruby Ridge, was at the forward command post just yards from the compound at that very moment.

Noesner set about the business of getting as many people safely out of the compound as he could. Over the next weeks, he would work not as the negotiator on the phone, but as the strategic co-ordinator making sure both teams of negotiators were well coordinated. It meant sixteen-plus-hour days. Two teams of five would work in twelve-hour shifts. Next to the negotiator on the phone, a "coach" would listen to the call and pass notes as required. A third team member operated the phone system and tape recorder. A fourth kept a log of key points discussed. Beyond this core group and a fifth negotiator (the shift team leader), only Noesner was allowed in the room during live negotiations. A speaker relayed conversations with Mount Carmel into an adjacent room, where the rest of the negotiation team and others could listen in. After each shift, the two teams debriefed and prepared for the next call.

By the night of March 1, the second day of the siege, Koresh had let four more children go. The kids were brought to the negotiators, who would then call the parents still inside the compound and confirm that their children were safe and being treated well. By the afternoon of March 2, negotiations had ushered the release of eighteen children and two adults. Even more promising, Koresh claimed that he'd surrender if he was allowed a national broadcast of his message about the Book of Revelation. The negotiators asked that the message be taped so that they could review it first. At 1:32 p.m., the Christian Broadcasting Network finally aired it. In what turned out to be the pivotal moment of the standoff, the Davidians prepared to surrender peacefully. Buses pulled up in front of Mount Carmel. Koresh was to be brought out on a stretcher by fellow Davidians, and Schneider would stay on the phone with the negotiators to ensure that the whole process went smoothly. The HRT was standing by.

"Everybody's lined up with their stuff, ready to go out," Schneider told the negotiator on the phone. But the HRT had reported that nothing was happening. No one came out. Schneider said that

Koresh wanted to give one final sermon before they left. Everyone waited patiently, hoping that Koresh would follow through on his promise. At about 6 p.m., Schneider informed the negotiators that Koresh had changed his mind. God had spoken to him and told him not to leave the compound.

Noesner was used to negotiating with all sorts of people, and he knew not to overreact. The bottom line was that the negotiations were working. He and his team had gotten a steady stream of people out of Mount Carmel safely. But Noesner also knew that Rogers and Jamar wouldn't react well to Koresh's backing out of the planned surrender deal. When Noesner walked into Jamar's office, Rogers was already there. Both Jamar and Rogers looked enraged at hearing the news, as Noesner recounted it:

> "This joker is screwing with us," Rogers said. "It's time to teach him a lesson."
>
> "I don't think that's going to advance our cause," I said. "It doesn't matter if Koresh is jerking us around. The point is, we're getting people out of there."
>
> "My people can get in there and secure that place in fifteen minutes," Rogers said.
>
> "Still too soon for that," Jamar said. "But I agree it's time to teach him a lesson."

Noesner's pleas for patience fell on deaf ears. "When Koresh reneged on that promise to surrender," he told me, "it didn't affect the negotiation team as much as others, because we understood that there's a potential for people not doing what they said they would. But the on-scene commander—I wish I had a videotape of when I told him that."

In a show of power, Jamar ordered armored Bradley vehicles to advance onto the compound property. From that point on, the negotiation team and the HRT were increasingly at odds with each other. HRT agents didn't seem fully aware of the negotiators' ongoing strategy. Noesner offered to brief members of the HRT after their shifts ended, but Rogers said no. Noesner proposed that he, Jamar, and Rogers have regular face-to-face meetings to coordinate strategy. Jamar didn't feel a need for that.

On March 3 and 4, two more children were released, followed by another on March 5. To personalize themselves, Noesner and the other primary negotiators who had spoken to Koresh sent in a videotape of themselves. In it, they each held up photographs of their families. On March 8, the ninth day of the standoff, Koresh replied with his own videotape, including footage of his wife Rachel and a number of his kids. The negotiators again seemed to be making progress, yet that very night, Jamar had turned off all the electrical power going into Mount Carmel. Noesner had just helped arrange for fresh milk to be delivered to the compound, and Schneider questioned why the power had been turned off. How were they now supposed to keep the milk cold? Noesner went to Jamar, who replied that there was nothing inconsistent about cutting the power.

At one point, on March 11, Jamar visited the negotiation room to discuss the capabilities of the M1 Abrams tanks the FBI had ordered. He seemed excited that the M1 could drive straight through Mount Carmel without stopping. The negotiation team was speechless, but an all-too-predictable pattern was now established. The negotiators would build rapport and arrange the safe exit of more people, and then their colleagues would undercut them. Rogers aimed high-power lights at the compound. Strange sounds were blasted from loudspeakers: dying rabbits, Tibetan chants, and Nancy Sinatra's "These Boots Are Made for Walking." Noesner had protested the plan, and Jamar had assured him that he'd stop it from going forward. But that didn't happen.

The bright lights and blaring noises made the nightly news. Why didn't Jamar make sure it stopped? Another special agent in charge who was helping Rogers apparently had nothing better to do during the night shift than to harass the Davidians. It took Noesner several more nights before he finally convinced Jamar to shut down the needlessly confrontational antics.

Despite the provocations, the procession of Branch Davidians leaving the compound continued. Two left on March 19, and seven more followed on the twenty-first. That same day, the HRT conducted "clearing operations" around the compound, crushing a gorgeous restored red Chevy Ranchero. Additional clearing operations were carried out days later. Schneider asked Noesner's team why this was happening, as the Davidians had been cooperating so dependably. The team had no satisfying answer.

On March 25, after twenty-six days, Noesner was rotated off as head of the negotiation team. No Davidians would leave Mount Carmel after his departure.

—

F. SCOTT FITZGERALD once wrote that the "test of a first-rate intelligence is the ability to hold two opposed ideas in mind at the same time, and still retain the ability to function." David Koresh, as Noesner recognized, was of two minds about surrendering. But Fitzgerald's quote better highlights the failures of Dick Rogers and Jeff Jamar.

The Waco siege turned catastrophic when Koresh promised to surrender and didn't. From that point on, Rogers and Jamar decided that Koresh couldn't be trusted. When confronted with a special form of ambiguity—someone else's ambivalence—they latched on to the easiest explanation they could find, namely, that Koresh was toying with them. Just as Israel's Zeira and Bandman denied critical counterevidence leading up to the Yom Kippur War, Rogers and Jamar obliterated the instability of Koresh's intention. Koresh both wanted to leave the compound and wanted to stay, Noesner knew. The negotiator didn't presume to have a fix on Koresh's motivations or beliefs, and told him so directly when they spoke: "I wouldn't begin to pretend to know everything that's in your mind and in your heart, David." Noesner knew that Koresh's plans were in flux, while Rogers and Jamar fixated on a snapshot. They picked out a fleeting moment in time and decided to treat an unstable and changeable intention as a stable, hidden one. There was no unequivocal answer to the question of what Koresh wanted. Like many hostage takers, he was caught in a situation that he didn't know quite how to get out of.

"My experience suggests," Noesner told me, "that in the overwhelming majority of these cases, people are confused and ambivalent. Part of them wants to die, part of them wants to live. Part of them wants to surrender, part of them doesn't want to surrender. And what I've found is that police officers and military people tend to want to say this person is a bad person, and therefore everything they do, everything they say, is bad and not believable. They assume the person has a specific purpose and manipulation in mind."

Rogers and Jamar felt that Koresh reversed his offer to surrender because he was intentionally "screwing" with them. Yet the reality was subtler than what the two FBI men believed. The Davidians had, after all, been fully prepared to exit, and even Steve Schneider seemed to believe that Koresh was on the verge of surrendering.

Noesner never claimed that Rogers and Jamar wanted to see anyone hurt or that they were somehow hell-bent on vengeance. He doesn't believe that. He just thinks that they saw the world too simply—that they were "black-and-white guys." They didn't know how to deal with ambiguity. Thinking about ambivalence, it turns out, causes a form of cognitive dissonance and risks the same pit-falls. Recent experiments looking directly at ambivalence showed that subjects who were made to think about contradicting opinions exhibited the same behaviors that we saw in Travis Proulx's research: people saw more patterns in obscure pictures, even where no pat-terns existed, and expressed their beliefs more fervently.

Good negotiators appreciate the role of ambivalence and can resist drawing conclusions from contradictory information. Like Noesner, they all have a quality of character that the poet John Keats made famous:

> At once it struck me, what quality went to form a Man of Achievement especially in Literature & which Shakespeare possessed so enormously—I mean *Negative Capability*, that is when a man is capable of being in uncertainties, Mysteries, doubts, without any irritable reaching after fact & reason.

Having negative capability means having a low need for closure, even in stressful situations. It's not the same as being indecisive. Negative capability just means not fixating or clutching on one aspect of a complex and shifting reality. It's a special form of restraint. As Jona-than Shay emphasized in *Achilles in Vietnam*, when discussing ber-serkers in combat: "Restraint is always in part the cognitive attention to multiple possibilities in a situation; when all restraint is lost, the cognitive universe is simplified to a single focus."

Jamar and Rogers couldn't cope with the uncertainties inherent in the Waco situation. When briefing the newly appointed attorney general, Janet Reno, during the siege, they made the same mistake that Major-General Zeira made when reporting to Israeli policy-makers. They didn't present the full, messy picture. They presented evidence that supported their preconceived appraisals. Jamar brought Rogers to the briefing but brought no one from the negotiation team.

Their presentation emphasized the allegations of sexual abuse—even though there was no evidence that such abuse was ongoing—and the need to act immediately.

Shown a one-sided picture, Reno approved a plan for tear gas. "Maybe the biggest disappointment," Noesner said of Waco, "was my failure to convince the bosses." Even though negotiations had been working, that somehow wasn't enough.

After the fact, the US government tried to learn from the Waco debacle. Former Missouri senator John Danforth would eventually be appointed to look into the causes of the fire that enveloped the compound. His report ultimately cleared the government of wrongdoing. Rogers was replaced as the head of the HRT. He would testify unapologetically that "had our crystal ball been working that day, there would not have been an insertion of gas into that compound." Reno called the approval of tear gas the most difficult decision she had ever made but declined to condemn the FBI briefings on which she had based it. Throughout Noesner's remarkable and distinguished career, he would continue to preach the benefits of patient, low-emotion negotiating, an approach that even today is underappreciated, he says.

In the spring of 1996, the FBI had a chance to prove what it had learned from Waco. A radical militia group known as the Freemen had settled on a group of ranches outside Jordan, Montana. Continually provoking local law enforcement, the Freemen claimed that the US government had no authority over them. They didn't pay taxes or get driver's licenses. They decided to commit financial, mail, and wire fraud and had threatened a federal judge. When an ABC news team arrived to interview the group, the Freemen pulled out guns and stole the reporters' camera equipment.

The FBI was able to draw out into the open two of the group's leaders, LeRoy Schweitzer and Dan Petersen, and arrest them. "You watch, folks—when it goes, it'll be worse than Waco," Petersen yelled out to reporters at his bail hearing. He was wrong. Dick Rogers's replacement, Roger Nisley, worked well with the negotiation team. Local cops helped the FBI set up a loose perimeter. FBI agents at the scene wore casual work clothes, not menacing combat gear. As Michel Thomas did in his classrooms, the agents lowered the overall pressure. Using third-person intermediaries, trust building, time, and patience, the agents wrapped up the whole thing eighty-one days later—after the longest siege in US history—with the Freemen's surrender. Not one bullet was fired.

⁓

MANAGING OUR DANGEROUS but natural urge to demolish ambiguous evidence or deny ambivalent intentions isn't easy. But it is possible. A good first step is to acknowledge that ambivalence is a far more common state of mind than most people assume. In a 2005 book on political ambivalence, psychologists Christopher Armitage and Mark Conner pointed out that "most people are not strongly committed to a specific ideology, meaning in principle they are open to messages advocating opposite sides of any given issue." High-pressure situations can make dealing with someone else's ambivalence more unpleasant, but that doesn't make ambivalence less real. Higher-ups can also make sure that people with a low tolerance for disorder aren't the ones calling the shots during acute or prolonged crises. The need-for-closure scale can be used as a personality assessment to identify people who might be most vulnerable to stressful situations.*

---

* To give you an idea of how gracious Gary Noesner is, he agreed to try his hand at the shortened need for closure scale we saw earlier. His rankings, in order, were as follows: 1, 1, 3, 1, 1, 1, 1, 1, 1, 2, 2, 1, 1, 2, 1. Do the math, and you'll see that his total comes out to 20. That's 5 points higher than the lowest possible score.

The special form of restraint Noesner exemplifies is not how we normally think about willpower. Nor does it have to do with delaying gratification. We can't really ascribe this type of restraint to confidence, either. Confidence can actually be a bad thing when it comes to confronting contradictions. People with a higher need for closure, like Zeira and Bandman, tend to be the most confident and report the least fear of being wrong. They're also the least likely to interpret behavior in multiple ways or to look at things from different angles. Remarkably, a person's innate need for closure also has no relationship to IQ. Restraint in the face of uncertainty is a hugely important variable in learning, and it's completely missed by common measures of intelligence. In discussing his related theory of open- and closed-mindedness, social psychologist Milton Rokeach noted how paradoxical this disparity was. "It seems," he complained, "that we *are* dealing here with intelligence, although not with the kind of intelligence measured by current intelligence tests." For Rokeach, the problem lay with IQ tests.

Beyond hiring more people like Noesner, organizations can, as we saw, also create a culture that respects ambiguity. At the right moments, organizations can underscore the consequences of bad decisions. Another critical step applies more broadly to high-pressure circumstances: crises require systematically imagining a variety of explanations and outcomes. That's what's behind the concept of red teaming in the intelligence world. When Central Intelligence Agency (CIA) analysts thought they'd pinpointed Osama bin Laden in Abbottabad, a different team of analysts was tasked with thinking up all of the reasons why it was someone *else* pacing in the garden. For this process to work, however, institutions must take it seriously and not simply go through the motions.

That's exactly what didn't happen at Waco. Noesner was never properly incorporated into the decision-making process. And that's why, on the morning of April 19, armored vehicles punctured the walls of the Mount Carmel Center and tear gas was pumped into the compound. That's why FBI covert listening devices recorded, over the course of that morning, these ominous phrases:

"Pablo, have you poured it yet?"

"You got to get the fuel ready."

"The fuel has to go all around to get started."

"Give me the match."

"Is it lit?"

"Let's keep that fire going."

FIVE

Overtested USA

WHEN TO RESIST MOMENTUM

IN LATE JUNE 2004, a fifty-two-year-old woman with short auburn hair and glasses noticed a lump on her torso. Her name was Trisha Torrey, and she was living in Baldwinsville, New York, north of Syracuse, running her own marketing company. The lump she discovered was about the size of a golf ball, firm, but not painful. Torrey's doctor couldn't be sure what it was without a test. So he referred her to a surgeon, who removed the lump that same afternoon and sent the tissue off for analysis.

One week passed. When Torrey still hadn't heard back about the results, she called the surgeon herself to check. The delay, he told her, was due to the long Fourth of July weekend. The lab doing the analysis was short-staffed. So Torrey waited some more, another week, until the surgeon finally called with the results. He delivered bad news. Apparently she had a very rare cancer called subcutaneous panniculitis-like T-cell lymphoma. Known as SPTCL, this particular cancer is so rare that the lab had ordered that the results be confirmed at a second lab. The doctor promised to make an oncol-

ogy appointment for her as soon as possible. She would need chemotherapy.

Torrey hung up the phone. She tried, as one does in vain at moments like these, to wrap her mind around what the diagnosis meant.
From what she was able to learn online, SPTCL was a death sentence. Her oncologist, Dr. Weiss (not his real name), was straightforward and frighteningly blunt. Without chemotherapy, he said, she
wouldn't make it to the end of the year. He sent Torrey off for a CT
scan and blood work. The results were negative. Still, he insisted that
the positive results from the previous lab tests trumped these newer
results. Besides, he told her, her records indicated that she had hot
flashes and night sweats, and hot flashes and night sweats are classic
signs of lymphoma. "But I'm fifty-two!" she protested. "At fifty-two,
all women have night sweats and hot flashes!" Weiss assured her that
her symptoms were unrelated to menopause.

She didn't tell many people about her diagnosis at first. Although
she had health insurance, it didn't fully cover all the doctor visits
and tests that she would need. She felt, moreover, that the diagnosis didn't make any sense. She was playing golf regularly. She felt
perfectly healthy. Was she in denial? Torrey put off treatment for
a few weeks. But she was spending so much time worrying that her
marketing business was suffering. August came, and she had to make
a final decision about chemotherapy. By that time, Weiss had taken
sick and his partner (let's call him Dr. Bateman) had taken over Torrey's case. He pressed her to start treatment at once.

Several days after her run-in with Bateman, Torrey was out with
a few business acquaintances. "I had way too much to drink," she
recalled. Tipsy, she told them about her diagnosis and her search
for a second opinion. One of her dinner companions happened to
have an oncologist friend who, it would emerge the next day, was
already treating someone with SPTCL. (Weiss and Bateman had

never treated such a patient before.) Torrey's friend helped her set up an appointment the following week. To speed things along and avoid any delays in transferring the paperwork, Torrey asked Weiss and Bateman's office for her medical records.

She picked up her records and waited for her new appointment. Then Torrey did something that most patients rarely do. She decided to carefully analyze her results. Page by page, she read through the records. She researched new medical terms and learned how to google Greek letters. When she looked closely at the two lab reports that led to her diagnosis, she noticed that neither seemed definitive. "One of the lab reports," she told me, "said 'most suspicious for,' and the other one said 'most consistent with.'" Were these hedges simply the way that the labs protected themselves against lawsuits? Or did they imply a very real uncertainty?

Torrey's new oncologist sent the biopsy tissue to Elaine Jaffe, a highly respected pathologist at the National Cancer Institute. On September 20, 2004, at a little before noon—halfway into her supposedly remaining six months—Torrey received a fax with the results. "I was standing right there at my fax machine," she said. "I didn't even understand it at first. It didn't say, you don't have SPTCL, which is what I expected. It said, basically, that there was no sign of malignancy." She didn't have cancer.

Her misdiagnosis would end up unexpectedly changing her life. For years afterward, she suffered from symptoms of post-traumatic stress disorder (PTSD). She would break down in tears at odd moments, sometimes after a mere mention of cancer on the evening news, other times while watching a movie character face a completely unrelated hardship. One fact in particular was hard to shake: the misdiagnosis had almost not been caught at all. She would have gone through chemotherapy and lost her hair. She would have gotten sick from the chemo, lost weight from not eating, and aged more rapidly. And—this was the most infuriating thought of all—had she survived the treatment, her doctors would have told her that she was now cancer free, all thanks to them.

After doing some research online, Torrey discovered that what might have happened to her *had* actually happened to others. In one heartbreaking case, a woman had died from her chemotherapy, only to have her husband learn, from a private autopsy, that she had never had cancer in the first place.

MISDIAGNOSES ARE DISMAYINGLY common. As symptoms can be ambiguous, important clues are too often missed or ignored. Delayed, botched, and missed diagnoses can affect 10 to 20 percent of cases. Every year, there are between forty thousand and eighty thousand preventable deaths in the United States from missed diagnoses alone, by one estimate. Given the faith we put in modern medicine, the numbers can feel a little bewildering. A 2014 study found that one in five breast cancers discovered by mammography and treated wasn't actually a health threat. In another study, pathologists identifying tissue samples as either normal, cancerous, or precancerous got it wrong up to nearly 12 percent of the time. In yet another study, radiologists judging chest X-rays disagreed with one another 20 percent of the time. Worse, when one of the radiologists reexamined the same X-rays later on, he contradicted *himself* up to 10 percent of the time. E. James Potchen, the study's author, wrote that observers tend to have "a characteristic way in which they manage the threshold of uncertainty in making decisions." Most disturbingly, some of the most poorly performing observers were also the most confident.

There's even evidence that doctors' diagnostic accuracy rates haven't improved in some areas of medicine. In the 1980s, researchers at Boston's Brigham and Women's Hospital compared missed diagnoses discovered in autopsies before the invention of ultrasound, CT, and radionuclide scanning. The researchers found that these new technologies hadn't seemed to improve matters. Whatever the decade—the 1960s, 1970s, or 1980s—about 10 percent of the time, physicians still missed major diagnoses that, if caught, could have prolonged patients' lives. Another 12 percent of the time, they missed diagnoses that wouldn't have changed the prescribed treatment. In 1996, in another study of autopsies, Wilhelm Kirch and Christine Schafii looked at diagnostic errors in 1959, 1969, 1979, and 1989. They found that misdiagnoses held steady at between 7 and 12 percent of cases over that time, and that false negatives (where the autopsy discovered a previously unknown diagnosis) remained between 22 and 34 percent. Autopsies aren't performed randomly among all deaths, of course, and our tools to detect mistakes have improved over time. But these are still startling numbers. In another sample of patients, the use of CT scans or ultrasound to diagnose appendicitis increased from under 10 percent at the start of the 1980s to over 30 percent at the end of the 1990s. But the rate of misdiagnosed cases held steady at around 15 percent.

Given the progress in medical science, how could doctors still be making so many mistakes? For one, doctors have to cope with an increasingly overwhelming amount of information. We have more knowledge and tools than ever before, and the challenge now is to develop systems to manage the complexity and uncertainty that this new knowledge brings. A related problem is that it's not always clear in precisely which circumstances a particular treatment is appropriate or not, as adequate research may not exist. As medical researcher David Naylor once put it, while it would be simpler if new technologies were "always appraised in rigorous studies . . . current data are often insufficient to guide practice." Combine technologies, Naylor pointed out, and the result is a "Malthusian growth of uncertainty." Two technologies can be used together to treat a patient in 2 different sequences. But five technologies can be used in 120 sequences. The surgeon and author Atul Gawande summed up the broader issue in 2002:

> The core predicament of medicine—the thing that makes being a patient so wrenching, being a doctor so difficult, and being a part of a society that pays the bills they run up so vexing—is uncertainty. With all that we know nowadays about people and diseases and how to diagnose and treat them, it can be hard to see this, hard to grasp how deeply uncertainty runs. As a doctor, you come to find, however, that the struggle in caring for people is more often with what you do not know than what you do. Medicine's ground state is uncertainty. And wisdom—for both patients and doctors—is defined by how one copes with it.

And yet, as professors of medicine Vera Luther and Sonia Crandall pointed out in 2011, "the culture of medicine has little tolerance for ambiguity and uncertainty." As others have, Luther and Crandall argued that ambiguity deserves a special place in medical education, for the simple reason that it causes "significant anxiety, frustration, disillusionment, self-doubt, and feelings of inadequacy." Even doctors don't like to think of themselves as artists who must improvise a fabric from ambiguous threads. It's more comforting for all of us to conceptualize medical practice as akin to repairing watches. Yet in reality, its certainties represent, to borrow a phrase from theorist Donald Schön, a "high, hard ground overlooking a swamp."

In a 2011 book on overdiagnosis, Gilbert Welch, Lisa Schwartz, and Steven Woloshin used the analogy of car warning lights to describe another dilemma of new medical technologies. Welch's first car, a '65 Ford Fairlane wagon, had only two engine sensors: oil pressure and temperature. But his '99 Volvo was another creature entirely. It was filled with diagnostic electronics. The only problem was, the warning lights didn't work perfectly. One told him that something was wrong with his coolant system every time it hit a big bump. There was even one that went off if another sensor wasn't sensing properly. His mechanic confessed that most of the lights should be ignored. As diagnostic technology grows more sensitive, the point was, our modern medical testing regime has more and more in common with Welch's Volvo—and the problems are proliferating.

———

TRISHA TORREY PENNED a letter to the thirteen doctors involved in her misdiagnosis. The letter was ten pages long by the time she was finished. She detailed what each doctor's role had been in her misdiagnosis and how it had affected her. Part of the problem, she suspected, was old-fashioned greed. In the United States, one of the only medical specialties that allows physicians to personally sell drugs to patients is oncology. That's one reason why so many oncologists have their own infusion centers. Torrey felt that Weiss and Bateman's certainty was motivated at least in part by the bottom line.

By the end of 2004, Torrey had grown passionate about the state of health care in the United States. She had read news article upon news article. She discovered an Institute of Medicine report indicating that as many as ninety-eight thousand Americans die each year because of medical errors. She began blogging on medical issues. She would read some news item and share her point of view. At one point, she even detailed her own story. The *Syracuse Post-Standard* came across it and ran a story about her. Before long, she was being asked to speak to the pharmaceutical industry about the patient's perspective. She became part of what's called the empowered-patient movement, helping others navigate their own health-care crises. The issue, she told me, is that "no one has ever expected us, nor helped us, to learn the skills to get the best out of the system."

The patient empowerment movement represented a seismic shift in the patient-doctor relationship. Through the 1970s and into the 1980s, most patients tended to regard doctors as ultimate authorities. People didn't question doctors' instructions, but simply followed directives. Doctors sometimes wouldn't inform patients of what the diagnosis was or even what drugs had been given. Patients didn't have access to their own medical records. In a 1984 landmark book, *The Silent World of Doctor and Patient*, Jay Katz emphasized how unethical it could be to leave patients out of medical decision making. By the 1990s, medical schools had begun training doctors to respect patient autonomy. When the Internet exploded, patients had ready access to medical information for the first time. By 2005, according to one poll, roughly half of the patients diagnosed with cancer were presented by their doctors with multiple treatment options. A third of those patients made the treatment decision themselves. In general, it has been a valuable shift. Informed patients do often have a better chance of making the right decisions in light of their particular circumstances. But the patient empowerment movement has also complicated the medical decisions currently facing both doctors and their patients.

Now patients, in addition to doctors, have to be aware of how ambiguity can undermine rational analysis. About two-thirds of primary care patients show up at their doctors' offices at some point with symptoms that remain inexplicable or ambiguous even after examination and testing. Patients who describe unclear symptoms to their physicians, as you might guess, can strain the patient-doctor relationship. One of the most telling experiments on the issue was published in 2005 by a group led by the University of Rochester's David Seaburn. Seaburn and his colleagues wanted to see how primary care physicians treated patients who reported medically confusing symptoms. Using detailed scripts and multiple test interviews, the researchers trained actors to describe specific symptoms. The researchers then recruited a group of local physicians and arranged for two different actor confederates to visit the doctors' practices unannounced. The visits were secretly audio-recorded.

Each physician saw one patient, either a man or a woman, who described the classic symptoms of gastroesophageal reflux. The first "patient" told the doctors that they suffered chest pains at night. They said that antacids helped a little bit and that different foods affected the pain in various ways. The second patient each physician saw described the symptoms unclearly: some emotional stress, dizziness, fatigue, and chest pains that were recounted in rather mysterious language. Seaburn and his colleagues transcribed these patient-doctor encounters and then categorized the interactions.

Clear patterns emerged from the twenty-three interviews with the second, ambiguous patient. Twenty-two percent of the time, the physicians simply ignored the ambiguity. For instance, after a patient described "vague symptoms of general chest pain," the doctor would respond with a statement of "fact": "Your pain is caused by gastroesophageal reflux." The researchers who later analyzed the interactions described most of these visits as "physician driven." The doctor was in charge, and the patient wasn't invited to offer much input. The patient was passive—the opposite of empowered.

But Seaburn's study revealed another troubling issue. Many of these doctors weren't just ignoring the ambiguous symptoms; 77 percent of the time, they *acknowledged* that the symptoms were unclear, only to follow up with a directive. For instance, in a sample dialogue provided in Seaburn's study:

Patient: What do you think this is?

Doctor B: I'm not sure what's causing the pain, so I think we should do an endoscopy to see if there is an ulcer or a tumor.

Ordering a test to get further information wouldn't be especially worrying, except for one small, incriminating detail. In only three instances did the physicians attempt to pry additional information from the patients who described the vague symptoms. Only three times out of twenty-three visits did the physicians continue prompting the patient to clarify the symptoms.

Ordering a test provided an escape from thinking about ambiguity. Tests, at least in this study, provided doctors an all-too-easy retreat from puzzling further over the patient's problems. In her book *Every Patient Tells a Story*, Lisa Sanders confirmed this premature rush toward closure: "By far the most common diagnostic error in medicine is premature closure—when a physician stops seeking a diagnosis after finding one that explains most of or even all the key findings, without asking . . . what else could this be?" When technology enters the picture, as Seaburn's experiment implies, the dilemma grows more vexing.

———

IN 2011, THE *New York Times* reported on a clever quasi-experiment run by James Andrews, a famous sports medicine orthopedist. Andrews has treated the likes of Drew Brees, Peyton Manning, Emmitt Smith, Charles Barkley, Michael Jordan, Roger Clemens, and Jack Nicklaus. Thinking that MRI scans might be giving doctors misleading results, Andrews took a group of thirty-one professional baseball players, all pitchers, and gave them MRIs. In twenty-seven of those pitchers, the MRI revealed abnormal rotator cuff damage. Twenty-eight of the pitchers showed abnormal shoulder cartilage. The problem was that the pitchers were all healthy. Andrews had deliberately selected players who weren't injured and hadn't reported any pain. It turns out that MRIs are extraordinarily good at detecting abnormalities but not always very good at revealing whether those abnormalities actually pose a problem.

"If you want an excuse to operate on a pitcher's throwing shoulder, just get an MRI," Andrews said. The story pointed to a critical downside of highly sensitive diagnostic tests. Pitchers, like all of us, have various physical flaws. But although the majority of these flaws are completely benign, the test's hyperactive warning lights go off.

Patients are practically drowning in diagnostic tests. And yet in too many cases, the results simply don't justify the rising number of CT, MRI, and PET imaging tests. In her 2007 book *Overtreated*, health policy expert Shannon Brownlee (and my colleague at New America) argued that "for every scan that helps a physician come to the right decision, another scan may cloud the picture, sending the doctor down the wrong path."

Seaburn and his colleagues showed that ordering a test can be a cheap response to unclear symptoms, providing a false sense of short-term closure. But if the test results are themselves unclear—if the warning lights aren't always working—couldn't that help propel a never-ending cycle of testing? A 2013 experiment run by Sunita Sah, Pierre Elias, and Dan Ariely suggests it could.

Sah speculated that ambiguous test results might lead doctors to order another test. In the case of the prostate-specific antigen (PSA) test for prostate cancer, she wondered, could an inconclusive result lead to another, more risky, test? Sah, Elias, and Ariely recruited a group of over seven hundred men between the ages of forty and seventy-five and randomly assigned them to one of four experimental conditions. The first group received information about the risks and benefits of a prostate biopsy. Then they were asked whether they would have a biopsy and how certain they were about their decision. The other three groups read about the risks and benefits of biopsies, too, but they also received background on the PSA screening test (which informs the decision of whether to have a biopsy) and were asked to imagine one of three PSA results: normal, elevated, or inconclusive. An inconclusive test result, subjects were informed, "provides no information about whether or not you have cancer." The men then had to decide whether they would proceed with the hypothetical prostate biopsy.

In theory, an inconclusive PSA result shouldn't make someone more or less likely to proceed with a risky biopsy. But that's not what Sah and her colleagues found. Only 25 percent of subjects who weren't given PSA screening results chose to proceed with the prostate biopsy. But 40 percent of subjects who received inconclusive PSA test results opted for the procedure. That's a fairly large increase among those who received a result clearly explaining that it "provides no information." Somehow, the very idea of not knowing something led to a panicky commitment to more invasive testing.

Since prostate biopsies are not only risky but also costly, the increased call for the biopsy is not insignificant. Sah described the problem as one of "investigation momentum." In this and other analogous cases, we commit to an investigative course of action and receive ambiguous results, and since we're especially averse to ambiguity under stress, we proceed with riskier diagnostic testing in the hopes of finding clear, anxiety-reducing answers.

Self-propelling momentum, Sah told me, results in "additional, potentially excessive diagnostic testing when you get a result that's ambiguous." She doesn't deny that there are many other causes of overtesting in the United States. The financial incentives involved are obviously a mammoth issue, as is *defensive medicine*, where doctors treat patients to avoid potential lawsuits. But one important and overlooked cause, Sah said, is the self-propelling cascade of tests encouraged because of inconclusive results, ambiguity aversion, and a disproportionate faith in testing. To the same point, in 2013 Deborah Grady cited evidence that in a US Department of Veteran Affairs (VA) medical center, the use of myocardial perfusion scans was inappropriate in about 20 percent of cases. That's roughly the same rate as in other practices. But Grady, an editor at *JAMA Internal Medicine* (formerly *Archives of Internal Medicine*), was pointing out that VA physicians are on salary and malpractice suits are rare. The matching rates imply that overtesting has deeper roots than financial incentives or defensive medicine.

In the past several years, medical journals have increasingly reported on instances where inconclusive test results led to additional risky tests or treatments. In one case, a man in his fifties with mild asthma needed hernia surgery. A preoperative evaluation came back normal, but as an extra precaution for a man of his age with asthma, a chest X-ray was ordered. It revealed a seven-millimeter *nodule*, a tiny mass of tissue, in the lung, which led a radiologist to order a CT scan. The lung nodule didn't show up on the CT scan, but the scan revealed a different nodule in the man's right adrenal gland. The radiologist then ordered another CT scan that was specifically focused on this area. The adrenal CT scan showed that the nodule was nothing to worry about. By the time he had his surgery, the man had endured the pain of a hernia for an extra six months, not to mention the worry that he might have cancer. What makes his case even worse is that the value of the first chest X-ray for patients fitting his profile has never been established. Yet the test spawned two additional tests, perfectly illustrating Sah, Elias, and Ariely's concept of investigation momentum.

MEDICAL PROFESSIONALS ARE aware of the overtesting problem and its various causes and are working to correct it. Roughly $200 billion may be wasted in the United States annually on overtreatment, by one recent estimate. In a 2014 survey of physicians, 73 percent said that unnecessary tests and procedures are a serious health-care issue. Asked why they might occasionally make the mistake themselves, 36 percent said it was "just to be safe." To be sure, medical uncertainties are especially emotional. The stakes are high, and we all know of situations in which persistent advocacy has paid off. The instinct to test "just in case" can't and shouldn't be entirely demonized. But we need a clearer weighing of risk and reward and a better balance between caring and overtreatment.

Leading the way, in 2010 *JAMA Internal Medicine* began running a series called Less Is More, detailing precisely when reducing medical care can have better health outcomes. The editors singled out diagnostic testing as one critical problem area. They know that abnormal but ultimately harmless findings on one test can lead to more testing and that every additional test or procedure imposes a psychological burden and carries a risk, often from complications or by exposing patients to radiation. As they put it in 2011, "no test (not even a non-invasive one) is benign, and often less is more."

The difficulty of helping doctors make smarter choices also speaks to the limitations of patient empowerment. If well-meaning and pure-hearted doctors struggle with when and how to apply certain tests, how can we possibly expect patients to do better? Even Trisha Torrey, by 2007, had begun to see the drawbacks of the movement. She had met several people who told her that they wanted to take more control over their health care, but that they were too sick to do it themselves. In many cases, patients who would have benefited the most from learning how to better navigate the system hadn't had the time or resources for it. And many patients aren't in the right psychological state to take full responsibility for their health-care decisions.

Beyond spreading awareness of how ambiguity can interfere with effective diagnosis and treatment, the simplest—not to say the easiest—answer is to provide the right resources to both patients and doctors. In Minnesota, for example, the cooperative HealthPartners noticed annual 15 to 18 percent increases in MRI and CT scans. So they started a program in which the national radiology guidelines appear on patients' electronic medical records every time a doctor orders a scan. After two years and change, the program had helped avoid an estimated 20,000 unnecessary tests and saved $14 million. Ratcheting up its less-is-more approach, *JAMA Internal Medicine* published top-five lists from the National Physicians Alliance, highlighting the key areas in which care could be markedly improved by less intervention. The lists are available online and often propose surprising don'ts. For instance, did you know that kids shouldn't take cough and cold medications? There's apparently little evidence that these over-the-counter medications reduce a cough or even shorten the duration of a cold. Yet one in ten American children takes these medications weekly. Initiatives like these are adding critical lessons that we, as a society, have already begun to acknowledge: that frequent mammograms aren't always needed, for instance, or that the dangers of certain drugs can outweigh their benefits.

Other recommendations speak directly to the epidemic of overtesting: don't automatically order diagnostic scans for kids' minor head injuries, don't order Pap tests for women under twenty-one years old, don't order annual electrocardiograms for patients with low risk for coronary heart disease, and unless there are red flags, don't do imaging for lower back pain within the first six weeks. The

ABIM Foundation, a nonprofit established by the American Board of Internal Medicine, set up a campaign called Choosing Wisely. The campaign asks various medical specialty societies to contribute top-five lists of things physicians and patients should question. So far, over sixty-five societies have helped identify more than 325 overused tests and procedures.

These efforts have been so successful that the Canadian Medical Association launched Choosing Wisely Canada in the spring of 2014. They've emphasized that the choice of fewer tests isn't about rationing. Rather, it's about the need to challenge the more-is-better mantra—about recognizing that despite technological advances, ordering tests isn't always the best way to resolve a problem. Far too often, tests are a harmful crutch. In 2013, one study of resident doctors revealed that computers garnered over three times more face time than patients did. Yet many diagnoses can be made simply by talking. As tempting as technological "certainty" feels, it's usually wiser to treat the patient instead of the scan.

———

MEDICINE IS NOT the only area in which new technologies appear to provide shortcuts out of uncertainty. Emerging technologies are often hailed as cure-alls, especially in the "developing" world. The One Laptop per Child program, which has distributed over two million laptops in thirty-six countries, provides an extreme example. It's comforting to presume that access to information (as opposed to deeply entrenched weaknesses in state institutions) is the primary barrier to empowering children who grow up in poor countries. A study of the program showed that while Peruvian students given laptops showed some improvements in general cognitive skills, they didn't attend classes at higher rates, spend more time on schoolwork, or improve their math and language skills. Similarly, the promise of free online education through MOOCs (massive online open courses) has been held up as a tool for social advancement. But for all antipoverty programs and social work, there are never any silver bullets.

Health-care technologies, especially imaging technologies, may be particularly tempting solutions to medical dilemmas because they promise to let us see previously hidden parts of the human body. We feel as though we've finally discovered a window into how things work, regardless of how blurry the picture is. But (despite the car warning lights analogy I borrowed earlier) the body and mind are not machines that we can simply hook up to a computer to determine what's wrong. Neither strictly follows the simple cause-and-effect rules of car parts.

The machine analogy has also led to serious problems in another field harnessing new technologies. *Neurolaw* applies brain imaging to criminal law. Neuroimaging evidence showing brain abnormalities has helped spare murderers from the death penalty. Evidence from neuroscience, according to a database created by Nita Farahany, of Duke University School of Law, was considered in at least 1,600 cases between 2004 and 2012. One San Diego defense attorney even boasted of introducing a PET scan as evidence of his client's moral innocence: "This nice color image we could enlarge. . . . It documented that this guy had a rotten spot in his brain. The jury glommed onto that."

Without question, scientists are learning a great deal using brain scans. We've covered some of their breakthroughs in this book. But images of the brain, like those of the rest of the body, do not always imply one-to-one causal relationships. Like lung nodules, brain abnormalities don't mean that anything is necessarily wrong. In a history of neurolaw, the University of Maryland's Amanda Pustilnik compared neurolaw to phrenology, Cesare Lombroso's biological criminology, and psychosurgery. Each theory or practice, Pustilnik wrote, "started out with a pre-commitment to the idea of brain localization of violence." But the causes of violence, like the causes of poor health, do not usually begin in the body. They pass through it, and the marks they leave are often subtle and vague.

James Fallon, a neuroscientist at the University of California at Irvine, has studied the brain scans of psychopathic murderers. He is skeptical of applying brain scans to criminal cases. "Neuroimaging isn't ready for prime time," he told me. "There are simply too many nuances in interpreting the scans." In an odd twist of fate, Fallon once subjected himself to a PET scan because his lab needed images of normal brains to contrast with abnormal ones. To his surprise, his prefrontal lobe scan looked the same as those of the psychopathic killers he'd long studied. The irony wasn't lost on him. That Fallon never hurt anyone isn't the core of the problem; it's that one nonviolent person's scan looked no different from a violent person's.

No one can blame doctors, scientists, or policymakers for their enthusiasm and excitement over new technological tools. But our new ways of seeing aren't necessarily clearer ways of seeing, and sometimes, the illusion of knowing is more dangerous than not knowing at all.

———

IN APRIL 2013, Trisha Torrey found another mysterious golf-ball-size lump. This one was low on her back hip, below the skin. It was round and hard as a stone, but this time the growth was painful, perhaps because of its proximity to more sensitive nerves and muscles. For a short period, for the first time in years, her PTSD symptoms reappeared, and panic set in. Then she reminded herself how much she'd changed since the first time around. If it wasn't cancer the last time, why should it be this time?

Torrey now had a different primary care doctor, Dr. Jennie Brown (actually her real name). Although a CT scan indicated that the lump probably wasn't cancerous, Brown said that small tumors can sometimes grow on the colon. She wanted to send Torrey to a general surgeon just in case.

But Torrey didn't remain passive: "I just said, 'I would rather not. Let's just see what happens if we don't do anything.'" Besides, Torrey added, "If I see a surgeon, he's just going to tell me I need surgery, right?" Brown laughed. "I can't argue with you there." Through all her experiences, Torrey has never, remarkably, received a correct diagnosis of the lumps. "No one knows," she told me. "Nobody can put a name to it." Yet she knew enough to suspect that the lump probably wasn't harmful and that it might simply go away. So instead of surgery, Torrey asked Brown whether there were any other feasible alternatives they might try out first. Brown prescribed a three-week course of antibiotics, and they waited to see what happened to the lump.

It was gone by the end of those three weeks.

SIX

The Hemline Hassle

A STRATEGY OF IGNORANCE

JOHN FAIRCHILD, THE dimpled-chin editor of *Women's Wear Daily (WWD)*, had helped turn the once-neglected pamphlet into one of the most powerful publications in fashion. Critics derided it as a "terror tabloid" and fashion's "bitchy bible," but designers knew to respect and fear its influence. *Vanity Fair* once described Fairchild as the "Citizen Kane of the fashion press." At the dawn of the 1970s, however, Fairchild was in trouble. He had risked his reputation—and that of *WWD*—by boldly predicting that 1970 would be the year of the midi, a skirt falling four inches below the knee. The months were ticking away, and Fairchild's endorsement of the midi seemed like a misplaced bet.

In London and Paris, the midi was in vogue. But in the United States, the skirt was slow to catch on, and in March 1970, *Life* magazine ran a cover article titled "The Great Hemline Hassle." The stumbling block for Fairchild and others with financial stakes in the midi was America's stubborn love of the miniskirt. "Those in the cruelest bind," *Life* noted, "are the high-volume apparel makers who must decide right now on their fall offerings, thereby running a serious risk of getting caught with their inventories down." Cautious designers were planning on devoting 5 percent of their fall collections to midi lengths. Bolder ones were thinking 40 percent or higher. By the beginning of summer, one Manhattan store, Bonwit Teller, had committed to a 95 percent midi-length inventory. Skeptical news stories didn't help, and just days after *Life*'s article, *Newsweek* followed with its own cover story on the hemline battle. It quoted midi haters like Paul Newman, who complained that it was "absolutely shameful that designers are able to get away with something like this." Arguing the other side was French president Georges Pompidou, who felt that the demure, elegant midi added "mystery to love."

Established designers claimed that the miniskirt's days were numbered. Coco Chanel was dying to bury it. She called the miniskirt "the most absurd weapon woman has ever employed to seduce men," dismissing short skirts as "indecent. An exhibition of meat." The miniskirt was popularized by the British designer Mary Quant in 1964. By 1966, the liberated length had moved from discotheques and eccentric boutiques to American offices and college campuses. Before the 1960s, young women tended to dress like their mothers. But the generation that saw Beatlemania, the first female cosmonaut, the Civil Rights Act of 1964, and the birth control pill had its own fashion preferences. Girdles disappeared, hemlines rose, vibrant colors replaced business grays, and cuts became bolder, freer, and foxier.

Outfits could now convey a sense of humor. Designers jazzed them up with snaps and zippers. For old-guard designers, these changes led to a loss in stature. Chanel wasn't alone in her disdain of the mini, which epitomized the new era and emerged, in her words, "from the street." In 1967, one top saleswoman at Bergdorf Goodman went as far as to claim that "those show-offs who wear dresses up to their bottoms know nothing about fashion." Famed designer

Norman Norell complained rather frumpishly, "Elegance is out. It's a fascinating, frustrating time to be a designer."

The question wasn't how low but rather how high hemlines might go. A poll by the Administrative Management Society found that 52 percent of firms' employees were okay with skirts two or three inches above the knee. But skirts kept rising. By the end of the decade, miniskirts were six inches higher. One designer from San Francisco explained coolly that "now there is the micromini, the micro-micro, the 'Oh My God' and the 'Hello, Officer.'" Hemlines could not be hiked any higher. Meanwhile, more women started to think of miniskirts and their "dolly bird" look as more exploitative than empowering. In an industry that craves novelty, the time seemed ripe for experimenting with lowering hemlines again. By 1970, couture designers sensed a window of opportunity.

Midi skirts didn't come out of nowhere. In the late 1960s, designers had already been experimenting with—and laying the groundwork for—a comeback of the longer lengths. One 1968 *New York Times* headline proclaimed, "Daring Now Means Mid-Calf." Husbands preferred their wives in midis, it reported, even if the same men still enjoyed minis on other women. By the fall of 1969, fashionistas like Gloria Guinness had already shifted their entire wardrobes to midi-length skirts. "What's more," Guinness added in an interview, "every smart woman in Paris is wearing her skirts midi length." Midis seemed to be replacing trouser suits, and hats might be on their way back, too, since they were needed for a complete midi outfit. The big-hair look that went with miniskirts would finally be banished. At Bonwit Teller, miniskirts were reportedly being left on the racks. Midi mania seemed ready to arrive in full force.

So in January 1970, when Fairchild proclaimed the midi, or longuette, the year's new look, he wasn't making some wild prediction. Dior, Givenchy, and Saint Laurent were lowering hemlines in their couture collections. Economic motives may also have played a role in the midi push. The economy was struggling, and fashion houses were losing profits as labor and material costs rose. If midis became must-buys, fiber producers and fabric mills could double their sales for skirts, and business on New York's Seventh Avenue might grow by over 30 percent.

In Washington, DC, midis hit stores in February. The arrival was not well timed. Spring was near, and midis had missed the chilliest winter weather. The *Washington Post* was quick to report that merchants were blaming "plunging profits on plunging hemlines." And while designers and European women were going gaga over longer lengths, Americans felt unduly pressured by the idea that miniskirts were a thing of the past. Nor did consumers look forward to replacing their entire wardrobes.

Various protest groups rebelled against what they saw as fashion dictatorship by the stuffy old guard. In Los Angeles, Juli Reding Hutner started an organization called POOFF (Preservation of Our Femininity and Finances). In a single week, membership shot to a thousand from just nineteen. "We're not going to let them pull the wool over our legs as well as our eyes," said Hutner. Bumper stickers read UP YOUR MIDI, and in Los Angeles, Mayor Sam Yorty agreed to celebrate an entire week in March as POOFF week. The group set up anti-midi petition booths outside department stores.

"We'll win by fall," Hutner predicted.

Men formed their own protest groups. Neil Kneitel, an investment banker, founded SMACK (Society of Males Who Appreciate Cute Knees). In Bellevue, Nebraska, an anti-midi rally was held at a shopping center. In New York, an International Council of Legmen rained letters on every member of Congress. Caught off guard, midi defenders blamed the media for these strange and sudden outbursts of antilonguette sentiment. Reporters who had never covered fashion before were writing about the midi-mini tug-of-war. David Frost was doing a TV show special on it. Designer Donald Brooks tried to maintain calmly that "women are ready for a change whether they realize it or not." Geoffrey Beene agreed, adding, "It's time for serious fashion."

———

IN THE LAST few chapters, we've examined how people cope with confusing experiences that have already occurred. But the future is also, of course, unclear. We have facts and data, some of which are very solid and clean, but how they'll combine to create a future scenario is often difficult to predict. Trends and emerging technologies don't usually develop according to discernable rules.

I've been using the term *uncertainty* to refer to the mind state caused by facing ambiguous information. But in forecasting, we should distinguish another cause of feelings of uncertainty: risk. Risky choices are those where the outcome isn't known but the odds of success are. Think of flipping a coin. You're certain of the probability of its landing on heads or tails, but you don't know the outcome of any particular toss. Ambiguous choices—the focus of this chapter—are those whose odds of success are unknown because the rules determining the outcome are unclear.

Daniel Ellsberg's famous thought experiment illustrates this distinction. Say you had to pick out a ball from one of two urns, both containing black and red balls. Each urn contains one hundred balls. Pull out a red ball, and you win a hundred dollars. Pick a black one, and you get zilch. But the two urns are different. Urn 1 holds anywhere from zero to one hundred red balls and from zero to one hundred black ones. All we know is that the total is a hundred. Urn 2 has fifty black balls and fifty red balls. Ellsberg realized that if you ask people whether they'd prefer to bet on pulling from Urn 1 or Urn 2, most people will choose Urn 2. The odds for both bets, as far as we know, are identical, and yet the majority of people prefer drawing from the known mix of balls over the unknown mix. That's ambiguity aversion.

Showing how fundamentally ingrained our preference for calculable odds is, a 2010 study replicated a variation of the urn experiment (using juice) with rhesus macaques. Led by Duke's Benjamin Hayden, the researchers found that monkeys also prefer known odds over unclear probabilities, even when that preference isn't rational. This preference holds for chimpanzees and bonobos, too. Recent research headed by Yale's Ifat Levy found that subjects were averse to the unknown even with *partial* ambiguity. One subject, given a 50 percent shot (with 75 percent of the odds unknown) to win $34 preferred a 50 percent chance (for certain) to win $5.

Evidence from brain science has shown that the amygdala and the orbitofrontal cortex are more active when people face ambiguous odds rather than merely risky ones, suggesting that ambiguity is fundamentally more emotional. The results held when participants were betting on whether a certain playing card was drawn or, in one clever study, when participants were asked to wager on either the high temperature in New York (involving known probabilities) or the high temperature in Tajikistan (involving unknown ones) on a given day. Even when precise odds exist, if they are unknown, then we treat the decision as ambiguous. In the real world, few big decisions have entirely known odds, and even when the likelihood of outcomes is relatively clear, we don't always know how to find that information. How we make predictions based on unclear odds affects a range of personal decisions. In the business world, mishandling ambiguous odds can be especially detrimental.

It can lead to bankruptcy.

—

MICHAEL RAYNOR, A business writer and strategist now at Deloitte, laid out an astounding fact in his 2007 book *The Strategy Paradox*. The highest-performing companies, he found, "often have more in common with humiliated bankrupts than with companies that have managed merely to survive." Firms that go bust, he showed, have the same characteristics as firms that go gangbusters. In certain markets, the opposite of sky-high success isn't abysmal failure but is mediocrity.

Raynor's linchpin study examined the business strategies of several thousand operating companies. The most lucrative tactics were *committed tactics*, that is, irreversible financial wagers on the future. Think of Bonwit Teller's bet to make 95 percent of its inventory midi lengths. When committed strategies do succeed, they pay off because of the lag time it takes for other firms to catch up. If midis became a runaway hit, Bonwit Teller would be fully stocked while sold-out competitors waited desperately for reorders. By the time rivals received new stock, Bonwit Teller would have presumably cleaned up. Raynor's study found that committed strategies either win big or lose big. Highly committed firms both made the most and lost the most. Since "strategies with the greatest possibility of success also have the greatest possibility of failure," he argued, breakthrough success often hinges on lucky bets.

Completely unanticipated events like the rise of the Internet or the widespread adoption of the MP3 format make winners and losers not necessarily of the wisest but often of the most fortunate firms. Wars, oil prices, natural disasters, a bolt of lightning that ignites a fire and burns down a semiconductor plant—the list of unknowns that can make or break a business is endless. In retail, the ambiguity stems largely from manufacturing products that take a while to hit the shelves. It's hard enough, in many businesses, to figure out what customers want. It's even harder to know what they'll want in six months. Whether you're aiming to sell a unique product or a cheaper version of something that already exists, it's frighteningly easy to make ordering decisions that result in inventory problems. Maybe you produce too little of a product and end up losing money when customers ask for more. Worse, you might make too much of a product and get stuck with surplus.

Cisco once wrote off a $2.2 billion loss in a "supply chain disaster," which, as the *New Yorker* explained, means it "spent two billion dollars on raw materials, parts, and products that it had no hope of either selling or using." The company also let 18 percent of its staff go, over 8,000 employees. In 2013, Target's sales in Australia were suffering under an estimated $100 million in surplus product that included unsold winter gear. The easiest way to liquidate extra stock is to discount it, dump it, or destroy it. One company even advertises its talents in destroying "expired inventory" like unsold board games, toys, and sports cards. In any case, you're losing money.

If you're forced to discount stock, moreover, you often have to take more losses to advertise the discounts. Treasury Wine Estates, one of the world's largest vintners, recently announced that it would have to dump $35 million worth of old and obsolete wine and increase discounts and rebates to the tune of $40 million. At the news, the company's shares fell 12 percent.

There are no easy answers in inventory management. Fads come and go with maddening unpredictability. In 2006, TMX Elmo dolls were a must-have, helping boost Mattel's profits. So Mattel tried to duplicate its success the following Christmas season. Toys "R" Us put up signs limiting customers to two per family. But the dolls ended up languishing on shelves. In December 2007, a market analyst joked that the new version, the TMX eXtra Special Edition, should be called the eXcess Inventory Elmo.

Navigating calmly between undersupply and oversupply can be

especially tricky in the ready-to-wear industry. In early 2012, for example, Abercrombie & Fitch was struggling with excess inventory. The company had made too many clothes and had to turn to large-scale promotions. Comparable store sales dropped by 8 percent during the first half of the year. By the end of 2012, the clothier had adjusted, slowing production and reducing its overall inventory by 35 percent of the previous year's inventory. But by the first fiscal quarter of 2013, A&F had clearly overadjusted. Now the problem was that it hadn't made *enough* clothes to meet demand. Sales dropped 17 percent below expectations. According to A&F, more than half the losses were the result of inventory issues.

Compounding the challenge of anticipating fickle customer demand is a particularly noxious demon of supply-chain management known as the bullwhip effect. This effect describes how variation in consumer demand is amplified as it travels up the supply chain, from consumer (cracking the whip) to retailer, to wholesaler, to manufacturer, and all the way to suppliers of raw materials and parts. Some years ago, for example, Procter & Gamble noticed a reasonable fluctuation in sales of Pampers diapers at retail stores like Kmart and Safeway. But in looking at orders from distributors, the executives noticed a surprising variability. When P&G examined their own orders to suppliers like 3M, they saw that these swings were even more pronounced. Hewlett-Packard discovered the same pattern in its supply chain. Printer sales at a major reseller were wavering, but the reseller's orders were fluctuating more, and HP's orders from its own printer division to its own integrated circuit division showed even greater ups and downs.

The bullwhip effect turns normal ebbs and flows in consumer demand into financial nightmares. In 1997, Stanford's Hau Lee and his colleagues described the result of these unpredictable swings in the grocery business:

Distorted information has led every entity in the supply chain—the plant warehouse, a manufacturer's shuttle warehouse, a manufacturer's market warehouse, a distributor's central warehouse, the distributor's regional warehouses, and the retail store's storage space—to stockpile because of the high degree of demand uncertainties and variabilities.

Fluctuations in demand led to a *series* of little buffers of excess groceries. Aida Velasco, a business professor at De La Salle University in the Philippines, estimated that for high-fashion, branded products, the bullwhip effect can lead to ten times more variability by the time demand hits the supplier. For example, if a company thought it would sell 100 leather jackets plus-or-minus five, then suppliers would have to be ready to provide materials for up to 150. That's too much leather. In 2012, researchers examining over 4,000 US companies found that 65 percent of them experience bullwhip effects.

At its root, overstocking is often caused by overreacting to ambiguous odds. Even in unpredictable industries like high-end fashion, businesses tend to assume that they can predict more about the future than is actually possible.

———

IN 1970, AS the fall fashion season approached, John Fairchild was about to have his own bold fashion predictions put to the test. By September, the mini-midi feud had turned into a serious financial worry. Fortunes, as well as reputations, were at stake. "Look, this isn't fun and games," Katherine Murphy, the fashion coordinator at Bloomingdale's, snapped to a reporter. "We have a multimillion-dollar business to run, and we're not laughing all the way to the bank. Our whole economy is based on planned obsolescence."

Critics said the midi was dowdy, that it added "instant age" (a favorite barb), that it made women look variously like a "bag of potatoes," a "brioche," "tea cozies," or that the reserved style was more suitable to the "covered wagon set" than to metropolitans. Cost-conscious women grumbled about the extra money for accessories that the midi seemed to require. A newswoman detailed the true cost of midis on a September visit to Saks Fifth Avenue: $23 for a midi skirt, $15 more for a sweater, $14 for a belt, $7 for a hat, and at least $28 for boots. By now the anti-midi lobbying had revved up, with FADD (Fight Against Dictating Designers) of Washington, DC, and GAMS (Girls/Guys Against More Skirt) of New York joining the cause.

Despite the onslaught, *Women's Wear Daily* and Fairchild stuck to their guns. They were committed and not about to retreat from their bold edict that the "whole look of American women will now change and die-hard miniskirt adherents are going to be out in the fashion cold." *WWD* had even ridiculed Jackie Onassis for wearing a shorter length, describing her acerbically as "the ghost of couture past." It had even run side-by-side photos of society women, noting that the woman not wearing the midi, as she "keeps those hems up," was lamentably dropping "down the fashion ladder."

Bonwit Teller's president, William Fine, who had bet millions of dollars on the midi, was growing nervous despite the influential *WWD*'s line in the sand. He mandated that store employees wear midis, and he sent a panicky September memo asking his salespeople to hold daily fifteen-minute huddles on their midi strategy. "The next four weeks will make or break our fall season," Fine wrote. "If you care about Bonwit Teller, there is only one choice—let us join together and 'make it.'"

By October, to Fine's dismay, the verdict was in. A reporter wrote of "hearing strains of Slaughter on Seventh Avenue." The *New Yorker* ran a cartoon depicting a woman in a miniskirt strangling a sales-woman wearing a midi. "Believe me, Miss," the saleswoman gasped, "if we *had* a mini I'd *show* you a mini." An apparel company president declared in the *Wall Street Journal* that "the midi is dead." In California, Saks Fifth Avenue in Beverly Hills was doing more alterations than it had ever done in its history. Women wanted the skirts they were buying hemmed shorter. At a fund-raiser for Governor Ronald Reagan, only 3 of the 450 women attending wore midis.

DEAD: THE MIDI DRESS, FROM ACUTE REJECTION BY THE AMERICAN WOMAN, the *Fresno Bee* announced with playful formality. Even the *WWD* apologist at the *Boston Globe* admitted defeat. "Bitterness is sweeping" along Seventh Avenue, she noted, as designers fumed over the midi's abysmal flop. A shop in Glen Ellyn, Illinois, held a mock funeral for the midi. Draped in black, the store was "decorated with thistles and mandrake roots." It displayed a coffin bearing a midi dress along with copies of *Women's Wear Daily*. Mourners drank Bloody Marys.

The mini-midi fiasco still echoes in the annals of fashion forecasting lore. Bonwit Teller ate huge losses. Malcolm Starr, Inc., one of the largest producers of high-priced dresses, went bankrupt after "taking a bath in heavy inventories." Nearly three years later, in May 1973, apparel producers still hadn't been able to liquidate their inventories of the longer hemlines. Department stores grew reluctant to gamble, remembering that brutal autumn, when, in one buyer's words, "we all went down the drain."

AROUND THE SAME time that the hemline hassle was unfolding so dramatically in the United States, a European businessman was on his way to building a clothing company immune to the prediction and supply-chain problems that had caused the fashion uproar. His success—and how he managed to cope so ingeniously with the perils of fashion forecasting—can be traced back to an insight borrowed from American supermarkets. It all began with the innovations of the supermarket chain Piggly Wiggly.

Piggly Wiggly's founder Clarence Saunders got a job in the wholesale grocery business at nineteen. He was a natural, and in 1916, he executed long-crafted plans of his own. Saunders had a vision for a new kind of store. In the early twentieth century, most grocery stores looked a little like butcher shops today. Clerks would stand behind display counters, and customers simply requested the items they wanted. The shop clerks would fetch things from back shelves, often one at a time. If needed, the clerk would grind coffee or cut and weigh cheese. Customers could pay in cash or put their purchases on a charge account after the clerk finally totaled it all up. Shoppers didn't get to choose their produce, and many stores didn't even have the prices clearly marked. Some customers phoned in orders and had them delivered for a small fee.

Saunders would radically challenge this approach. He figured that having salespeople fetch customers' items was an incredible waste of labor. To deal with rush hour, shops had to employ multiple clerks and delivery boys. During slack hours, the same employees were being paid to do nothing. Saunders saw a work-around: shoppers might be just as happy to select their items themselves. He filed his first patent for this strange new self-serving store in October. The patent revealed a store design shaped like a blocky M, with the entrance at the bottom left and the exit at the bottom right. Saunders's store had *aisles*. He had constructed a path that customers could walk along to select their canned goods and produce. Where once massive flour barrels stood behind counters, Saunders sold flour in small, ready-to-go packets. After converting an old grocery store to the newly formatted Piggly Wiggly, he lowered the cost of doing business from 15 to 4 percent—this by operating out of the same space.

Piggly Wiggly transformed the storeroom into the store, removing a barrier between product and customer and cutting out a link in the supply chain. There *was* no more back room. By the end of the 1950s, Saunders's self-service concept was the norm, and when an engineer from Toyota named Taiichi Ohno visited America in 1956, this model of the US supermarket is what left the greatest impression on him. Toyota had already begun applying insights from US supermarkets to its production system, but Ohno was still struck by how successful the self-service model had become. In theory, by cutting out the storeroom (and intermediary), you could reduce the uncertainty of not having full control over your purchases.

Ohno would later contrast the supermarket model with how someone in Japan might traditionally have purchased tofu. Ohno explained that in the morning, the tofu seller walked his route, playing a flute to announce his approach. Fresh tofu was brought right to your door. But it wasn't always available. If tofu was sold out, you had to rush off to the store. If you ordered home delivery, on the other hand, and wanted some scallions, you couldn't really just order the two stalks you needed. You would ask for a bunch. "You think," Ohno wrote, "'I might as well buy some daikon, too,' so in the end this is an uneconomical way of shopping." Tofu aficionados, like P&G's distributors, would add buffers to their orders just in case. To manage tomorrow's unknowns, they'd buy a little extra.

Stockpiling as a flight from ambiguity is one driver of the bullwhip effect. All sorts of purchases, in fact, can serve to reduce the anxiety of various mental conflicts. We'd all like to buy our way out of life's troublesome trade-offs. Maybe we want to buy two pairs of pants but only have cash for one, or maybe we have to make a mortgage payment but also desperately need a vacation. Or maybe we don't have enough time to both achieve our career goals and raise a family. Only the well-off have the means to purchase their way out of these inner conflicts, while low-income families are stuck grappling with the unresolved stress such contradictions cause. P&G's purchasing managers, in this comparison, were like rich shoppers who buy a little more than they needed to escape uncertainty. They soothed the anxiety of the unknown by buying their way out of it, in the same way insurance buys peace of mind. Ambiguity aversion does, in fact, lead to higher insurance premiums than risk alone justifies. People are willing to pay more for earthquake insurance than they should, for instance, compared with what they pay for life insurance, where the odds of disaster are clearer.

Ohno saw supermarkets as a place for customers to get exactly what they need, in the exact quantity they need, at the exact time they need it. Shoppers no longer had to stockpile, because they had more control over the process. Supermarkets had reduced uncertainty by shortening the supply chain. At Toyota, similarly, Ohno strove to cut supply-chain inefficiencies by reordering automobile parts only when customers ordered particular cars. In his words, this meant that "for every ten parts that are taken away, simply make ten parts." He stopped trying to anticipate demand and instead instituted a simple rule that Toyota would only restock what had been purchased. Forecasts wouldn't trigger production—consumers' decisions would.

By intimately linking production to purchasing, Toyota avoided the costs of trying—and inevitably failing—to predict customers' shifting preferences. The company would gradually stop producing cars for unknown buyers and shift to a build-to-order system. While it took decades to perfect, the tactic made Toyota one of the most efficient car companies in the world. The approach became known as the just-in-time system. In the early 1990s, in an eccentric move, Toyota consultants were hired to help implement this system at a clothing company.

AMANCIO ORTEGA GAONA was the youngest of four children. He was born to a poor family living in a tiny Spanish hamlet of around five dozen people. His father was a railway worker, and the family often moved around when Amancio was still a child, eventually landing in A Coruña (or La Coruña), a city on the northwest coast of Spain. Regularly blanketed by fog and mist, A Coruña is situated near the rocky Costa da Morte, or Coast of Death, so called because its legendary history is littered with morbid tales of shipwrecks. A Coruña's mythology, for good measure, also includes folktales of dark magic and witchery.

Ortega decided to drop out of school at the age of twelve, after his mother had been denied credit at a grocery store. He'd witnessed the episode, and as he later recalled it, he instantly understood what had to happen. He stopped attending classes—marking the end of his formal education—and took a job at a local shirt maker. He'd spend his life in the fashion industry.

One day years later, as the story goes, Ortega and his fiancée saw a gorgeous silk negligee in a shop window. But it was wildly expensive. A skilled tailor by then, he reproduced one like it at a smidgeon of the cost. His fiancée adored it, and before long, Ortega had started his own business manufacturing clothes.

Ortega's eventual success would hinge on solving the same puzzle that had occupied Taiichi Ohno. Could Ortega remove some of the troublesome links in the supply chain? Like Ohno, he wasn't interested in trying to predict customers' needs. His aim was to perfect a system of rapid reaction. He was looking for a way to make clothes without stockpiling, a method, in his words, that had "five fingers touching the factory and five touching the customer."

From selling to wholesalers, Ortega knew that customers ended up paying more than double his price by the time the clothing hit stores. Shops often added margins as high as 80 percent to cover their overhead and to hedge against losses on unsold items. Ortega thought that he could easily trim retail margins by 30 or 40 percent. First of all, he'd get into retail and start distributing his clothes directly. More generally, he wanted—and this would be a lifelong project—to streamline the supply chain, which he viewed as too long and too lax. As it stood, making clothing was essentially a separate business from selling it in stores. Shops routinely ordered clothes that customers didn't want and misestimated quantities on items that did sell. Ortega believed the solution was to create more-direct feedback loops between customers and manufacturers.

Starting in the 1970s, Ortega would impose a forty-eight-hour rule on his businesses. Orders placed by his retail stores to the distribution centers had to be delivered within two days. He saw clothes as perishable products, akin to fish or yogurt. Fresh fish is irresistible, he'd say, but it quickly goes bad. Of course, speedy delivery wouldn't help matters much without more variety, so Ortega's retail outlets would also offer a far greater assortment than what other shops offered. Every few weeks, Ortega's outlets would completely swap out their inventory. This was unheard-of. It meant producing up to five times as many garments as his rivals did.

Making more styles faster had upsides that even Ortega might not have envisioned. Each style was now produced in a smaller batch. Smaller batches and faster turnover gave his clothes an aura of fleeting exclusivity. Customers weren't dressed in uniforms, and if they liked something, they knew to buy it immediately because it might not be there in a few days. But Ortega was surely aware of two other critical benefits of his more-styles-faster approach. One was a far greater flexibility in reacting to shifting trends. The other was that smaller batches reduced the downside of bad bets. If a style didn't sell well, the flop wasn't too costly. Successful styles could be quickly ramped up, and unsuccessful ones just as quickly discontinued. To pull all this off, Ortega had to build a logistics machine previously unseen in the ready-to-wear business. His brand of "fast fashion" would revolutionize the industry.

———

NEW YORK CITY'S Fifth Avenue north of 50th Street embodies the disruptive changes unsettling fashion's old hierarchy. Ortega's flagship store, Zara, is on the corner of 52nd Street. At 51st, there's an H&M, Zara's chief rival in fast fashion. Sandwiched between Zara and the Japanese fast-fashion brand Uniqlo is a store called Hollister, owned by Abercrombie & Fitch. As of March 2014, A&F was exploring how to reposition Hollister as a fast-fashion brand to compete with the likes of H&M, Zara, and Uniqlo. Nearby along Fifth Avenue is the venerable Versace, and across from Zara, esteemed Salvatore Ferragamo, Ermenegildo Zegna, and Rolex.

Zara's design ideas come from all over, including its higher-priced rivals. Hundreds of trend spotters around the world scour fashion and business districts, clubs, bars, and university campuses for the latest styles. Dominant lines, colors, and materials aren't forecasted but instead emerge from what customers are buying at the moment. Many of Zara's designs are cherry-picked from high-end competitors' successes and reproduced at more affordable prices. Over the last decade, the success of Zara's supply chain has led to the complete remaking of New York's fashion strips, as fast-fashion brands invade the once-sacred prime real estate of elite couture.

Globally, Zara is now opening at least one new store a day. Although it has a relatively low profile in the United States (Europe accounts for most of its profits), Zara's store on Fifth Avenue cost more than today's equivalent of the Louisiana Purchase, a stunning testament to how far Ortega has come from his early days. When he first opened a Zara store, in 1975, he had intended to call it Zorba, after the film *Zorba the Greek*. They had already cast the mold for the letters. But a bar a few blocks away was already called Zorba, so Ortega played around with the letter combinations before hitting on the final name. (The Spanish pronunciation is "Thara.") Zara expanded from Spain to Portugal, then across Europe, and eventually worldwide. As the company grew, it kept its philosophical pillars constant: design and deliver styles quicker, more flexibly, and in smaller batches; react to, don't predict, what customers want.

If a retailer can halve the lag time between manufacturing products and selling them, the company has also halved the amount of time it needs to forecast. By owning his entire production line, Ortega cut the time from design to sale to as little as two weeks, an unmatched turnaround. Ortega could produce high-fashion styles with breakneck speed at easy-on-the-pocketbook prices. In 2000, his holding company, Inditex, logged a whopping $2.4 billion in sales. Like Toyota, Zara linked production directly to customers' purchases. And like American supermarkets, Ortega did away with needless stockpiling by removing a link in the supply chain. In fact, Ortega's stores wouldn't have stockrooms. The stores *were* the stockrooms.

Ortega avoids forecasting fiascos by committing in advance to as few styles as possible. Six months ahead of time, Zara binds itself to only 15 to 25 percent of that season's inventory, compared with 40 to 60 percent for other retailers. At the start of any given season, Zara still has to design up to *half* the total styles, versus the only 20 percent wiggle room other fashion chains have to handle emerging fads. Inditex can react so quickly, partly because over 60 percent of its production takes place in either Spain, Portugal, or nearby countries like Turkey and Morocco. Eight-five percent of its in-house production capacity is reserved for in-season clothes.

"We have the ability," Ortega told journalist Covadonga O'Shea, "to completely undo any production line if it isn't selling; we can dye the collections with new colors and we can create styles in just a few days." Zara's designers, when they fail, do so quickly and inexpensively. Ortega actually assumes that his designers will occasionally fail. He built that expectation into the business model. Inditex's designers work up over 30,000 styles a year, some 18,000 of which are made for Zara stores. If a product takes off, designers will have three or four variations on that style ready to produce.

Tales of Zara's legendary flexibility sometimes sound as mythic as the fog-shrouded legends of A Coruña. One well-known example followed the tragedy of 9/11. After the attack, Zara's equestrian fall themes suddenly seemed inappropriate to the city's somber mood. Within two weeks, as other stores struggled with unsold wares, Zara had successfully replaced them with quieter, darker shades.

When the film *Marie Antoinette* was released in October 2006—later winning an Oscar for costume design—Zara quickly incorporated gold buttons, cropped collars, and velvet motifs. When Madonna did her final concert of a Spanish tour, teenagers could already buy the outfit she'd worn at the first performance. When Crown Prince Felipe (now the king of Spain) announced his engagement in 2003, his would-be bride wore a striking white trouser suit. Within weeks, women across Europe were wearing the suits, thanks to fast fashion. If a one-shouldered cocktail dress is suddenly hip, Ortega's nimble supply chain can have it in stores at a supersonic pace. If it falls out of fashion a few weeks later, that's not a problem, either. In 2001, Zara produced a killer khaki skirt that sold out in only a few hours. They had sent out just twenty-eight hundred of the skirts to stores to test the market. Within a day, the company knew the skirt was a hit, could quickly produce variations, and could ship them out. Even if the skirt had flopped, it would have flopped cheaply.

Zara's fast-fashion approach has also seemed to change the way people shop, increasing the number of impulse purchases. Since styles are always changing, customers visit Ortega's stores more often. His stores' climate of scarcity has paid off. According to one study, Zara's Spanish customers visit on average seventeen times a year, compared with three for rivals. And because of its tiny batches—three to five pieces of every design, in each size—Zara only has to discount 15 to 20 percent of its inventory, and the average discount is only 15 percent. Inditex's European competitors, by contrast, are compelled to sell an estimated 30 to 40 percent of their stock at 30 percent off.

Nelson Fraiman, a Columbia Business School professor, has trumpeted Ortega's success as one of process—not product—innovation. Inditex's speed comes from its mastery of logistics. Zara's main distribution center outside A Coruña is located between its manufacturing plants and connects to them by over two hundred kilometers of underground tracks. Inside the 400,000-square-foot building, conveyer belts extending up to five stories high drop clothes into over 400 chutes and package them into cardboard boxes. The system can handle the distribution of 2.5 million garments a week. At Inditex's headquarters across the street, nicknamed "The Cube," market specialists and designers work collaboratively in large, open spaces. Prototypes of garments can be made on the same day they're designed, on site—a costly but critical advantage.

Rivals have done their best to compete with Ortega's model. When Esprit announced in 2012 that its new CEO was Inditex's former distribution and operations manager, its shares rose 28 percent. Prada, Louis Vuitton, and other high-end fashion companies began producing four to six collections a year rather than two. Patagonia doubled the number of styles it puts out every year. Benetton started shipping new styles to stores once a week. Uniqlo and Forever 21 (an American fast-fashion brand) managed to deliver new looks to stores within six weeks, nudging closer to Zara's two-week standard. But Inditex's supply chain took decades to put together. You can't replicate it overnight. Gap and H&M, for instance, don't have the same central manufacturing capacity that Zara enjoys. That makes them less flexible. As one Gap executive complained, "I would love to organize our business like Inditex, but I would have to knock the company down and rebuild it from scratch."

———

ORTEGA ONCE CALLED self-satisfaction "a terrible trap if you want to achieve anything important." He described optimism as "a very negative emotion." Although he no longer plays an active role in managing Inditex, he clearly wasn't keen on being praised when he was in charge. When admirers lavished compliments on Zara's designs, he'd interrupt to ask what they didn't like about the styles. He was never satisfied with what he already knew. Forcing himself to stay close to his designers, to literally roam the halls of the building, he decided early on that he would never have a physical office. This from a man who, in 2012, was dueling with Warren Buffett for the title of the world's third-richest person, behind only Carlos Slim Helú and Bill Gates. By then, Inditex had become the largest clothing retailer in the world.

For small companies in volatile markets, a CEO's capacity to tolerate ambiguity is crucial to a firm's success. One Swedish study in the late 1990s found that ambiguity tolerance was one of the most critical variables linked to higher financial performance. The researchers looked at CEOs' confidence levels, too. Confidence had no effect whatsoever on a firm's profitability and productivity, although it seemed to increase customer satisfaction. But Zara's triumph reflects much more than Amancio Ortega's personal attitude toward what he can't predict. Being humble and flexible as a matter of character is one thing. Constructing a new business model predicated on not knowing is another.

Ortega showed that in the world of fashion, professionals who were paid to foresee trends were so bad at it—and so blind to their cluelessness—that he could build the biggest fashion retailer in the world by admitting he couldn't predict fads. Zara's spectacular success is based in Ortega's bald admission that we often don't know the odds, even in the short term.

Fashions will no doubt continue to be unpredictable. In May 2013, the midi, almost inexorably, looked to be trending again. One of the United Kingdom's biggest online fashion shops reported a 200 percent rise in midi sales over the same period the year prior. Liz Jones, a fashion writer, predicted that the midi would be an even bigger hit come fall, and by December 2013, Jones seemed to be right. Thanks to stars like Victoria Beckham and Nicole Scherzinger, midi dresses were, another columnist wrote, "a must have fashion item for this winter." *Mail Online* gushed that "the mini has officially been replaced by the more demure midi." Sales of midis by the brand George at ASDA were up 174 percent over 2012's "party season."

"The age of the mini dress," a George spokesperson decreed, "is over."

———

IN PART 2, we've explored how the urge to resolve ambiguity is deeply rooted, multifaceted, and often dangerous. In times of stress, psychological pressures compel us to deny or dismiss inconsistent evidence, pushing us to perceive certainty and clarity where there is neither. Unpleasant anxiety can compel us to seize and freeze on ideas and beliefs in areas of life completely unrelated to the source of that anxiety. When we feel that something is off balance, we've seen that we can try to uncover the origin of the imbalance in conflicting or unresolved ideas or events. As we make decisions, we need to recognize both the consequences of a decision and our current need for closure. In so doing, we can avoid grasping for new solutions in panic or sticking too rigidly to old ones.

We've seen how easily we can misinterpret genuine ambivalence as calculating duplicity. When we're trying to pin down someone's intentions—whether the person is an employee, a boss, a customer, or a friend—we need to realize that ambivalence is a more natural state of mind than we ordinarily assume. Wanting and not wanting the same thing at the same time is so common that we might even consider it a baseline condition of human consciousness. When interpreting someone's intentions, we should take into account that stressful circumstances make us more likely to ignore our natural human ambivalence. More broadly, organizations that are consistently forced to deal with ambiguity under pressure can ensure that people with a low need for closure play a central role in decision making.

We also need to recognize that we can't always resolve ambiguity by seeking out more information. As we've seen in medicine, sometimes the search for more detailed evidence carries its own hidden risks. The ambiguity inherent in the problems of human health will never be eliminated by technology, just as there are no silver-bullet solutions to poverty. There are simply too many variables. And yet doctors can refrain from ordering that one last test, and patients can help stop them. Tools like top-five lists are important steps toward reducing overtesting in cases where less care is more.

Our need for closure is a powerful force. It's so deeply ingrained in everyday living that cultivating an awareness of how it works isn't enough. Combating its dangers means designing institutions and processes that make us less likely to succumb to our natural tendencies toward resolution when it matters most. The right negotiators will stay calm in the face of fluid, incomplete, and seemingly contradictory information. The right reminders at decision points will lower our need for closure. We can build an awareness of what we don't know about the future into our approach to the world by crafting methods to react quickly to change rather than trying to predict it. Ambiguity doesn't have to be paralyzing or distasteful. Under the right conditions, as we will see, embracing uncertainty can in fact provide opportunities to innovate. It can inspire creative solutions, and might even help make us better people.

PART THREE

Embracing Uncertainty

SEVEN

Building a Better Ducati

THE USES OF UNCERTAINTY

FOR THE ITALIAN manufacturer Ducati, 2004 was supposed to be a banner year in the premier class of Grand Prix motorcycle racing, MotoGP. Ducati had earned competitors' respect in 2003 with its GP3 motorcycle, and team director Livio Suppo reported that the new model, the GP4, had already clocked faster times at three tracks.

MotoGP motorcycles are high-tech prototypes produced in single-digit quantities. The official teams Honda, Ducati, Kawasaki, Suzuki, Yamaha, and Aprilia (among others) field two riders each and run through exorbitant sums in a globe-trotting R&D face-off. Private teams can also compete by buying and racing previous years' models, although that usually puts them at a competitive disadvantage.

Because MotoGP bikes crack over 200 miles per hour on straightaways, riders have to be daring and surprisingly agile. Imagine corralling a three-hundred-plus-pound machine motored by a 230-horsepower engine around a hairpin turn. Your bike is at a sixty-degree slant. Your knee scrapes the track, and you're surrounded on all sides by rivals trying to outwit, outrisk, or outright intimidate you into a potentially fatal error. Crashing, if you're lucky, means skidding across the loose gravel (or "kitty litter") beyond the tarmac with only your kangaroo leathers, body armor, and helmet as protection. Lap by lap, it takes racers around forty to forty-five minutes to complete an average of seventy miles.

Victories are team efforts. As certain tracks have more grip, sharper turns, or longer straightaways, manufacturers set up their bikes uniquely before each race. Struggling teams sometimes make major design changes midseason, but bike setup usually involves small—millimeter, not centimeter—adjustments to the suspension, chassis, or wheelbase of the motorcycles, among other components. After races, analysts gather precise data on lap times and top speeds, tire temperature, fuel consumption, and engine speed. Riders work closely with engineers to identify problems and enhance the bike throughout each season.

Ducati's 2004 team, in short, faced what many businesses do: trade-offs to weigh, problems to fix, and solutions to invent. The central role of R&D is why MotoGP awards three Grand Prix championship titles: one for riders; another for teams; and a third title for manufacturers, which counts official team scores and finishes from private teams. It also explains why the mechanics can have bigger egos than the racers and why Ducati's engineers referred to the racers as the bikes' "most expensive sensors."

When the 2004 season began in April, the team's loyal fan base, the Ducatisti, was as optimistic as ever. Reigning champion Valentino Rossi had left top-class Honda to accept a multimillion-dollar contract at downtrodden Yamaha, and the hope was that Rossi's switch would create an opportunity. Loris Capirossi, one of Ducati's two riders, enthused that 2004 would "be the most wide open," and predictions were that his fellow rider, Troy Bayliss, was set for a breakthrough season.

At the first race in South Africa, as the *Sydney Morning Herald* reported, "the expected Ducati challenge didn't materialize." Capirossi came in sixth, and Bayliss was fourteenth. The Spanish Grand Prix was a greater debacle, and the pair fared little better in Le Mans, France. Ducati had such a dismal start that the team felt compelled to switch to a different engine midseason. By September, Bayliss was musing that it had "been a strange year, really." By October, he was telling journalists that Ducati's GP4 wasn't fast enough and that Rossi was unbeatable: "I don't know what's going on—I'm not an engineer. . . . I know when the bike is about to say 'You are going to crash today.' I'm an experienced rider and I don't have stupid crashes." Capirossi would finish ninth overall, and Bayliss wouldn't complete eight of sixteen races. In one early stretch, Bayliss failed to finish in four straight races, crashing in three of them.

In 2011, Harvard's Francesca Gino and Gary Pisano revisited Ducati's 2004 MotoGP season in a *Harvard Business Review* issue devoted entirely to failure. Thematically, the issue explored an idea that was relatively novel at the time: failure brings benefits. Formulated broadly, the thesis was that failure forces us to revisit old certainties when things don't turn out as planned. It requires us to *impose* ambiguity on causes we assumed we understood.

Ducati's 2004 to 2007 run fit that narrative nicely. After the team was humiliated, it improved steadily over the 2005 and 2006 seasons, and in 2007, its rider won the Grand Prix championship title, the first time in over thirty years that a non-Japanese manufacturer produced a championship bike. By the end of the 2007 season, Rossi was threatening to quit Yamaha if they didn't build him a faster motorcycle. Ducati's Suppo described it as a victory of ideas.

And yet Gino and Pisano, in telling Ducati's story, weren't focused on the standard failure-to-success narrative that filled much of the special issue's pages. They had noticed a more complicated—and more revealing—pattern.

Ducati's entrance into MotoGP had actually begun in 2003. It was meticulously planned. Some 19,000 hours of engineering effort went into the GP3, over 1,000 hours of controlled-road simulations, 120 hours of wind-tunnel tests, and some forty days of testing at ten racetracks around the globe. "The 2003 season will be mainly a preparation for 2004," CEO Claudio Domenicali said. It would be a learning year.

Very soon, however, Ducati exceeded its own expectations. In a test qualifying session in March, Capirossi was clocked at 204 miles per hour, then a record speed for a Grand Prix motorcycle, and Bayliss was second-fastest. Rossi called Ducati's performance "spectacular." It was, a reporter wrote, a "psychological blow" to competitors "that suggested this could be more than just a development year."

Ducati's surprising success continued at the first race of the season, the Japanese Grand Prix in Suzuka. Capirossi came in third—a podium finish—and Bayliss was fifth. "The result we wanted was a podium from the whole year, [and] now we're ahead of our dream schedule," a Ducati spokesperson said. "We're very excited and are trying to keep our feet firmly planted on the ground. We mustn't get carried away. . . . We were always confident after testing that we could compete, but now we've put the cat among the pigeons." In Spain, Bayliss would notch yet another podium finish.

In the season's sixth race, Capirossi won.

Ducati had stunned the field. But as Gino and Pisano astutely observed, its failures in 2004 seemed to be caused by the unexpected successes of 2003. Only after a string of victories did Ducati fail, and only after failing did it start improving again. Remarkably, this rendering of events combines two stories that now populate business

books and articles and are usually told separately: that failure can be
a good thing, and that success can be detrimental.

If both of these narratives seem a bit odd, they are even stranger
when combined. How can letdowns always be good and achievements always be bad? Triumphs don't inevitably lead to flops, just
as botched efforts don't always inform victories. And if both story
lines were right, then businesses would be stuck in the up-down-up
cycle that Ducati experienced. But some stay successful, while others
remain failures.

So what's really happening?

Taken together, Ducati's MotoGP trials actually reveal a third
narrative in which neither success nor failure has a starring role.

⁓

WE'VE LOOKED AT the dangers of a high need for closure, whether
spurred on by trauma or unrelated anxiety, a high-stakes negotiation,
inconclusive medical results, or a changing business environment. In
Part 2, we focused on avoiding mistakes under pressure—those situations in which we're forced to react to ambiguity—and often feel
compelled to avoid uncertainty. Part 3 will spotlight moments where
uncertainty can be useful. Rather than explore how to minimize the
harm that can come from dismissing ambiguity, we're going to look
at how to maximize the benefits of harnessing ambiguity, sometimes
even imposing it, and always training to face it. How can teachers
help students better solve problems that have no clear answer? What
is the best way to react to both failure and success? How can embracing the mind state of uncertainty—which requires accepting and
cultivating ambiguity—help us innovate?

Zara's tactic, we saw, is to limit the amount of damage caused
by not knowing what garments would sell. The strategy works be-

cause the company offers a far greater number of designs and can shrink the time to reproduce a winning product to mere weeks. But Zara doesn't create innovative products. Its supply chain is novel, but there's nothing all that original about Zara's clothes. MotoGP engineers, on the other hand, can only field their motorcycles in a high-stakes competition eighteen times a year. They can't race a thousand motorcycles on each track and then stick with the fastest ones. They can't freely borrow competitors' designs and see what works. On the contrary, Ducati was challenged with inventing the best motorcycle to *ever* hit the racetrack—with innovating. MotoGP bikes could never be produced using Zara's strategy, just as Apple could never have invented the iPhone by reducing its time to market to two weeks.

Nowadays, failure is much praised—the failed start-up has become a badge of honor among Silicon Valley entrepreneurs—and rightly so. Failure is part of the process, the error in "trial and error." Originality requires venturing out into the unknown, dwelling in uncertainty, and learning from missteps. And the more inventive a product, the less you know about its chances of success. "Innovation drags you into the realm of ambiguity," Pisano said. In some scientific fields, experiments fail more than 70 percent of the time. Between 70 and 80 percent of new food products flop. Venture capitalists, film producers, book editors, video game programmers, and pharmaceutical researchers all face extraordinarily high average failure rates. Failure is central to discovery and creativity, and as Columbia Business School's Rita Gunther McGrath has pointed out, during uncertain times, "failures are more common than successes." Today's economic instability and globally competitive markets have also made staying on top harder than ever. The average time that a company spends in the S&P 500 index, *The Economist* reported in 2011, is one-fifth of the average time in 1937.

In 2012, education expert Tony Wagner underscored that the "long-term health of [the American] economy and a full economic recovery" depend upon finding ways to encourage "far more innovation." Thomas Friedman and Michael Mandelbaum, as Wagner noted, argued that only innovators and entrepreneurs will be safe from losing their jobs to automation or outsourcing. In a world where, say, a refrigerator instruction manual can be edited cheaply and proficiently by an English teacher in Turkey, and where tax preparation can be done by algorithm, the people most likely to succeed and flourish are those who are creating new economic opportunities.

Tomorrow's workforce needs to handle the uncertainty and failure that go along with innovation. Unfortunately, today's students are woefully unprepared.

A sports analogy helps us get at the root of the problem. Picture the way most golfers practice at the driving range. They choose a club, execute a few practice swings, spill some balls from a tall bucket, and then start hitting. After a while, they switch clubs and smack another batch. Golfers call this automatic thwacking "beating" golf balls, and some years ago, a sports psychologist named Bob Christina noticed that it was a poor approximation of tournament play. Practice conditions didn't match how unpredictable real-world conditions were. When you're playing eighteen holes of golf, you have to be *inventive*. You don't hit the same shot twice in a row with the same club. You're switching clubs, the slopes of the course are changing, and the ball is always in a different position relative to the hole. A better way to practice at the golf range, Christina saw, would be to train to face new and shifting challenges.

The practice range has its uses, of course. For building basic skills, repetition is great. Hitting buckets of balls is what you should be doing. Golfers have to learn the baseline mechanics before they can apply them, just as physics students need to memorize basic equations. But Christina distinguished between learning skills and another, equally important kind of learning that he called *transfer practice*. Instead of treating technique as the be-all and end-all, he emphasized training to face playing situations. Ideally, he'd want players to practice on the widest range of golf courses under different conditions, but that's not so realistic in terms of resources. But Christina could viably transform the driving range into a place where golfers didn't just learn to hit shots mechanically, but also prepared to adjust fluidly on the fly.

Fifteen years ago, transfer practice wasn't widely known among golf teachers. In 2002, when Christina first presented its benefits to *Golf Magazine*'s top hundred PGA and LPGA teachers, as he told me, "you could hear a pin drop." Now it's common practice. These days—he affectionately calls it his retirement—he spends much of his time as an assistant coach for the University of North Carolina at Greensboro men's golf team, helping Spartan golfers apply his techniques. He has the students simulate the unpredictability of the golf course by switching clubs, alternating distances, and playing out different scenarios.

He helps them in another way, too—by *not* helping. Whenever we hire an instructor, whether it's for cello or calculus or bowling, we usually think we're paying for close attention and constant advice. But Christina helps golfers prepare for competition by withholding feedback, something that many pupils and even fellow teachers were initially uncomfortable with. Whenever a golfer hits a shot, he or she gets nonverbal feedback from how the body feels, how the ball moves, and how it sounds. Since Christina wanted golfers listening to this kind of feedback, he had to suppress his own. He knew that golfers often perform better during training if they can adjust to a coach's constant feedback, but that very feedback can be a crutch, hurting them later on when they have to think for themselves. Christina was eventually asked to help revise the LPGA and PGA curriculum for training its pros. He changed how top golf instructors teach.

Higher education faces a problem not unlike the one Christina addressed. Graduates are confronted with a labor market that increasingly puts a premium on creativity, exploring uncertainties, and learning from failure, yet many college professors still act like old-school golf instructors focused on automatically applying skills, rather than helping students learn to deal with the challenges of invention. Creativity expert Ken Robinson famously argued a few years ago that "the current system of education . . . was designed and conceived and structured for a different age." Another education-reform guru, Sugata Mitra, claimed further that the Western educational system has become obsolete. Its emphasis on rote learning, he said, is preparing workers for a world that no longer exists.

Can't we do better?

———

TODAY'S PEDAGOGIC DRIVING range is the university lecture, the standard form of teaching in higher education for six hundred years. In a typical college classroom, students are neatly arranged in rows facing the professor. The teacher runs through the material using clear, declarative statements. Lectures are not usually designed to help students grapple with ambiguous problems. Professors don't generally include gaps in logic for students to fill in, or contradictions to work out, or pauses that encourage students to reflect. Most lecturers do ask questions to engage students, but their questions are too often rhetorical. That's because teachers get nervous or impatient and then answer their own queries. In one study, teachers estimated that ten seconds had usually elapsed between their question and when they resumed speaking. The true average elapsed time was two seconds. Another study revealed a stunning ratio of teacher-to-student questions: an instructor in one case posed eighty-four questions, while students asked only two.

In 1971, Donald Bligh's *What's the Use of Lectures?* exposed the downside of the traditional technique. As normally given, lectures do little to inspire interest, encourage conceptual or active thinking, change students' minds, or help students learn how to respectfully disagree with their peers (since they're not discussing material with one another). Lectures are often as good as, say, reading a textbook. They convey facts. That role is fitting, since in the Middle Ages, a lecture meant that a teacher would read aloud from an original source. "The problem is not with the lecture," educator Dominik Lukeš wrote, "but with the idea that receiving information is the key part of learning."

Think about how you learned something that you know how to do very well. Did you learn it because you were *told* how to do it? Or did you learn it by doing, by figuring it out yourself or with help? As access to information is democratized, the value of the old-fashioned lecture seems likely to decay further.

Traditional lecturing, more importantly, encourages an approach increasingly at odds with the challenges graduates face. Have you ever had a lecturer highlight the necessity of stumbling, errors, and luck in developing breakthrough innovations? Or is the messy process of creativity usually sanitized after the fact? Have you ever been given a classroom assignment that you were 80 percent likely to fail at, matching an entrepreneur's odds? Have you ever confronted a school problem that might have no solution? Have you practiced overcoming how it feels to fail?

Claire Cook, a cognitive scientist who has studied the instructional value of ambiguity, agrees that helping students deal with uncertainty is particularly important today. "When you're in a workplace, typically," she told me, "the really valuable skill is to be able to approach a problem that doesn't have a single right answer." We need graduates who can tackle problems without obvious solutions, and yet educators are doing too little to prepare students to navigate unknowns.

Some teachers, of course, are training students for vague challenges like those faced in innovative fields with high failure rates. Other instructors have long felt a need to help pupils tackle such assignments because they teach subjects that more obviously require high degrees of creativity. Jim Lang of Assumption College is one of the latter. Beyond being a tenured professor at Assumption, Lang is also the founding director of the Center for Teaching Excellence at the college and a columnist for the *Chronicle of Higher Education*. That makes him a very rare and useful species: a practitioner, a researcher, and a journalist. When he encounters new research, he teases out what's practical in his classrooms.

Lang teaches creative nonfiction. He tries to surprise his students—keep them a bit off-kilter, as he puts it. His goal, he wrote in one of his columns, is to "make them drive on the wrong side of the street." While Michel Thomas took care to remove all irrelevant anxieties from the learning environment, Lang, like Bob Christina, seeks to add relevant ones. "Every time they come into class," Lang told me, "I want them to be thinking, 'What the hell are we going to do today?'" Students in the class I observed divided their essays into sections and experimented with narrative structures; Lang offered just enough guidance to help them discover the answers themselves. Lang's classrooms are a testing ground for thinking, not accumulating facts that much of the world now has access to at any time. By keeping students slightly off-balance, he's preparing them to transfer what they've learned to the outside world, where it really counts.

At a 2012 teaching conference, Lang and other pedagogical experts composed a list of techniques to prepare students to actively face uncertainty and all that comes with it. Most methods, they found, fell into three categories:

1. Ask students to find or identify mistakes.
2. Have students argue on behalf of unfamiliar positions.
3. Give students tasks that they'll fail at.

A math teacher at the conference told Lang that he sometimes inserted mistakes into assigned problems and asked students to find them. An architecture professor said that he occasionally made mistakes while doing calculations on the blackboard and that his students had learned to watch out for his errors and correct them. A chemistry teacher suggested giving students some experiments that were designed to fail—exactly the kind of task that mirrors real-world challenges and that is so rarely used as a teaching tool. Manu Kapur, a researcher at the Learning Sciences Laboratory at the National Institute of Education in Singapore, describes this last approach as "designing for productive failure." In his experiments, students who were given less feedback and allowed to fail did far better on later tests than those who, like golfers, received constant feedback, had more help, and appeared to be learning more during the tutoring sessions.

Lang and his colleagues aren't alone in honing in on the uses of failure as one way to help students prepare for uncertainty. Edward Burger, now president of Southwestern University in Texas, used to grade his students on what he dubbed their "quality of failure" throughout the semester. As a mathematics professor at Williams College, the University of Colorado at Boulder, and Baylor University, Burger found that by reframing failure as an opportunity, he could remove some of its stigma and help students learn more from their mistakes. The approach also made them more willing to take risks and engage in discussions. In one assignment, he deliberately asked students to write their drafts of a paper quickly and poorly. By failing quickly, Burger knew, the students would be forced to spend time analyzing their mistakes. Anne Sobel, who teaches filmmaking at Northwestern University, has further argued that the best way to help students innovate is to move beyond standard grading measures and reward students for their willingness to experiment, tolerate failure, and take calculated risks.

Another approach to helping students prepare for ambiguous challenges is to focus more directly on the emotions involved. A person's comfort with confusion, the ability to admit that he or she is wrong, resilience, and the willingness to take risks are primarily emotional skills. Students have to grow comfortable not just with the idea that failure is a part of innovation but with the idea that confusion is, too. Harvard physics professor Eric Mazur even added to his class syllabus a section on embracing confusion. The section explained that "being confused can be very disconcerting, especially when you are under pressure to perform." But he urged students instead to "think of confusion as an opportunity to learn, not as a failure or an obstacle to understanding." Whether we try to avoid an ambiguity or seek to explore it, as Michel Thomas knew, hinges partly on whether we feel threatened. Since the emotional experience of ambiguity is highly sensitive to stress, making it safe for students to feel confused is an important first step.

Piotr Winkielman, a University of California, San Diego, psychologist, has studied the same approach-versus-avoid switch that Thomas learned to manipulate. "With kids, you can clearly see the tension," Winkielman told me. "Kids like the familiar. If it's early in the morning, they'll run to their familiar toy, or familiar doll, or familiar adult. But they also get bored very quickly. So they have this funny preference for familiarity that quickly wears out, and then they'll go for novelty. But they only go for novelty if they're in a *safe* environment." In 2010, Marieke de Vries, Winkielman, and other researchers ran a study that confirmed a similar phenomenon in adults. When people were in a bad mood, they found comfort in the familiar. Happy adults, on the other hand, lost their taste for the recognizable as the warm glow of familiarity deteriorated into a yawn. Novelty was threatening only when the adults were in a defensive state of mind. An upbeat mood can apparently turn a confusing idea into an interesting one. By rebranding failure and confusion as not merely normal but also indispensable, teachers can go a long way toward changing students' emotional attitude toward uncertainty.

Ideally, students should treat the feeling of uncertainty— whether brought on by failure or confusion—as an indication to keep thinking. "People come alive when the world breaks down," said Sidney D'Mello, a psychologist at Notre Dame. Instead of denying ambiguity, he told me, you want students to treat confusion as "a signal that [they] need to attend to information at deeper levels of comprehension."

Ducati's admirable response to its 2004 failures stemmed from its ability to view its decision-making process in just this way. Failure was an alarm bell begging Ducati engineers to scrutinize their assumptions, and that's what they did. And yet, the reason that disappointments don't always lead to deeper learning is even more instructive.

———

IN 2014, CHRISTOPHER Myers and his colleagues (including Francesca Gino) published a series of experiments investigating when people learn from failure and when they don't. Their studies shed light on the deeper reason why letdowns can send helpful signals, while triumphs can send harmful ones. Myers's group described the key variable as the "ambiguity of responsibility," or the degree to which the causes of an outcome are unclear.

In one study, the researchers asked participants to pretend that they were members of a race-car team. Facing the risk of engine failure due to a gasket malfunction, the subjects had to decide whether to go ahead with an upcoming race. They were told that the gasket had failed during a certain number of races, but (as the experiment was conducted online) they had to click on a link for "additional information, if needed," to learn how many times the gasket *hadn't* failed. Clicking the link would let them in on a truly dire statistic: there was a 99.99 percent chance of gasket failure. After choosing to race or not, subjects were informed that their decision paralleled the one engineers faced before the fatal 1986 launch of the Space Shuttle *Challenger*. Seventy nine percent of the subjects made the mistake of electing to go ahead and race, generally because participants failed to seek out the additional information.

Myers and his colleagues then asked people to name the key factor that led to their decision and explain why. Here was the ambiguity of responsibility in action. Participants who failed might blame the experimenters for withholding vital information by requiring them to click the link. Or they could excuse themselves by pointing out that a race-car engine malfunction is safer than an O-ring failure in a shuttle.

In the second part of the experiment, the researchers sent the same participants another challenge the following week. This time the subjects were asked to play the role of a security analyst and identify a potential terrorist threat. Just as with the race-car question, they had to actively seek out additional information to answer correctly. Would people who took responsibility for flunking the race-car puzzle do better this time? In fact, subjects who had blamed themselves for their race-car error had a 40 percent chance of correctly identifying the terrorist threat. Those who had first blamed external factors had a 15 percent chance.

The study mirrors what Ducati learned after its 2004 failures. First, the engineers were forced to admit that they'd made mistakes. The GP4 hadn't performed up to expectations, and now they had to find out why. They also had to uncover where their design decisions had gone awry. They discovered that they'd started the design process too late, giving themselves too little time to test and experiment. Adjusting, they began designing their 2005 model, the GP5, in March 2004, more than a year ahead of time. They would also complete it sooner. Ducati would begin work on the GP6 a year and a half before the 2006 season.

Another realization Ducati engineers came to was that they needed a more adaptable bike design. Both the GP3 and GP4 were fully integrated systems, in which every major part was designed in concert. While—in theory—integrated systems allow you to optimize overall performance, they're also inflexible, since changing one component requires redesigning others, which is costly and time-consuming. For 2005, the engineers shifted to a modular design, which allowed them to change and test one component at a time. Finally, they learned how to interpret rider feedback. They hadn't understood, while winning consistently in 2003, that a racer's poor performance could bias their analysis of what might be wrong about the motorcycle. From the ups and downs of 2004, they grasped how racers' moods affected their suggestions about the bike.

But Myers and his colleagues also examined the 21 percent of subjects who got the race-car gasket problem right. The researchers found that subjects who took *credit* for choosing not to race performed slightly worse in identifying the terrorist threat later on. It was a mistake to deflect blame after choosing to race, but it was also a mistake to be too self-congratulatory.

Ducati's early victories in 2003, similarly, led the team to stop learning because it thought it already had the answers and took undue credit. In July of that year, as the London *Independent* reported, the emphasis within Ducati's shop had shifted dramatically. "The project and the bike are new, and we just wanted to gain experience this year," Loris Capirossi said at the time. "But at the start of the season we see that the bike is strong, and now we have the chance to win races." Technical director Corrado Cecchinelli confessed that success in 2003 moved Ducati away from its usual approach to racing. "You look at the data when you want to understand what's going wrong. You do not look at the data because you want to understand why you're performing well," he said. "Our 2003 learning season was, in some way, too successful. So, our strategy was we ride, we go home, and we do not need to analyze the data. It was not important to have information at that point." When Ducati's design changes and modifications seemed to be working, the engineers stopped asking why.

Ducati's GP4 failed because the team focused on winning rather than learning. "We were confident based on the results of the season and we gambled," Filippo Preziosi said. "We changed several things in the bike for the 2004 season." Over 60 percent of the 915 parts in the GP4 were completely different from those in the GP3. The designers were so confident in their decision making that they believed the GP4 would work out even better than the GP3 had. That's what led to Ducati's dismal start in 2004.

In other research, Gary Pisano looked at a range of businesses that have high failure rates and that depended on innovation, and he uncovered the same pattern. "Companies often do debriefs when things go badly," he told me. "But we found that folks let their guards down when they succeed. They drop out of learning mode." Unexpected successes led companies to grow overconfident and less creative.

Taken as a whole, Ducati's exploits tell us that people are more likely to respect causal ambiguity when they fail than when they succeed. But by definition, there is often more causal ambiguity than we can perceive. If that weren't true, success wouldn't be detrimental. It would mean that we'd found the answers. What counts, then, isn't so much success or failure but whether we stay in learning mode, continue to seek out ambiguity, and view uncertainty as the doorway to invention. The reasons for success can be just as ambiguous as the reasons for failure, but they are usually even harder to discover, since we're even more unlikely to look for them.

"There are very few cases where we can say with 100 percent certainty that we are or are not completely responsible for an outcome," Christopher Myers told me, of his study. "Whether people succeeded or failed—and how they attributed that outcome—changed what they did with the moral of the story moving forward." An amusingly wide range of research on what's called the *hedonic bias* shows that people do indeed tend to take credit for successes while blaming their failures on others. Athletes attribute wins to effort and skill but pin losses on rotten luck, and teachers blame their students' poor performance on insufficient talent but interpret high marks as evidence of their own instructional gifts. Politicians think victories stem from their personal characteristics but imagine that losses are the fault of their party label. Yet when the causes of a lousy outcome are unclear to us, improvements depend on accepting that we have more to learn. When we don't understand what caused a success— which is more often than we'd like to admit—we need to accept the very same thing to prevent future failures.

In 1992, Duke University's Sim Sitkin published a now-classic analysis on the uses of failure and the liabilities of success. On the one hand, Sitkin wrote, "errors fuel . . . [an] 'unfreezing' process, in which old ways of perceiving, thinking, or acting are shaken and new ways can be accommodated." At the same time, he also saw that successes made organizations complacent, less exploratory, and less flexible. Sitkin recommended that businesses train employees to face novel, surprising situations and encourage small failures.

But Myers's research and Ducati's story imply yet another strategy. If fiascos lead to victories just as often as conquests precede flops, then as Gino and Pisano emphasized, organizations should treat successes with the same scrutiny normally applied to failures. They should look for ambiguous causes even when—especially when— decisions worked out. Embracing uncertainty after success means that businesses should always question the role played by unforeseen factors. They should ask, Are we misinterpreting which aspects of the product made it a hit? Which parts of the production process can we improve? What are the issues that success may have encouraged us to ignore and that could affect future decisions? What was the role of luck?

—

IN THE DOCUMENTARY *The Pixar Story*, Steve Jobs, who co-founded the animated-film enterprise, described how initially prosperous companies are often ruined by their own successes. The danger, he said, arises when executives stop questioning what they already know—when companies "have a really successful first project, but they don't quite understand why that product was so successful. And their ambitions grow and they get more grandiose, and their second product fails." Jobs was describing his experience not with Pixar but with his blockbuster computer company, Apple. The company's first real product, the Apple II, was wildly popular, as one of the first affordable microcomputers available to the average consumer. Yet the Apple III flopped. Applying this earlier experience with failure to the situation at Pixar, Jobs believed that "if we got through our second film, we'd make it."

Pixar obviously made it. In an industry with a wildly high dud-to-hit ratio, they reeled off fourteen straight number one box-office wins. The studio did it by embracing doubts, by remaining afraid of failure. It conducted postmortems after each *success.* Early on, Pixar's cofounder Ed Catmull learned that employees would rather just celebrate their victories and move on. He had to find creative ways of encouraging them to look harder at possible mistakes made or at practices that could be refined. In his book *Creativity, Inc.*, Catmull detailed the importance of always seeking out what he dubbed "the Hidden." He used the metaphor of a door, behind which is "the universe of all that you do not and cannot know," a vast world "far larger than we are even conscious of." To foster a creative culture, he wrote, you have to actively find ways to grapple with and discover these unknowns—a quest that "becomes even harder when you are successful . . . because success convinces us that we are doing things the right way."

Pixar understood the risks of apparent mastery. Brad Bird, who directed *The Incredibles*, described the culture he encountered when he was first hired. "Any company that had four hits in a row would not be open to changing anything. This place was the exact opposite. They were saying, look, we've had four hits in a row—we are in *danger* of repeating ourselves, or of getting too satisfied." Pixar figured out how to harness the benefits of rethinking "frozen" certainties—which most companies only take advantage of when they fail—and apply them to triumphs.

An even more powerful example of the role of uncertainty in innovation comes from science. The greatest asset of the scientific tradition, after all, is its persistent self-scrutiny and skepticism. Embracing uncertainty—at least at the level of scientific communities—is the defining feature of science. It's not a defect. Two giants of the philosophy of science, Karl Popper and Thomas Kuhn, both emphasized this point in different ways. For Popper, intellectual honesty means trying to *refute*, rather than prove, a theory about the world. For Kuhn, science leaps forward when contradictions pile up and lead to the abandonment of a prevailing theory. In each view, the acceptance of uncertainty precedes new ideas and discoveries. Uncertainty, as climate scientist Tamsin Edwards put it recently, "is the engine of science."

The editors of *Nature* once wrote that if science didn't "progress darkly, up and down many blind alleys and false trails, from hypothesis to hypothesis, [then] science would soon end." That's why great psychological insights are cumulative and why it is the responsibility of scientific journals (and science writers) to be distrustful. The openness at the heart of the scientific spirit means never taking error personally, seeing success as provisional, and welcoming criticism with dispassionate grace.

On the surface, there may appear to be a paradox between the confidence of entrepreneurs like Jobs and companies like Pixar and the need to embrace uncertainty. Innovation requires boldness and self-assuredness, but it also depends on being able to dwell in uncertainty. How can we square these seemingly opposed traits? How are we supposed to gain enough confidence to start a business, chase a dream in Hollywood, or launch a new product while simultaneously cultivating doubts, especially after we have done well?

One answer is that lasting knowledge earns its keep by allowing itself to be persistently questioned. In any field, we gain true confidence when we allow our ideas and successes to be continuously challenged. Our most important beliefs, John Stuart Mill wrote, should "have no safeguard to rest on, but a standing invitation to the whole world to prove them unfounded."

In MotoGP racing, the question every winning engineer faces is whether that invitation remains open after the accolades.

EIGHT

The Puzzle Man

WHERE TO FIND HIDDEN ANSWERS

BEFORE BASIC MOBILE phones took off, migrant laborers across the world had to endure long bus rides back to their countryside villages to hand-deliver money to their families. The trips were time-consuming and costly. If you wanted, you could ask someone to deliver the money for you, risking that they might spend a little on the way. Access to basic financial services simply wasn't an option for many. People didn't have bank accounts, but then, increasingly, they did have cell phones. In the Philippines in 1998, customers had an insight about the uses of rechargeable airtime minutes. Prepaid users would buy a scratch card at the local store, scrape off an opaque strip concealing a unique multidigit code, and type it into their phone.

Filipinos figured out that these codes could be used to transfer money. What was an activation code, after all? It was a unique number attached to a dollar amount. Prepaid airtime cards could serve as digital currency. All you had to do was buy an airtime card and, instead of uploading the code into your own phone, you could text it to a loved one or friend somewhere else in the country. Then you could simply destroy the card without using it. Your friend now had a code with a cash amount linked to it. They could upload it to their own phone and save the money they would have spent. Taking the logical next step, the friend could use the code as payment to a third party or even exchange it for cash, minus a reasonable commission. Prepaid airtime codes, combined with the mobile's texting function (usually transmitted by SMS, or short message service) could turn any corner candy, cigarette, and soda shack into a Western Union.

It was a transformative idea. Even the most remote villages had stalls selling airtime cards. In December 2003, the largest telecom company in the Philippines commercialized the breakthrough, launching PasaLoad (and addressing one downside of the scratch cards: once you punched the code into your phone, you couldn't transfer any of the airtime again). Researchers in Botswana, Ghana, and Uganda described how people there were also using airtime as a virtual currency. In 2004, a service in Mozambique allowed airtime swapping, and in 2007, Kenya's Safaricom launched M-PESA, allowing users to deposit, send, and withdraw money using their cell phones. By certifying existing airtime vendors as licensed M-PESA agents, the service soon became Kenya's top vehicle for money transfers—not surprising, since the ratio of M-PESA agents to banks surpassed fifty to one. As of 2013, M-PESA had over seventeen million customers in Kenya, or more than two-thirds of the adult population.

The floodgates were open. Airtime could serve as virtual currency, and text messages could be something else, too, something greater than a simple spinoff of the mobile phone. In May 2011, Coca-Cola's director of international media, Gavin Mehrotra, declared that for mobile advertising, "SMS is [our] number one priority," shocking his audience of seasoned marketers. Mehrotra's emphasis on SMS was telling. By the end of 2013, by one estimate, SMS was in use by 5.78

billion people, making it the most popular two-way communications platform on the globe. That made it practical not only for texts, advertising, and sending money but also for many other things that people in wealthier countries had started doing over the Internet.

In the Philippines, President Gloria Macapagal-Arroyo was quick to set up a range of SMS-based government services. In 2001, she set up a citizen complaint service with her initials: TXTGMA. SMS services were opened to solicit reports on crime, government corruption, and pollution-belching vehicles. By 2008, the country was helping citizens send text messages to fifty-four national government agencies. Eighty-seven percent of Filipinos preferred communicating with the government this way, according to one study, compared with 11 percent who favored the Internet. Governments in Ghana, Bahrain, and Indonesia launched an array of services that used the text function as a data channel. In Malaysia and Laos, it would now be possible to send out flood warnings by text. In India, citizens could check their application status for their passports by SMS, avoiding bribe-seeking intermediaries.

The possibilities seemed endless. You could offer people agricultural, educational, and health information. With mobile money, you could sell products via SMS. Services soon let you pay your taxes via SMS. A company in Nigeria sold clean water at mobile-payment vending pumps. In Kenya, crop insurance payouts based on automated rainfall measurements were sent directly to mobiles.

Who was driving these innovations? Carnegie Mellon University researchers reported in 2014 that an astonishing 85 percent of innovations in mobile financial services (a now multibillion-dollar global industry) came from emerging markets, and that at least half were pioneered by users. Ordinary citizens were inventing new applications, and telecoms were reduced to playing catch-up. It was as if multinationals were somehow blind to the range of emerging possibilities of mobile technology—just as prior expectations of red hearts and black spades blinded Bruner and Postman's subjects, causing them to miss the trick cards in front of them.

One key upside to seeking out ambiguity, as we've seen, is that it can aid learning even when success tempts us to take more credit than we deserve. But what if there were a systematic way of forcing ambiguity onto an object's *function*—and exposing our own blind spots? For inventions, for instance, what if we deliberately tried to see beyond our assumptions of a device's conventional use, just as migrant laborers started seeing mobile airtime cards and the SMS function in wholly unanticipated ways? Mobile money's origin story implies that shedding preconceptions and finding new uses for available tools can spark commercially revolutionary changes. Remarkably, the story of mobile money—and the key role of recognizing the functional ambiguity of SMS—holds striking parallels to one that played out when Alexander Graham Bell first patented the telephone. It's the story of how groundbreaking inventions are usually hatched.

———

BEFORE THE TELEGRAPH took off, train stations made lucrative hunting grounds for pickpockets. Trains were the fastest way for information to travel, so unless a cop caught you in the act, you were always one step ahead. You could rob people at one station and hop on a train, and there was no way for authorities to alert anyone at the next station. But in 1844, an incident on the Paddington-Slough train changed all that. The telegraph line set up along the tracks was advertised as a way that commuters could order horses to be ready on their arrival. The Paddington-Slough telegraph was merely a neat way of promoting the train service, and not much more. The thought that the telegraph could be used to fight crime simply hadn't occurred to anyone.

Surprisingly, then, an encoded message from Paddington to Slough nabbed a pickpocket. The telegraph book from that August day describes a policeman arresting a dumbstruck thief with the unfortunate name of Fiddler Dick after the train pulled in. The lawman found a woman's stolen sovereign in the pickpocket's watch fob. Other suspicious characters, accomplices, "lurk[ed] about" the station "uttering bitter invectives against the telegraph." Who knew that the telegraph would give police wings?

Over the next thirty years, the telegraph extended across the US. In 1848, there were just 2,000 miles of telegraph line. By 1852, there were over twenty thousand. A decade later, the telegraph had become a critical tool for businesses, politicians, and journalists. In 1872, Western Union figured out a way to use numbered codebooks to allow for wire transfers of up to $100 between select cities. It didn't take long before the company raised the maximum to $6,000, and about $2.5 million—almost forty thousand transactions' worth—was soon being transferred annually by wire. Telegrams had become a mainstay of modern life.

For inventors of the era, one of the most promising avenues to fame and riches involved finding new ways to make the telegraph more cost-effective. In 1858, Charles Wheatstone patented a technique that enabled a prepunched tape to be fed through an automatic Morse-code transmitter. The Wheatstone automatic telegraph allowed you to send messages ten times faster than even the best human Morse key operators typing manually. Another major innovation was the *duplex*, which allowed two messages to be sent simultaneously in opposite directions over the same wire, doubling the efficiency of existing lines. In 1874, Thomas Edison invented the *quadruplex*. Now you could send four messages, two in each direction, over a single wire. Edison's gadget apparently saved Western Union a cool half million annually.

Two inventors caught in the thick of these high-stakes horseraces were Elisha Gray and Alexander Graham Bell. By 1874, Gray was an established inventor and cofounder of an electrical equipment company that would become Western Electric. Bell was still in his twenties, a young man searching eagerly for his first big break. Both Gray and Bell were interested in the possibility of creating a "harmonic" telegraph that could transmit messages at various tones or frequencies. A harmonic device, both men thought, might send even more messages along a single telegraph line. Gray believed that his design would be able to send sixteen messages simultaneously.

On June 2, 1875, Bell was working on his version of the device when one of the reeds became stuck. When his assistant pulled it free, it made a twanging sound at the other end of the wire. Nine months later, in March 1876, building on that breakthrough, Bell was able to transmit human speech. The patent application for his new invention, a "speaking telegraph," was titled "Improvements in Telegraphy."

Gray had arguably been a step ahead of Bell in inventing the telephone. His eureka moment came in early 1874 in what was later called the bathtub experiment. His nephew was playing with some of Gray's electrical equipment in the bathroom, "taking shocks" to amuse the younger children. Two lines had been attached to an induction coil. One ran to the dry zinc lining of the bathtub. Gray's nephew held the other. Touching the zinc lining, the boy could connect the circuit and get a little jolt of electricity. But Gray noticed something bizarre. Rubbing one's hand against the zinc produced a noise—the same pitch being made by the induction coil. When Gray changed the pitch of the coil, the sound under his hand changed, too. Accurate sounds were somehow being transmitted electrically. Gray soon grasped that it should be possible to transmit human speech over telegraph wires, if he could figure out how to convert them into electrical vibrations. But he could truly not envision the benefits of transmitting sound. He decided instead to focus on improving the telegraph.

Bell's funder, Gardiner Hubbard, was hectoring him to focus on the harmonic multiple telegraph as well. Hubbard, like Gray and the bigwigs at Western Union, saw the telephone as a distraction. "You had better throw that idea out of your mind," he told Bell, "and go ahead with your musical telegraph, which if it is successful will make you a millionaire." But Bell couldn't let it go. "In spite of my efforts to concentrate my thoughts upon multiple telegraphy," he remembered later, "my mind was full [of the idea of transmitting speech]." Gray boasted to his patent lawyer that Bell was wasting precious hours on a project with no commercial value: "I don't want at present to spend my time and money for that which will bring no return."

Nevertheless, on February 14, 1876, Gray filed a caveat, a document meant to stake a claim on his forthcoming patent. Bell filed a patent application the same day, and Gray ultimately had a chance to file a full patent to contest Bell's claim. But Gray's lawyer advised him that the matter wasn't worth fighting over.

By June 1876, Gray was ready to show off the fruits of his labor at the Centennial Exhibition in Philadelphia. He demonstrated to judges his ability to send eight messages at once over a single wire. But Bell was in Philadelphia, too, and stole the show by reading parts of Hamlet's soliloquy into his magnetoelectric telephone. Gray was upset enough after Bell's demonstration that he immediately asked his lawyer for a copy of his caveat. Still, Gray insisted to his lawyer that Bell's device wouldn't be too consequential: "I am working on an Octoplex between Philadelphia and New York—four [messages] each way simultaneously—eight [messages] at once. I should like to see Bell do that with his apparatus." To his other lawyer, Gray added, "As to Bell's talking telegraph, it only creates interest in scientific circles, and, as a scientific toy, it is beautiful; but we can already do more with a wire in a given time than by talking."

The financier Hubbard pleaded with Bell, throughout 1876—even after the Centennial Exhibition—to focus on multiple telegraphy. One big breakthrough on the telegraph could secure Bell's annual income, Hubbard felt, and *then* Bell could spend time tinkering with the telephone. Bell was initially ambivalent, but by October, he had decided firmly to ignore Hubbard. Four years later, some thirty thousand telephones would be in use globally. His patent would be one of the most lucrative in US history.

Bell's breakthrough wasn't merely technical. After all, Gray had grasped the same insight over a year earlier. But Gray was stuck on the idea that the sole function of a telegraph wire was to send telegraphs. Bell's true insight was conceptual. He imagined how the "speaking telegraph" could be more than a novelty gadget.

The invention of the telephone and the creative use of phones' SMS function reveal the same underlying pattern. Innovation usually happens when an inventor grasps the potential of an existing technology's previously neglected function. It happens when he or she recognizes that something that seemed to have a clear function actually has an ambiguous function. For the telegraph, one of the aha moments came when the new system helped catch pickpockets. For the telephone, the shift began when Bell understood that talking to someone far away had collateral benefits beyond the speed of transmitting information. For mobile money, it came when Filipinos realized that airtime cards were actually coded cash amounts and that texts could transfer money. All of these cases required people to liberate themselves from old, powerful, and unspoken assumptions about what something is. As one contemporary psychologist and inventor has shown, these insights reflect a style of thinking similar to that used to solve puzzles.

———

IN 1766, A London cartographer mounted a map onto a thin board of mahogany, took out a fine marquetry saw, and cut out the shapes of countries, creating what some call the world's first jigsaw puzzle. The idea was for kids to learn geography. Anne Williams, in her recent history of the hobby, notes how unlikely a fascination jigsaws are. We take a perfectly good image, dismember it, and scramble it into a confusing mess. Then we spend countless eye-straining hours reassembling it, embarking on a journey with shifting phases, each prompting a different strategy. Maybe we start with edge pieces, then seek out certain colors or distinctive patterns. Perhaps, near the end, we arrange the missing pieces by type: one-pronged, two-pronged, and so on. We encounter unexpected twists along the way, when what seemed like a hand turns out to be a foot, or when what seemed like a cloud turns out to be an old man's hair, or when we realize that we've been looking at a piece upside down for the past three days.

Absolut ads function, as we saw, like two-piece puzzles. They set in motion our voracious drive to make sense of things. But many puzzles do more than bait the impulse to resolve a contradiction or fill in a blank. Brainteasers often force puzzlers to fight *against* the mind's natural tendency to close. They ask us to battle our reflexive assumptions. Clever crosswords make us wade through multiple word meanings: if the clue is "fire," are we looking for a synonym for enflame? Shoot? Terminate? Passion? Likewise, good detective stories take advantage of our assumptions about who commits crimes to conceal the culprit under our noses. Avid puzzlers, jigsaw lovers, and mystery aficionados take special pleasure in challenging their own tendencies to reduce ambiguity. They enjoy lingering long hours over what they do not yet know, even though, of course, they want and expect a solution in the end. The strange appeal of the jigsaw may lie here. The act of puzzling is in part a protest against the mind's reduction of ambiguity.

Art students face a similar hurdle. Just as the mind reverts to stereotypes and drilled-in word associations, the eye reduces objects to their prototypes. Ask a room of amateur art students to sketch a cup and saucer on their notepads, and you will get a series of archetypal images. Any art teacher will tell you the same thing. Even if you place a cup and saucer in front of a set of beginner students, some of them still will draw their idea of a cup and saucer. But some students may draw the set as it actually appears.

Henri Matisse once said that when he ate a tomato, he looked at it like anyone else would, but that when he painted a tomato, he saw it differently. To draw or paint objects accurately, you have to look at the tomato or cup and saucer as if for the first time—as a collection of unique colors or shades. Only then can you paint it faithfully. Friedrich Nietzsche observed the same phenomenon at work in how we observe nature: "Little do we see a tree exactly and completely with reference to leaves, twigs, color, and form; it is so very much easier for us simply to improvise some approximation of a tree." That's as it has to be. Given the hypercomplexity of the world, the mind has to make aggressive guesses. A basic function of all organisms, psychologists at the University of California, Berkeley, wrote, "is the cutting up of the environment into classifications by which nonidentical stimuli can be treated as equivalent." When we spot a tomato at a supermarket, it's good that we recognize a tomato and don't fixate on an irregular oval of unique colors and shades. We couldn't function properly if we did.

And so we order the world according to categories, and if objects we encounter are close enough to a given category, a kind of magnet kicks in, "effectively pulling them toward the prototype," as one researcher put it. From everything that we saw in Part 1, this tendency toward order is on par with what we'd expect. We have to reduce the messy world to manage it. But resolving something—fitting it into a mental box—also means that you stop scrutinizing it. Recognition means closure, and it marks the end of thinking, looking, and listening. That's true whether you're painting a peach or listening to a lecture or prematurely pinning down, like a desiccated butterfly in a display case, someone's vibrantly ambivalent or fluctuating mind-set. For inventors, in particular, our need to simplify can be bothersome. That's because when we recognize an object, we make unconscious assumptions about it. We're recognizing the conventional *function* of that object, too, usually automatically.

German psychologist Karl Duncker once conducted an experiment to test this idea—which he called *functional fixedness*—and to explore the nature of problem solving. On a table, Duncker put out three small candles, some matches, tacks, and three small pasteboard boxes. He asked his subjects to affix the candles to the door at eye level, side by side ("for visual experiments," it was explained). For one group of participants approaching the table, the three boxes were empty. For the other group, the boxes had been filled: matches in one, candles in another, and tacks in the third. In hindsight, the solution seems simple. You empty the boxes, attach them to the door with thumbtacks, and set the candles inside the boxes. Yet the subjects who approached filled boxes were over 50 percent less likely to solve the puzzle than those who found the boxes empty.

So why was the answer so elusive?

Duncker grasped that the perceived function of the box—as a container for tacks, matches, or candles—obscured its potential use as a tray. Like an SMS function used exclusively for texting, the box had a single role to play. Even with the boxes staring them in the face, few people could imagine a different use for them.

—

ON THE NEXT page are three logic puzzles known as the stuck truck, desk lamp, and three lightbulbs problems. You can try to solve them or just read through them:

1. A truck driver was driving his delivery truck under an overpass when suddenly he came to a screeching halt. He wasn't paying attention and inadvertently drove under the overpass that was just barely as high as his truck. The truck top was wedged so tightly that he could not go forward or backward. Without damaging either the top of the truck or the overpass in any way, how can he get his truck unstuck all by himself so he can drive away?

2. For some bizarre reason, a desk lamp is screwed to the wall by its base. You need to remove the lamp from the wall without damaging either the wall or the lamp. The room is empty, except for you—and your pockets are empty. You cannot leave the room and no one can bring you anything. How can you remove the lamp from the wall?

3. A room has three lightbulbs. Outside the room are three switches that are all in the off position. You cannot see the lightbulbs from the switches. The lightbulbs are in a room with no windows behind a solid door that leaks no light around it. How can you determine which switch turns on which lightbulb? You can only open the door once, and once you open the door, you cannot change the position of any of the switches. They are ordinary lightbulbs and you are completely by yourself. How can you do it?

It's best to treat these riddles like tricky crossword clues. First, you need to recognize and dismiss your instinctual answer. Then you have to dig deeper to unearth other possible solutions. For the stuck truck problem, people usually focus on the top of the truck. That's a red herring. The solution is to deflate the tires a little, so that the truck can either drive through the overpass or back up from under it. There's a second possible solution, too. Assuming the truck is jammed into the overpass behind the cabin, you could shift the weight of whatever's inside it toward the front axles. For the first so-lution, you have to see that one function of tires is to give the truck height. For both solutions, you have to stop thinking about the part of the truck that's actually stuck.

The second problem is a bit thornier. If only one screw fastens the lamp to the wall, you can keep it from spinning while rotating the base of the lamp. If two screws have the lamp pinned, you have to be a little more creative and use the electrical plug. Unplug the lamp, and you can use one of the plug's metal prongs as a screwdriver. The screw isn't the only object that can be turned, and the plug isn't just a "plug."

Puzzlers tend to struggle most with the final brainteaser. When we think of a wall switch and a lightbulb, we can't help but imagine flipping the switch, and watching the room light up. Our first im-pulse is to try to arrange the switches so that two lightbulbs are on when we open the door and we can still somehow figure out which light corresponds to which switch. That's a dead end. Think instead about being able to flip the switches on and off as many times as you want before you open the door. If you disregard a lightbulb's ten-dency to light up, you might hit on the fact that when bulbs illumi-nate, they grow hotter. Flip on one of the switches for five minutes, flip it off, flip on a second switch, and open the door. You now have two different indicators.

Starting in 2005, and building on Karl Duncker's work, a psy-chologist at the University of Massachusetts named Tony McCaffrey wanted to see whether he could devise a scientific approach to solving these and other insight problems. McCaffrey and his colleagues re-viewed a hundred recent inventions and around a thousand historical inventions and noticed a pattern. Nearly all of the breakthroughs involved a progression very similar to the toy-insight problems that we just encountered.

Almost all inventions, McCaffrey found, involve a two-step process. The first is to notice an obscure feature of an object. The second is to build a solution based on that feature. Drawing on this two-step process, McCaffrey developed the first systematic and highly effective way to overcome functional fixedness. He laid out his method, called the *generic-parts technique*, in a 2012 issue of *Psychological Science:* "I propose that subjects should create function-free descriptions for each part [of an object]." Describing each part of an object without specifying its function overtly forces us to step outside our prototypical classifications. Instead of seeing the truck as having tires, for instance, we need to reconceive the vehicle as a metal box containing shifting objects sitting on air-filled rubber tubes.

McCaffrey's technique involves asking two questions about each part of an object and constructing a diagram. First ask, "Can this be decomposed further?" If yes, you should create another hierarchical level on your diagram. Second, ask yourself, "Does this description imply a use?" If yes, you should articulate a more generic use. For example, if you were to break down a tea kettle until none of its parts imply a use, then you'd list a handle, lid, kettle, and spout. Then you'd break the elements down further.

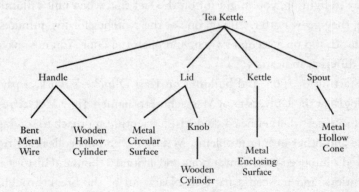

For his study, McCaffrey gave subjects logic puzzles like the ones earlier and taught some of them the generic-parts technique. Here is one of the insight problems tested in the study. Using the technique, you should be able to crack it:

> You need to connect two rings together so that when you grab the top ring and lift it up, the bottom ring will follow and remain securely fastened. Each ring weighs three pounds, is six inches in diameter, and is made of solid steel. You do not want to damage them. You have a long, thin candle, one long wooden match that will light almost anywhere, and a two-inch cubic block of steel. How can you connect the two rings?

Equipped with the generic-parts technique, the question gets a little easier. First, realize that melted wax won't work. But by decomposing the candle into multiple parts, you get wax and wick. Both imply functions. Break them down into parts that don't, and wax becomes, in McCaffrey's words, "cylindrically shaped lipids," wick becomes string, and string becomes "long interwoven fibrous strands." Now the solution is obvious. Break the candle on the steel cube, scrape the wax from the wick, and use the string to tie the rings together. Subjects trained in the generic-parts technique, McCaffrey found, solved 67 percent more problems.

Finding new uses for objects isn't just helpful for solving toy-insight problems or understanding how inventors think. As one of McCaffrey's favorite examples shows, it could conceivably save your life in an emergency. Newspapers reported that the iceberg that sank the *Titanic* was 400 feet high and hundreds of feet long. The ship could have had time to pull alongside it and use it as a raft. But the captain probably saw the iceberg as a destructive force, not as something that floats. "If you call something an iceberg," McCaffrey pointed out, "it's not even going to occur to you that, hey, oh my gosh, this thing could be a flotation device, this thing could be a lifeboat."

———

"WHAT MAKES PUZZLES puzzling?" McCaffrey asked me over lunch, letting the question linger. "Puzzles irk us," he said, adding cryptically, "and they confound our identity." McCaffrey received his PhD in cognitive psychology several years ago, in his forties. In his dissertation, he drew inspiration from Arthur Conan Doyle's crime-scene puzzles, where any minor detail might betray the incriminating clue. For McCaffrey, puzzle solving requires deliberately rethinking our routine assumptions.

"I'm addicted to these kinds of aha moments you get from seeing a new meaning in something," he said. He recounted a story about having to take a holey window screen from his house to the hardware store about three miles away to have it repaired. But after trying every possible angle, he still couldn't fit the screen in his car. He thought maybe he could tie it on the roof, but the air would flow underneath and might lift it off while he was driving. Then he realized what to do. Instead of strapping it atop the car, he put the screen on the windshield. McCaffrey used the tension of the wiper blades to clamp it against the windshield so that the wind couldn't rip it free. Seeing through the screen, it turned out, wasn't a problem. He drove down the highway three miles that way.

Before earning his PhD, McCaffrey had already collected three master's degrees: one apiece in computer science, philosophy, and theology. For eleven years he had been a Jesuit, working as a grade school teacher for several of those years. His interest in the psychology of inventing truly began there. "I would give my students puzzles all the time," he said. "I'd give them verbal puzzles, mechanical puzzles, or math puzzles. I would observe how they got stuck, and think about how I might get them unstuck, not by giving them specific hints but by giving them more general strategies. After doing this for a couple of years, I started to develop a theory about how to help people be more creative."

After publishing his generic-parts technique, McCaffrey won a National Science Foundation grant and has since been building his invention tool-kit and starting a related business. The generic-parts technique was just the beginning. More than anything, he wanted to help actual inventors.

"What frustrated me was that the previous research in my field wasn't able to generalize to help with real complex problems," he explained.

To that end, another strategy in McCaffrey's tool-kit is the feature-spectrum technique. He developed it by taking fourteen common objects such as an umbrella, a flashlight, eyeglasses, a button, a pillow, a candle, and a wristwatch and asking people to list as many features of the objects as they could. Think of features as common associations that include but go beyond an object's functions—physical properties, like what an object is made of, but also functional characteristics, like what occasion it's usually used for, the place it's usually used, whether it moves or not, and what energy is involved in its use. By combining their responses to all fourteen objects, he was able to develop a thirty-two-category system (which he has now expanded to fifty) for all types of features of physical objects. He also discovered which categories people tended to neglect for which objects.

When McCaffrey asked subjects to write down all the common features of candles, for example, people, of course, reported that the objects are cylindrical and made of wax. But they also noted that candles emanate light; that lit candles have flames; and that candles can be scented, lend atmosphere, burn, melt, are warm, are used for holidays, and are decorative. He compiled the results across the various objects and found that subjects tended to overlook twenty-one of the thirty-two types of features of the physical objects they considered. McCaffrey had previously guessed that people would overlook a third of an object's features, but in fact the participants were missing two-thirds. Inventors, McCaffrey grasped, were probably also looking at an excessively narrow range of features to improve on, or vary, in any given product.

Afterward, almost as a thought experiment, he took the data from the study and invented some new candles. "I sat down and I said, 'Let me see how many designs I can make in two hours.'" He created a simple graph comparing people's lists of the features of candles and aligned them with his thirty-two-feature taxonomy. That way, he could see exactly which features people don't think about when they think about candles.

"The first one I focused on was motion. No one wrote down motion. The category was completely blank. No one wrote down anything such as 'candles are motionless,' because it would never occur to anybody to write down that candles are motionless! I mean, they might notice that the flame flickers with motion, but nobody wrote that down, either. So I said, let me try to make candles that move."

To accomplish this, McCaffrey turned to another category that was completely blank in people's features list: weight. Nobody had noted that candles lose weight as they burn. Couldn't he use a candle's weight loss to make it move? What if he created a "scales of justice" device, with a weight on one side and a candle on the other? In a nice finishing touch to his concept, McCaffrey added a candle snuffer. He called his design the self-snuffing candle.

The design allows you to adjust how long the candle burns by changing the weight on the other side of the scale. You could set a candle to burn for one hour so that it puts itself out as you go to sleep, for instance. McCaffrey invented ten candle designs over a two-hour period. He even showed his self-snuffing idea to a candle company, Pilgrim Candle, which confirmed that it had never seen a design remotely like it:

In adapting his puzzle-solving insights to real-world challenges, McCaffrey also understood that most inventions are unlike toy-insight problems in one key aspect. Inventors, he knew, do not generally have in front of them all of the objects that they need for a solution. With the whole world at their disposal, they have to sniff the right answer out of an overwhelming number of possibilities. That's different from solving a puzzle. McCaffrey also knew that almost all inventions involve importing a solution from a different domain into the context of the problem at hand.

"I'd estimate," he wrote, "that nearly 90 [percent] of new solutions are really just adaptations from solutions that already exist—and they're often taken from fields outside the problem solver's expertise." By way of example, he told me about a sporting goods company that was recently having problems with its skis. At high speeds, when skiers made sharp turns, the edges of their skis would lift into the air a little, making the skiers more likely to fall. The company needed to reduce the ski's vibrations. It eventually found a solution in violin manufacturing. To reduce the vibrations in some violins, violin makers had inserted a thin metal grid. The ski company adapted the grid for its skis.

Looking for a way to systemize the process of pulling insights from other fields, McCaffrey devised an "analogy finder" technique. The best way to explain it is through a real-world solution that the technique recently helped uncover. Not long ago, a materials science company came to McCaffrey with a problem. Its designers wanted to adhere a coating onto Teflon, a nonstick surface. McCaffrey didn't ask why, because he didn't want the intended use to bias his search. The analogy-finder method, like his other techniques, is based on revealing the hidden biases in our everyday descriptions and associations. In this case, the bias was the company's described goal: "adhere coating to Teflon." The word *adhere*, McCaffrey found in searching through patent applications, implies (1) a chemical process (2) between two surfaces (3) which are in direct contact. These suppositions were limiting the search for solutions in other fields.

His analogy finder employs a sort of super-thesaurus technique to shed these assumptions. Instead of just searching research publications and patent databases with the word *adhere*, it also searches for synonyms: *fasten*, *connect*, and so on. "This is basically a word technique in which you describe what you need," McCaffrey said. "Let's say you want to reduce chatter in skis. If you're stuck on your wording, you would overlook all the inventions where people described it as, well, 'diminishing vibrations,' or 'lessening oscillations,' or 'dampening turbulence.'" McCaffrey's research has found that people can generally come up with about eight synonyms for a verb like *fasten*. "If you go to a nice thesaurus," McCaffrey said, "there are 61 synonyms for *fasten*, and for other verbs, there can be 80 or 120. So there are all these different ways of phrasing the same goal, and people are very narrow in how they can rephrase it. This thesaurus technique just blows that wide open and then allows you to do searches for the same goal described in various ways."

For adhering a coating to Teflon, the critical breakthrough was finding synonyms, like *fasten*, that didn't imply a chemical process, as the verb *adhere* does. The trick was using three surfaces instead of two. If you put a magnetic surface behind the layer of Teflon, you can "adhere" a coating with enough metallic content to remain attracted to the magnet on the other side. The solution was a sandwich.

———

ON APRIL 1, 1880, Alexander Bell and his twenty-five-year-old assistant, Charles Tainter, tested a wireless telephone over a distance of 700 feet, from the window of their lab on L Street in Washington, DC, to the roof of the nearby Franklin School.

"Mr. Bell," Tainter said, "if you hear what I say, come to the window and wave your hat." Robert Bruce, in his biography of Bell, disclosed how fondly the inventor later remembered the moment. "It is unnecessary to say that I waved with vigor, and with an enthusiasm which comes to a man not often in a lifetime." Bell and Tainter's "protophone" worked by transmitting speech on beams of sunlight, enabling wireless calls two decades before the electrical engineer Reginald Fessenden is credited with broadcasting the first human voice by continuous wave radio.

The protophone came as a relief to Bell, who described it as his greatest invention in terms of "the principles involved" despite its lack of practical success. Writing to his wife in April 1879, he confessed he worried that people would remember him as the man who more or less accidentally discovered the telephone: "I can't bear to hear that even my friends should think that I stumbled upon an invention and that there is no more good in me." Bell's imagination ranged widely. He would read encyclopedia entries before retiring for bed. "Find this makes splendid reading matter for night," he noted. "Articles not too long—constant change in the subjects of thought—always learning something I have not known before." Driving that curiosity was a happy insistence that there was always more to puzzle over. As his son-in-law, David Fairchild, remembered:

Mr. Bell . . . [had] an indefinable sense of largeness about him, and he so radiated vigor and kindliness that any pettiness of thought seemed to fade away beneath his keen gaze. He always made you feel that there was so much of interest in the universe, so many fascinating things to observe and to think about, that it was a criminal waste of time to indulge in gossip or trivial discussion.

Fairchild recalled one moment when a grandchild came to give Bell a good-night kiss, bringing along a balloon. "Isn't it wonderful!" Bell said, turning to Fairchild. "See how it rises!" Fairchild remembered that "wondering to him was almost a passion." Bell's inventiveness drew its strength from his extraordinary capacity to be puzzled. As the psychoanalyst and philosopher Erich Fromm observed, "The capacity to be puzzled is indeed the premise of all creation, be it in art or in science."

Thomas Edison, one of Bell's long-standing rivals, was a less romantic figure. With just a few months of formal schooling, he emphasized hard work, persistence, and experimentation. His record of 1,093 US patents remains unsurpassed. He liked to juggle multiple projects, letting one influence the other. In his biography of Edison, Paul Israel described another of the inventor's peculiarities:

A related characteristic was Edison's tendency to conceive seemingly endless variations in the design for a particular device. Edward Dickerson, a Western Union attorney, later described him as possessing a "remarkable kaleidoscopic brain. He turns that head of his and these things come out as in a kaleidoscope, in various combinations, most of which are patentable."

Not long after the invention of the telephone, Edison patented the principles underlying his incandescent lightbulb. New electrical innovations—like using sparks to light gas lamps—were at first considered, Tom Standage wrote in *The Victorian Internet*, "mere spin-offs of telegraphy." But with Edison's brainchild and other breakthroughs like the use of electricity to power trams and elevators, a new reality dawned on people. Telegraphy was not the fundamental category. Telegraphy was just one use of electricity.

Moving beyond existing conceptual categories and importing solutions from other domains seem central to innovation. Both are certainly at play in artistic creativity. John Gardner, the author and literary theorist, called the mixing of two artistic forms "genre crossing." He described it as one of the principal means by which new artistic forms are invented. If, for example, a composer is looking for novelty, Gardner wrote, "he may try to borrow structure from some other art, using film, theatrical movement, or something else." Gershwin and Stravinsky blended jazz and classical music. Shakespeare combined comedy and tragedy in his dark comedies. Edgar Allan Poe combined his interests in puzzles and true crime stories to create the detective story form. Franz Kafka later inverted Poe—Kafka's protagonist K. is a detective who cannot unravel the mystery—to pen some of the most dynamic and haunting literature ever written. What would happen if artists or writers constructed tools like Tony McCaffrey's to uncover possibly overlooked combinations? Or if other professionals looked systematically at how their assumptions were limiting the search for solutions?

I asked McCaffrey what characteristics he thought defined inventive minds. By chance, he'd just been to the Thomas Edison museum in New Jersey. He was astonished by Edison's persistent questioning of everything: How does this work? Is there another way to do this? Does it have to happen that way? From McCaffrey's perspective, the successful inventor requires two traits. The first is a wide horizon. If 90 percent of inventions are, as he found, analogous solutions, then it's essential for inventors to pull from everywhere. Second, inventors seek to understand things deeply. They aren't eclectic dabblers. They really want to know how things work, and they are unafraid to ask obvious questions. "Inventors," he said, "think both broadly and deeply. Specialists tend to think deeply but not broadly. Dabblers tend to think broadly but not deeply. Inventors do both."

Chatting with McCaffrey, it was difficult to ignore the central thread running through many of the invention-facilitating techniques in his tool-kit: the hidden constrictions embedded in everyday descriptions. Grasping that tires are tubes filled with air, that the word *wick* implies a use, that candles might move, and that *adhere* suggests a chemical process, the successful inventor is always looking to escape the narrowing assumptions buried within day-to-day language. That argues, broadly, for treating conventional associations with suspicion. It suggests that having a playful disrespect for norms—no matter how authoritative they seem—can be unexpectedly valuable.

———

CREATIVITY CAN'T BE bottled like a summer firefly. Flashes of insight wouldn't be flashes of insight if they could be manufactured on an assembly line. But by inventing methods to reveal the possible solutions we've overlooked, McCaffrey has (along with other entrepreneurs like him) taken important steps toward upping our odds of finding new solutions to old problems. Even the most humble insights can help people improve their lives.

In Brazil, a mechanic recently figured out that a one- or two-liter bottle filled with water (and bleach) could work as a lightbulb. Since water refracts light, sunbeams entering the top of a clear bottle of water will scatter in every direction. Fit the bottle into a hole in someone's roof, and the inside is brightened far more than a mere hole in the roof could illuminate it. The bottles can give off the equivalent of a fifty- or sixty-watt bulb and dramatically reduce the electricity bill or light up homes not reached by electrification. In 2012, in another remarkable innovation, the government of Haiti rolled out a partnership with the mobile company Digicel to dole out aid payments via cell phones. The program, Ti Manman Cheri, electronically paid a monthly stipend to women who kept their children in school. The program allowed much-needed subsidies to reach some of Haiti's poorest citizens. And it all began with airtime cards.

Concern Worldwide, an international humanitarian organization, illustrated a creative way to make aid payments without even having to distribute cell phones to beneficiaries, as Digicel had in Haiti. In a 2008 pilot program in Kenya, the organization made payments to over 3,000 people in the Kerio Valley using the M-PESA infrastructure. Not everyone had a phone, but Concern understood that it didn't have to purchase mobiles for everyone. Groups of ten could share phones. All the recipients needed was their own SIM card—the tiny removable plastic chip inside cell phones—since every SIM card has an embedded circuit that stores a subscriber's unique ID number.

Concern Worldwide repeated the practice in a later program in Nairobi. Irene Okoth, a program beneficiary and mother of five, explained how the system worked. "I will go to the M-PESA person," she said. "I will give her the SIM card to put . . . in their phone." Okoth could simply use the vendor's mobile. Then she would only have to enter her secret PIN and collect her money. Someone at Concern figured out that people didn't even need a phone to receive money safely. SIM cards, they realized, had a more ambiguous function than normally assumed. Among other uses, SIM cards could be debit cards, and the shacks at the ends of roads with no electricity could be ATMs.

NINE

The Art of Contradiction

WHAT DIVERSITY OFFERS

JERUSALEM IS A metropolis of barriers and boundaries. Its walled historic core, the Old City, is itself divided into cragged quarters: Armenian, Christian, Jewish, and Muslim. Divisions are further subdivided according to time-honored rites. Stark linguistic and cultural differences separate the New City less obviously. More subtle contrasts, for example, indicate the border of the Jewish neighborhood of Patt in southern Jerusalem. Take a right off Yaakov Patt Street and head down Berl Locker Road, and you'll see a residential neighborhood of palm and lemon trees, rose and roof gardens. You'll see four-story buildings in beige brick, many with decorative walls and gates, along with a few larger, eight-story apartment buildings. Colorful clothes hang outside next to air conditioners. Magenta bougainvillea flowers climb a cypress tree.

Below the mouth of Berl Locker is A-Natr Street, which leads into the Arab community of Beit Safafa. A-Natr soon becomes A-Safa Street and passes Al-Qada'il Road just north of the 1949 Green Line. In Beit Safafa, high-rises seem conspicuously absent. Building rights are more complicated in the Arab areas of Jerusalem. Beyond this flattening of the skyline, the homes themselves look similar to those in Patt. Olive trees are nestled in brown dirt. Children play in a soccer field. When I visited, work crews had begun constructing a controversial highway through Beit Safafa to connect Israeli Jews in the southern West Bank to the center of Jerusalem and to Tel Aviv on the coast. In January 2014, the Supreme Court upheld Israel's right to build the highway. Residents of Beit Safafa view the highway as part of a plan to force them off their land.

Throughout Jerusalem's history, there has never been a single religious truth. Inhabitants hold starkly conflicting views of what Jerusalem itself means. One-sided narratives can be comforting and appealing in a land marred by a history of sieges and attacks, captures and recaptures of property, and ethnic and religious conflict. Arabs and Jews generally live disconnected lives, and most schools in Jerusalem are operated in the service of either Arab or Jewish children, not both.

Yet in Patt today, across from a bus stop in a little park and down a redbrick road, a school is conducting a bold experiment in shades of gray. The school's name is Hand in Hand, and its Jerusalem location is one of five in Israel. Hand in Hand schools are integrated, with each class made up, to the extent possible, of equal numbers of Jewish and Arab children. Students here do more than confront the contradictions—the deep ambiguities—of daily life in Jerusalem. They linger in the gap between two supposed certainties and cultivate two ways of speaking about the world. Every school day, the children embrace the inconsistencies of accepting two ostensibly opposed ways of seeing the city. In classes here, two teachers work in teams. One instructs in Arabic, and the other in Hebrew. Hand in Hand students are bilingual.

NONSENSE

STUDYING THE EFFECTS of bilingualism is notoriously tricky. For one thing, people who speak two languages don't always speak them with equal skill or use them with the same frequency. Different languages overlap in distinct ways, and bilinguals also have varied bicultural experiences that can be more or less incongruent. Italian and Romanian are more closely related, linguistically, than Arabic and Norwegian. And it's one thing for a bilingual child to grow up in Paris and Rome, and another to come of age in Moscow and Buenos Aires. Through the clutter, however, psychologists have noted a positive correlation between bilingualism and creativity. One literature review found that twenty of twenty-four studies comparing bilinguals with monolinguals revealed a bilingual advantage for creativity. Its author, psychologist Lina Ricciardelli, suggested that the advantage depends on bilinguals' high proficiency in both languages.

Dean Simonton, a psychologist at the University of California at Davis and an expert on creativity, has done illuminating work showing that eras of artistic creativity often follow periods of openness to outside influences. Simonton's interest in creativity began in the mid-1970s, with his doctoral dissertation. Back then, he was trying to figure out exactly why creative geniuses tended to cluster in specific periods. Why, he wondered, were there so many brilliant people in the golden and silver ages, but not in the so-called Dark Ages? What explained the seemingly disproportionate number of creative minds in Renaissance Italy, or in Islamic Baghdad during the reign of the Abbasids? In searching for the sources of societal and cultural creativity, Simonton eventually narrowed in on multiculturalism and bilingualism.

In one historical study of Japan, Simonton spliced the period between 580 and 1939 into twenty-year intervals. In each generational period, he gauged the number of eminent immigrants, the amount of travel abroad, and whether natives were influenced by outsiders. Then he compared these ebbs and flows with fourteen measures of national achievement—in religion, business, medicine, philosophy, and art, among other areas. Openness to outside influences and the frequency of travel abroad, he found, was correlated with simultaneous gains in achievements in business and religion. Most strikingly, he also discovered that the more diversity there was in Japanese society, the more creative the society was two generations later in the areas of medicine, fiction, poetry, and painting. Diversity can be painful initially, it seems, but it pays off decades later. While at first most immigrants occupy a marginal position in society, as Simonton explained, "after a generation or two not only do they become integrated but their culture becomes part of the 'melting pot'—as we start eating pizza or chow mein."

Rodica Damian and Simonton, in a chapter in *The Wiley Handbook of Genius*, described the sources of creativity, in the broadest sense, as "diversifying" experiences. These experiences "push people outside the realm of 'normality' and help them see the world in multiple ways," which in turn aids the "cognitive flexibility necessary for coming up with creative ideas." One well-known study looked at high-achieving individuals such as T. S. Eliot, Graham Greene, Jimmy Carter, Carl Jung, and Margaret Mead and found that a huge proportion of them were first- or second-generation immigrants. A study of distinguished US mathematicians found that 52 percent were foreign-born or second-generation citizens. Even though foreign-born immigrants represent just 13 percent of the US population, they account for 30 percent of the nation's patents and a quarter of its Nobel laureates. In 2009, an experiment showed that simply coaxing subjects to remember their time spent living abroad made them more creative. The more time people had spent living abroad, similarly, the more likely they were to solve Karl Duncker's candle problem.

The finding that deeply absorbing a foreign culture makes people better at solving puzzles reinforces an important point that Jerome Bruner (the lead author on the reverse-colored playing card study) has emphasized throughout his entire career. Our ambiguity-reducing preconceptions, he has argued, are culturally driven.

Bruner was born in 1915. He was ninety-seven when we talked, and he remained marvelously lucid. How we collectively deal with ambiguity, he told me, serves as "one of the founding elements of what we speak of as human culture." He said that our shared, distorting preconceptions *constitute* what we call culture: that culture is a shared warping of the world, a communal papering-over—or collective denial—of ambiguity. It can be partly defined as a set of instructions for the contradictions we should blot out, and the brand names, technologies, and geniuses we should have faith in: guidance for how our beliefs should bend perception.

That's why living in a foreign country can make people more inventive. And why soaking up a new culture or shuttling back and forth between two different ones can shake up our expectations. It can help us to think beyond our normal assumptions, even in the simple case of realizing that a box can be used for more than just holding tacks. That language is one of the ways in which culture achieves its simplification of the world also hints at why bilingualism can aid creativity. Just as McCaffrey saw that the limits of language can hinder innovation, learning to speak in other tongues can promote it.

———

BILINGUAL KIDS USUALLY experience two cultural views of the world. But speaking two languages has other remarkable advantages, even purely at the level of brain function. Ellen Bialystok of York University is one researcher at the forefront of studying the cognitive effects of bilingualism. Bilinguals, her research shows, outperform monolinguals on various tests in three key areas: the ability to focus, the capacity to inhibit previously acquired information, and the ability to hold information in the mind. Since both languages are active, or available, at the same time, bilinguals not only have to remain aware of which language to use in which circumstances, but also have to select that language and suppress the other.

Bilingual people, for example, perform better at the Stroop test, a classic experimental tool. In one of the original versions of the test, published in 1935 by J. Ridley Stroop, subjects were timed on two tasks. On one task, they had to look at squares of different colors and identify the color: red, blue, green, brown, or purple. On a second task, subjects saw words printed in these same colors and had to, again, identify the ink color. The trick was that the words spelled out the names of conflicting colors. The word *red*, for instance, might be printed in blue ink. As Stroop explained it, "where the word 'red' was printed in blue it was to be called 'blue,' where it was printed in green it was to be called 'green,' [and] where the word 'brown' was printed in red it was to be called 'red,' etc." In black-and-white, Stroop's test would look something like this:

BLACK WHITE **WHITE** BLACK
GRAY **WHITE** BLACK WHITE
WHITE BLACK GRAY BLACK
BLACK WHITE BLACK **GRAY**

The task here would be to move from left to right, and then row by row, and name the shades of "ink" aloud: "white, gray, black, gray, white, black, white," and so on. You should feel yourself slow down a little to get the text colors right. In the original, Stroop compared how long it took subjects to describe the color blocks with how long it took them to name the ink colors when the words conflicted. People took over 70 percent longer to identify the colors when the words named other colors.*

Imagine the kind of mental control it takes to switch quickly between reading the word and then the letter color in the Stroop test, and then imagine never adapting to doing it one way or the other. That's a bit like the situation that fully bilingual people face when they're switching frequently between languages—it's a never-ending workout. In one study, even seven-month-old babies who had been raised in a bilingual home had better control over their attention than did babies raised in a monolingual one.

Bilinguals are constantly sorting conflicting information. Young bilingual kids even intermix languages early on—a phenomenon called *code switching*. Bialystok described this mental tussle in terms of Piaget's conception of learning. You "expect things to be a certain way," she told me, "and if you encounter a new situation that's similar to one that you expect, you apply that scheme. That's assimilation. But every now and then, the new situation doesn't quite fit. You can't quite apply that schema. The only way to move forward is to slightly change the schema. That's accommodation. And that's exactly what's happening here. Something is slightly different. [Bilingualism] works like a little *irritant* that requires you to think a little harder."

Managing the conflict between two languages even seems to have long-lasting, protective effects on the brain. In 2011, a study

* During the Cold War, the CIA reportedly employed a modified version of the Stroop test in order to detect Soviet spies. In their version, the words were in Russian. The idea was to uncover whether someone was secretly fluent in the language. If suspected spies didn't speak Russian, identifying the color wouldn't slow them down, because there would be no conflicting impulse to read the word. If the task slowed them down, they knew Russian. The test may have been particularly effective in uncovering spies because it's difficult to suppress the automatic reaction to read the word. You'd have to practice.

of Spanish-English bilinguals showed that more-proficient bilinguals were less susceptible to symptoms of Alzheimer's disease. The mental workout, over a lifetime, builds up a kind of cognitive reserve. Bilingualism, it's important to note, isn't a one-way street. One downside is in reduced verbal fluency. Bilinguals have more word gaps and more tip-of-the-tongue experiences. Their vocabulary in each language is a bit smaller than monolinguals.

The benefits, however, outweigh the costs. Researchers continue to debate the precise cognitive mechanisms involved, but as the European Commission reported in 2009, hundreds of studies support the link between bilingualism and creativity. In 2005, Bialystok and Dana Shapero also reported that bilinguals cope with ambiguity better. In one experiment, they showed five-year-old bilingual children variations of the ambiguous figures pictured here, each of which contains two distinct images:

Children have a very difficult time seeing both figures in these images, partly because they tend to seize and freeze on the first image that they recognize. "Having decided it's a rat," Bialystok said, "it's very hard for a child to give up on that. Once an image is labeled . . . it has been fixed in space, so to speak." Yet bilingual children were more than three times better than monolingual kids in identifying both the rat and the man, more than twice as good at distinguishing both the vase and the profiles, and significantly better at picking out the saxophone player and the woman. Having learned to process the world using two languages—having grown comfortable with linguistic ambiguity—bilingual kids were able to get unstuck more easily.

Bilinguals are also better at grasping the arbitrary nature of words and symbols. Some years ago, the researcher Sandra Ben-Zeev asked monolingual and bilingual children (ages four to eight) to think about objects as if they had different names. Testing Hebrew-English bilinguals, for example, children were told: "You know that in English this is named airplane [experimenter shows toy airplane]. In this game its name is *turtle*." Then the kids were asked, "Can the *turtle* fly? [Correct answer: Yes.] How does the turtle fly? [Correct answer: With its wings.]" Bilingual kids had an easier time answering questions when using the bizarre substitute words. Jean Piaget once devised a similar test for kids known as the sun-moon problem. Suppose, he offered, we decided to switch names for the sun and the moon. When we go to bed at night, what would be in the sky? And how would the sky look? When the test was later put to bilingual children, both partially bilingual and fully bilingual kids again performed better than monolinguals, who were more likely to describe the night sky as bright.

Simonton has suggested a clever little exercise that helps explain how this kind of conceptual flexibility might affect creativity. Pick out twenty nouns, he suggested, words that people use frequently, and find a good two-way dictionary. Translate the English words into all their possible meanings in the foreign language. Then translate each of those foreign words back into English, and repeat. Let's try French, starting with the English noun *window*. In a room, a window is a *fenêtre*. In a car, my dictionary tells me, it's *glace*. In a shop front, the word is *vitrine*. At a bank, it's *guichet*. If we translate *fenêtre* back into English, we find two new meanings: "fenestra" and "inlier." *Fenestra* is an anatomical term referring to a small opening or perforation, particularly between the middle and inner ear. *Inlier* is a geological term for a formation encased by rocks of a younger age. *Glace* also means ice, ice cream, icing, or mirror. *Vitrine* can also refer to display cabinet. *Guichet* also means ticket office. You can imagine that being able to access different meanings like these simultaneously could help expand the kinds of things that come to mind when we think of the word *window*. Simonton is suggesting, in short, that bilinguals have a built-in version of Tony McCaffrey's thesaurus technique. They aren't as confined by language, because they viscerally understand how flexible it is.

When a person is fully bilingual, as Simonton put it, "all concepts have representations in both languages, but the representations cannot be identical." That's why computer translations aren't perfect. The implication, he explained, is that "the concepts themselves must become more open and flexible." Colin Baker, an expert on bilingualism, offered a nice example of how multiple languages can offer bilinguals a richer and more complex conceptual experience of the world. In Welsh, the word for "school," *ysgol*, also means "ladder." So if you know both Welsh and English, you have a richer conceptual notion of school—as a place to move up in the world.

That's partly the idea, of course, behind Jerusalem's Hand in Hand. The education it offers is both cognitively and culturally valuable. The teachers know that theirs is a long-term project. One second-grade teacher, Yaffa Shira Grossberg, has taught for twenty-one years, including eleven at Hand in Hand. When I visited, the children ran around us wildly during a break as she described the school's philosophy. For her classes and for all others, from prekindergarten through sixth grade, pairs of teachers work in tandem.

"We teach through conversation," she said. "It's a dialogue between my coteacher and me, and we include the children in that conversation. When I speak to my class, I speak to them in Hebrew, and when I speak to my coteacher, I speak to her in Hebrew and she answers me in Arabic. We encourage the students to answer in whatever language they're comfortable with while they're younger.

As they get older, we encourage them to answer in the language in which the question was posed. By the end of second grade, their passive comprehension is completely bilingual." Starting in first grade, students learn both alphabets and the basics of reading and writing.

Grossberg's affection for her students is palpable. In part, she said, they're like any other kids. They fight and complain about stolen chairs and pencils. But the cultural dimensions of speaking both Arabic and Hebrew aren't lost on them. "They notice that there's a different mix of Jewish and Arab students," Grossberg said. "They sense that this is different and unique. But they're too young to make that a barrier. Then later on, by the time that they're old enough to realize that their differences could have been a barrier, the barrier is already gone." As if perfectly timed for the end of our conversation, a sea of small girls swept Grossberg away and back to her class, holding on to her as if to a raft.

———

ACROSS FROM JERUSALEM'S Yad Vashem Holocaust museum, on a rocky hill, I met a family with three little boys. Tristan, eight, was the oldest, Andrei was six, and Amos was just three. Tristan and Andrei were Hand in Hand students. Grossberg was Tristan's teacher. Their father, Philip Touitou, is a French-Algerian Jew, and the boys have beautiful golden skin that seems to mirror the brown tones of the earth here. His partner, Danae Elon, is an American-Israeli filmmaker.

Touitou is funny and engaging, with a sweet temperament made even more charming by an aura of irony and resilience. Elon has dark hair and striking eyes, brown-gold around the pupils, but green and almost turquoise at the rim of the irises. She has a relaxed and almost neutral humor about her. Her wit sneaks up on you.

Amos was still learning Arabic, but Tristan and Andrei were well on their way. In addition, they spoke Hebrew, French, and English in varying degrees. The boys were relaxing at the end of the school day. Amos sat on the couch fitting a toy car inside of a toy truck. Andrei told me that he had made a kite and began singing a song about a bird in Hebrew. Tristan, between racking up high scores on an iPad game, assured me that switching languages is "easy-peasy" and that his four best friends are Arab boys.

Watching her children figure out and play with multiple languages has often surprised Elon. "They say funny things. For example, there's an expression in Hebrew, 'I love this,' and it's like, *ani met al ze.* But *met* means 'dead,' so Tristan will say, in English, 'You're dead about that, aren't you?' They make funny translations. I think that it enables them to have a wider outlook on life. They can navigate not only the language barrier, but the national and religious and color barriers."

Elon herself grew up trilingual, speaking Hebrew, English, and Italian and moving among different social worlds. The clash between these worlds informed and inspired her filmmaking. "You grow up here with lots of contradictions in-built," she said. "It gives you a way of looking at things."

She first discovered her love of film by accident. Kicked out of school, she was saved by a unique arts academy that happened to have a film department. With funding for Israeli filmmakers scarce at the time, the school was able to hire some of the best filmmakers in the country—artists who would make their mark on the national filmography. Every Friday, they'd take students to see a classic film, and one day, Elon saw *Seven Samurai.* Walking out of the theater, she knew the career she wanted. She graduated from New York University's Tisch film school in 1995, having won a class award for cinematography and a National Eastman Scholarship.

Her breakthrough film was a documentary called *Another Road Home*, which explored her childhood in Jerusalem. Not long after the Six-Day War, in 1967, a Palestinian man from the occupied village of Battir knocked on the Elons' door. He was hired on the spot as Danae's caretaker and would stay with the family for twenty years. His name was Mahmoud, but he was known to the Elons as Musa. In the film, Elon scours the streets of Paterson, New Jersey, looking for Musa's sons, who had emigrated, without their father, to start businesses in the United States. Musa himself, at seventy-six, flies to America for a reunion, navigating a dangerous, multiday journey through checkpoints and Jordan. "It's unlikely," a *New York Times* review remarked, that "there will ever be a more moving portrait of the shared selfhood, usually veiled by politics, common to Palestinians and Israelis." *Variety* praised the documentary for its "unflinching simplicity." In the film, Elon asks Musa how, in one of her most poignant memories of him, he had so carefully and tenderly ironed her Israeli military uniform for her. "Don't worry," he tells her. For him, it was merely an act of affection.

In 2009 came Elon's *Partly Private*, which somehow explored the pros and cons of circumcision in a documentary shaped like a romantic comedy. The film opens with Tristan's birth, ends with Andrei's, and follows the debate she and Touitou had over what to do. Touitou wanted to have the boys circumcised—the tradition in his family. Elon was unsure. *Partly Private* won the 2009 Best New York Documentary at Tribeca. Both *Another Road Home* and *Partly Private* grapple with contradictions, be they religious, political, or personal. *Another Road Home* was built around Elon's memory of Musa ironing her military uniform. She couldn't understand the contradiction, and the film doesn't resolve it. Elon doesn't answer the questions she raises in *Partly Private*, either. She merely poses them in human terms. She has said that she "wasn't interested in exploring who was right and who was wrong in the argument." Her films are wonderful elaborations of complex questions.

One of Elon's current film projects focuses on raising Tristan, Andrei, and Amos in Jerusalem. In one scene, she puts microphones on Tristan and a Palestinian friend, another Hand in Hand student, as they roam through the Jerusalem streets at night with a few other boys. It was Israel's Memorial Day, which commemorates those who have fallen in Israel's wars.

"They took their skateboards," Elon said, describing a scene that took place along the borders of Patt and Beit Safafa, near Hand in Hand. "And they went out. It was around seven o'clock at night, and they were walking through all these dark alleys. There were women, Arab women, around, and Tristan's friend says, 'Tristan, don't speak Hebrew here, because if you speak Hebrew here, you're going to get cursed and you won't know it.' Then the siren goes off for [Memorial Day], and the group of boys stands up straight, and they say, 'This is about the Holocaust.'" The boys were confused, because Holocaust Remembrance Day was only a week prior. "The Palestinian boy explains to the group that the siren is about the Holocaust. And they all stand still. Then the whole group heads back and passes down another street, and Tristan and his friend say, 'Okay, don't speak Hebrew, don't speak Hebrew here.' A hundred meters farther along, they say, 'Okay, now we don't speak Arabic, we don't speak Arabic here.'"

They were seven years old, navigating this cultural minefield, switching between languages, trying to understand both worlds and attempting to move fluidly between them. As Elon recalled the scene to me after dinner, Andrei interrupted her, to tell her, in Arabic, that he loved her. "This guy's accent in Arabic is flawless," she said. "It comes from his guts, you know?"

"Andrei has lots of Arab friends and lots of Jewish friends," she said, holding her middle son. She told me about a family visit to the Palestinian town of Jericho and how comfortable the boys felt there: "They are free with Arabs. They don't grow up claustrophobic in their environment, and they don't grow up with fear of the other." Hand in Hand parents, she admitted, may have different motivations. The Arab parents want their progeny to speak Hebrew without an accent, so the children can participate in Israeli society. The Jewish parents are liberals. For a Jewish child, speaking Arabic without an accent is a political act.

"If you want to talk about politics of the weak," Elon said, "Arabs make fun of the way Jews speak Arabic. That's their way of getting back at you. There's a whole social statement in the way Jews speak Arabic. I speak Arabic, but I cannot speak Arabic in public. Because when I do, I feel the weight of the whole story kind of sink in. I can hear it in the way I pronounce 'ha' or 'huh.' It's a big deal. That's why, when I hear Andrei speaking like this . . ." She shook her head, overcome with emotion, and slipped into a proud silence. Andrei began to show off his Arabic. His father brought out a bowl of watermelon for dessert.

MONTHS BEFORE MY visit, a group of sixth-graders from Hand in Hand were accosted verbally and attacked on a public bus. The children were doing nothing wrong. They were merely talking among themselves in Arabic when a pair of Jewish teenagers overheard them. "You should be thankful that we allow you to live here," one said. An older woman joined in. "Shame on you that you are still alive," she said. "You are monkeys." She added, "I will send someone to murder you . . . You have no right to live." She pulled a student's hair and slapped her. When another bus rider protested, one of the teens replied, "I'm not embarrassed to be racist. I hate Arabs. So what?" The bus driver called the police, who detained the woman.

Hand in Hand supporters put up fliers in Hebrew across Jerusalem:

Yes: It is possible that we will have a different color.

Yes: It is possible that we will have a different religion.

Yes: It is possible that we will speak a variety of different languages.

Yes: It is *essential* that we ensure that all children can ride the bus safely.

A year earlier, someone sprayed DEATH TO ARABS across the outside of Hand in Hand Jerusalem, apparently a price-tag crime by Jewish Israeli radicals—payback for government action against illegal West Bank settlements. Tristan's homework assignment, the night before I arrived, was to write a letter to Superland, a local amusement park that had decided that it didn't want Jewish and Arab children attending on the same days. Certain days would be for Jews, others for Arabs. In November 2014, a fire burned down part of the school one Saturday night. It was started in the preschool.

⁓

IN 2011, PSYCHOLOGISTS Arne Roets and Alain Van Hiel compared Arie Kruglanski's concept of the need for closure with Gordon Allport's descriptions of the prejudiced mind. Roets and Van Hiel found that the roots of prejudice can be traced to a general cognitive outlook characterized by the hunger for certainty. Prejudiced people, Allport wrote in his landmark work, *The Nature of Prejudice*, "seem afraid to say 'I don't know.'" They have an "urge for quick and definite answers," "cling to past solutions," and have a preference for "order, but especially *social* order." Such people "adopt concrete, if rigid, modes of thinking," "cannot tolerate ambiguity" when making plans, "latch on to what is familiar, safe, simple, definite," and fail "to see all relevant sides to [a] problem."

Gordon Allport was Jerome Bruner's and Leo Postman's teacher. Years ago, Allport ran a study that mirrored Bruner and Postman's reverse-colored playing card experiment. Instead of testing card suits, Allport's experiment tested stereotypes. He flashed subjects a picture of a black man and a white man engaged in an argument; the white man is holding a razor. When, later on, Allport asked subjects to recall who in the picture had been holding the razor, half erroneously remembered it in the black man's hand. "Expectancy," Allport's colleague Robert Buckhout later wrote, "is seen in its least attractive form in the case of biases or prejudices."

Thinking about prejudice as entrenched in the high need for closure might help us see the problem in a slightly different light. We are all stereotypers. Our rapid-fire assumptions are how we achieve the miracle of simplification. Culture determines the "style" with which we reduce complexity and ambiguity. Since we can't have no style at all, we can't avoid relying on preconceptions. We can fight one version of snap judgments—bigotry—but we can never graduate morally from crudely categorizing other people. We aren't normally comfortable thinking of perception this way, I suspect, because we don't consider positive snap judgments stereotypes. But we must lose just as much information when our stereotypes are generous as when they are judgmental. Ultimately, everything is more mysterious than we can imagine. But while none of us can escape our limited mental maps of the world, we can sample from other cultures and subcultures and discover new ways of looking at things. We can, in a sense, begin to triangulate the truth. We can refine our necessarily aggressive preconceptions (as what we learn morphs into habit), but life is too short to learn everything. Inevitably, there remain vast areas of knowledge—of ideas, people, and places—where our mental models are poorly informed. Yet we can be bighearted and acknowledge these gaps. We can struggle, persistingly, to seek out the contradictions our minds naturally work to eliminate.

Just as great artists or scientists are inspired by contradictions, the prejudiced person seeks to eradicate them. That's what is so striking about Hand in Hand and Tristan, Andrei, and their friends. Elon doesn't romanticize or idealize either side, but she understands both sides, as do her kids. She knows that having an open mind doesn't imply having no opinion. It often implies having both opinions. It means not denying the supposed contradiction that victims can be victimizers and vice versa, a simple truth that dogmatists refuse to accept. Such contradictions fuel Elon's art. The open-minded person, likewise, cultivates those tensions.

GEORGE SAUNDERS ONCE said that "in art, and maybe just in general, the idea is to be able to be really comfortable with contradictory ideas." Wisdom, he said, might be "two contradictory ideas both expressed at their highest level and just let to sit in the same cage sort of, vibrating." In *Seven Types of Ambiguity*, William Empson showed that much of the power in the poetry of Shakespeare, Donne, Chaucer, Tennyson, Yeats, and Milton comes from contradictory, mystifying, or parallel meanings.

Part of the bilingual person's advantage in creativity seems to stem from an understanding of the arbitrary and hidden biases of language. But another advantage comes from having at least two cultural views of the world. John Gardner, in *On Moral Fiction*, offers the best description of the origins of artistic creativity that I've read: "Art begins in a wound, an imperfection—a wound inherent in the nature of life itself—and is an attempt either to learn to live with the wound or to heal it." In Gardner's framework, dissonance can come from different conflicts. Living in two places, being a part of two cultures, and social alienation are just some of the possible sources of creative work:

> This alienation . . . is often reflected in another, more ordinary alienation, the social displacement which occurs when . . . Joseph Conrad leaves Poland, Joyce goes to Paris or Faulkner to Hollywood, or the contemporary novelist leaves Harlem, Brooklyn, Texas, Ohio, or Nebraska for Academia. Such displacement is so common in the lives of artists as almost to be a law of artistic success. (For the roaming Celtic bard, in fact, it *was* a law.) . . . In the unlucky, social displacement leads to maladjustment and to art that whimpers or snarls. In the lucky, it leads to a healthy doubleness of vision, the healthy alternative—crucial in art—to disorientation and emotional insecurity, the anxiety and ambivalence of the neurotic. . . . The two most eminently sane poets who have ever written in English, Chaucer and Shakespeare, are both people who moved from one locale and station to another, somewhat more prestigious; and a part of their greatness lies in their having found, through the medium of poetry, ways of reconciling conflicts between the old and the new.

Mark Twain argued that "travel is fatal to prejudice, bigotry and narrow-mindedness." The claim holds because both empathy and creativity spring from the same source: diversity. Empathy, after all, is a fundamentally creative act by which we connect previously unimagined lives to our own. The path to embracing other cultures has to traverse the imagination. That's why studies have shown that a high need for closure hurts creativity. And it's why reading fiction—which puts us in other people's shoes—can both lower our need for closure and make us more empathetic. Spending time among diverse social groups has the same effect. Hand in Hand Jerusalem, aimed at instilling those ideas deeply, has the psychology exactly right. Since people who naturally crave neatness tend to get nervous around unfamiliar "others," positive intergroup experiences help those with a high need for closure feel less anxious. In fact, intergroup experiences benefit these people the most.

Jerome Bruner emphasized this same thought when we spoke. He talked about how cultivating ambiguity helps us keep an open mind and empathize with different viewpoints and how contradictions are a kind of fuel for human imagination. Travis Proulx has developed a similar thesis. Creativity, he argued, is a fifth reaction to contradictory, ambiguous experiences. In keeping with the other four *A*'s— assimilation, accommodation, abstraction, and affirmation—he calls the fifth reaction to anomalies *assembly*. When we assemble, we take the uncertainties in our lives and create something out of them. It's no accident that periods of artistic production—in Hellenistic Greece or in New York City in the 1970s—occur during eras of social upheaval. Art can be cathartic because the accurate depiction of irresolvable conflicts is itself a form of soothing truth-telling. Creativity, as Bruner put it, often results "when the ambiguity *wins*."

Hand in Hand, in that sense, is its own artistic triumph. In 2013, even as the Education Ministry took parents of another bilingual program to court because the program was formally "unapproved," Hand in Hand was set to open its fifth bilingual school, a kindergarten. There is no civil marriage and practically no interfaith marriage allowed in the country, so it is virtually illegal for Jews and Arabs to marry one another inside Israel. Yet in classrooms at the seams of Jerusalem, Hand in Hand's children paint and draw together, play basketball together, study religion together, and sing together in Arabic and Hebrew.

EPILOGUE

HERE'S A SIMPLE thought experiment. Take a guess as to how much you've changed over the last ten years on a scale from 1 to 10. Now, on the same scale, estimate how much you will change over the next decade. How do your two ratings compare? Do you assess your past changes differently from how you predict your future ones?

It turns out that most people do, and that the inconsistencies are glaring. A team of psychologists led by Jordi Quoidbach recently recruited almost twenty thousand subjects between the ages of eighteen and sixty-eight to explore such disparities. The subjects were asked how much their personality, values, and preferences had changed over the past decade or would change over the next one. For instance, eighteen-year-olds filled out a personality questionnaire as if they were twenty-eight years old. Twenty-eight-year-olds answered the same questions as if they were eighteen or thirty-eight. Nineteen-year-olds and twenty-nine-year-olds did likewise, and so on. For a fifty-year span, Quoidbach could compare people's predictions of personal evolution with their reports of actual change.

In terms of values and preferences, people predicted significantly less change than they recalled experiencing, although the predictions improved slightly in older subjects. The results on personality changes were more consistent—and provocative—across all age groups. Folks reported that their personalities were starkly different ten years earlier, yet they foresaw little change ahead. Most people, the psychologists wrote, "expect to change little in the future, despite knowing that they have changed a lot in the past." We create a sharp division between our present, fixed self, and our past, evolving selves. We always think we've settled into ourselves, and we're always wrong.

"The most interesting finding is that at every age, we feel like we're done with our own evolution," Quoidbach told me. "It's like the present is what you've achieved after all those long years of changing. And now you're done."

The paper was titled "The End of History Illusion."

Quoidbach's heading was a nod to Francis Fukuyama's well-known 1989 essay, later developed into the book *The End of History and the Last Man*. Writing at the end of the Cold War, Fukuyama claimed that history had a direction, a theme, a natural progression, and that we were witnessing its culmination. The world was watching, he wrote, "not just the end of the Cold War, or the passing of a particular period of postwar history, but the end of history as such: that is, the end point of mankind's ideological evolution and the universalization of Western liberal democracy as the final form of human government." The claim made Fukuyama famous.

The end-of-history concept was widely criticized and debunked, and even the author moved on. But Quoidbach's study illustrates one reason why the argument was so powerful in the first place. We're inclined to conceive of the past as a story, as some plot that's heading inevitably in one direction. The problem is that thinking this way robs the past, present, and future of their mystery. It treats the "us" of ten years ago as evolving and the "us" of now as finally developed, and it loses sight of how wonderful and frightening both the present and future are in their potential. Our impulse to deny the unpredictability of the future favors neatening the past into a tidy narrative.

Misconceptions and misunderstandings of this sort, stemming from aversion to uncertainty and our craving for order, have occupied us throughout this book. We've seen how troubling mental conflicts, under a high need for closure, can lead us to seize and freeze, to grow servile or increasingly dogmatic. Dick Rogers and Jeff Jamar, at Waco, couldn't handle David Koresh's wavering because they were bad at dealing with ambiguity. They were more comfortable interpreting ambivalence as deception. As we stand queasily at the dawn of a new globalism, advancing technologies also tempt us to envision permanent solutions to unsettling unknowns. In medicine and poverty-fighting programs, that tendency can be downright harmful. In business, likewise, our attempts to predict the future in light of ambiguous odds often backfire.

The brain does much of its necessary resolving and categorizing unconsciously, in the same way that we recognize an ordinary tomato at a grocery store or eliminate the conflict between moving lips and sounds without realizing it. Our working models of the world are like the air we breathe. We usually don't notice them. But as Travis Proulx has shown, even when we don't consciously pick up on anomalies, we remain exceptionally sensitive to them. Something as subtle as a seen-but-unrecognized trick playing card can trigger an attempt to restore a cognitive balance between sense and nonsense. Our perceptually powerful expectations don't merely guide how we simplify ambiguity. When violated, they also determine when we look for meaning.

Yet something more—another persistent and powerful theme beyond our tendencies toward closure—is embedded in the stories and examples we've examined. When we work at puzzles, we're engaging with the shortfalls of our instinctual answers. When we laugh, we're partly taking pleasure in the whimsical inadequacy of our assumption-projecting minds—in the mistakes we make as we constantly fill in, filter out, or extend our ideas. All of the remarkable men and women we've followed in this book found ways to unshackle themselves from the mind's compulsive desire to eliminate ambiguity. They resisted simple, edifying stories that suggested a neatly categorized world. Even within psychological science, we've seen that progress is not necessarily neat and linear.

The heroes of this book are all protestors, and what they are protesting is the premature destruction of the world's mystery. They include Arie Kruglanski, who refused to pathologize the worst outcomes of aversion to uncertainty in Weimar, Germany, and Travis Proulx, who would not accept the rigid silos of a fragmented psychology. There is Gary Noesner, the hostage negotiator who was able to dwell calmly in contradictions, and Trisha Torrey, a patient advocate who pushed back against a medical system taking the quest for certainty too far. Linguist Michel Thomas and English teacher Jim Lang, master instructors, learned to help their students brave the swampy grounds of uncertainty. Francesca Gino and Gary Pisano, too, showed that the causes of success in business are more ambiguous than we perceive and that there is always more to question. Tony McCaffrey, an inventor with a kaleidoscopic mind, devised a system to help us break free of the vise grip of our suppositions and be more creative. Psychologist Jerome Bruner emphasized that culture determines how we reduce ambiguity and make sense of nonsense. Danae Elon's films and life have been dedicated to cultivating an empathy born of resisting that very reductionism.

Each of them has shown that we can push back against our own mind's need to reduce and simplify and dispel all remaining doubts. Learning two languages, or living in two cultures, helps us do just this.

End-of-history thinking is yet another example of how our minds try to order the untidy world. The tendency to airbrush away ambiguity is so deeply ingrained that it is not so surprising that we streamline history, too, or view the past as important only for the role it played in getting us to where we are now. We tend to think that only *we* are developed, fully realized, complete. This way of thinking treats the past the way that too many people treat "developing" countries. How can we have anything to learn, after all, from people who have not yet developed into us? Our natural tendencies blind us to how people in Nepal or Niger are just like anyone else; we forget that in the most important ways, people ten or a hundred years ago were exactly like us, too.

FOUR THOUSAND PEOPLE began to walk in a procession from Moscow's train station to Novodevichy Cemetery. It was July of 1904. One week earlier, in Germany, Anton Chekhov had died from tuberculosis, at the age of forty-four. At two in the morning, he had awaken in a delirium, and his wife, Olga Knipper, sent a Russian acquaintance staying in their hotel for a doctor. She later recalled the "sound of retreating footsteps on the crunching gravel in the stillness of that unbearably sultry July night." She put ice over her husband's chest, to which he replied, "Don't put ice on an empty heart." The doctor came and administered a shot of camphor. Then the doctor ordered a bottle of champagne.

Chekhov smiled at Olga. "It is some time since I have drunk champagne." He drank his glass slowly, and then he lay down on his left side and died. A large black moth slapped its wings against an electric lamp. The cork popped out of the unfinished bottle of champagne. Several days later, his body was transported back to Moscow in a filthy green railway car labeled FOR THE CONVEYANCE OF OYSTERS.

Maxim Gorky would pen one of most insightful and tender trib-

utes to his friend. Gorky recalled how Chekhov had spoken animatedly about helping teachers and about how it was "ridiculous to pay
in farthings the man who has to educate the people." Chekhov told
him that if he had the money, he'd "put up a large, bright building—
very bright, with large windows and lofty rooms. I would have a fine
library, different musical instruments, bees, a vegetable garden, an
orchard." He would invite teachers from the village there. "There
would be lectures on agriculture, mythology," Chekhov told him.
"Teachers ought to know everything, everything, my dear fellow."

"I think that in Anton Chekhov's presence," Gorky wrote, "every
one involuntarily felt in himself a desire to be simpler, more truthful, [and] more one's self." Often, intimidated visitors would try to
impress Chekhov, launching into abstract, philosophical speeches.

"From such impressions of existence within the space of the tutorial session there comes a psychical conglomeration," one would say,
"which crushes every possibility of an objective attitude toward the
surrounding universe. Of course, the universe is nothing but our
presentation of it. . . ."

"Tell me," Chekhov interrupted, "who is that teacher in your district who beats the children?" The man, Gorky writes, "who had just
been mercilessly belaboring Chekhov with his store of clever words,
suddenly . . . began to speak simple, weighty, clear-cut words."

Chekhov was disarmingly simple. He had, as he put it, "peasant
blood flowing in [his] veins." Before the emancipation of the serfs,
his grandfather Egor managed to purchase his father's freedom. He
wrote over a dozen plays and hundreds of short stories. Trained as a
doctor, he treated peasants at free clinics, fought cholera outbreaks
and famine, donated thousands of books, and built several schools.
His letter to the editor Alexei Pleshcheyev revealed his true nature:

> The people I am afraid of are the ones who . . . are determined
> to see me as either liberal or conservative. I am neither lib-

eral, nor conservative, not gradualist, nor monk, nor indifferentist. . . . Pharisaism, dullwittedness and tyranny reign not only in merchants' homes and police stations. I see them in science, in literature, among the younger generation. That is why I cultivate no particular predilection for policemen, butchers, scientists, writers or the younger generation. I look upon tags and labels as prejudices. My holy of holies is the human body, health, intelligence, talent, inspiration, love and the most absolute freedom imaginable, freedom from violence and lies, no matter what form the latter two take.

For Chekhov, morality lay not in our relationships with what we know, but in how admirably we deal with what we don't. In the face of what we don't understand, his stories ask, how curious are we? How fearfully strict? How deferential to others? It's this sort of morality that we need more of in our whirlwind era. It's a morality distinct from IQ and common notions of confidence or self-control. Chekhov showed that not knowing doesn't leave us without a compass, in some relativist nether land. Owning our uncertainty makes us kinder, more creative, and more alive.

He had an almost-radical belief in the limits of what it is possible to understand in this world. "It is time for writers to admit that nothing in this world makes sense," he once wrote. "Only fools and charlatans think they know and understand everything . . . and if an artist decides to declare that he understands nothing of what he sees—this in itself constitutes a considerable clarity in the realm of thought, and a great step forward." Tolstoy, after meeting Chekhov in 1885, noted that "he is very gifted" and "must have a good heart, but up to now he has no definite point of view on things." Even Tolstoy bridled at not being able to pin the young author down.

Many of Chekhov's short stories explore forms of freedom and constraint. "The Betrothed," Chekhov's final story, is a good example. Nadya, the protagonist, is in a garden. The sweet smell of May is in the night air. She is twenty-three and engaged, but now she feels unsure of herself, and anxious. She imagines that "far away under the sky, above the trees, far away in the open country, in the fields and the woods, the life of spring [is] unfolding now, mysterious, lovely, rich, and holy beyond the understanding of weak, sinful man. And for some reason she wanted to cry."

Nadya sits down for dinner. Her mother Nina Ivanovna is there, as is her fiancé, Andrey Andreitch, and his father, Father Andrey. Her mother, for some reason, "looked very young" in the moonlight. The group begins to discuss hypnotism:

> "So you believe in hypnotism?" said Father Andrey to Nina
> Ivanovna.
> "I cannot, of course, assert that I believe," answered Nina Iva-
> novna, assuming a very serious, even severe, expression,
> "but I must own that there is much that is mysterious and
> incomprehensible in nature."
> "I quite agree with you, though I must add that religion dis-
> tinctly curtails for us the domain of the mysterious."
> A big and very fat turkey was served. Father Andrey and Nina
> Ivanovna went on with their conversation. Nina Ivanovna's
> diamonds glittered on her fingers, then tears began to glit-
> ter in her eyes; she grew excited.
> "Though I cannot venture to argue with you," she said, "you
> must admit there are so many insoluble riddles in life!"
> "Not one, I assure you."

Later, Nadya's fiancé takes her to the house that has been prepared for their marriage. On the wall is a painting of a "naked lady and beside her a purple vase with a broken handle." Nadya realizes that she does not love him. He holds her tightly, and "his arm round her waist felt as hard and cold as an iron hoop."

Nadya secretly leaves town, which thrills and frightens her. She starts a new life for herself. Eventually, she returns home for a visit. The town seems old, small, out of date. That's the climax of the story. Chekhov ends the tale with this line: "She went upstairs to her own room to pack, and next morning said good-bye to her family, and full of life and high spirits left the town—as she supposed for ever."

The story, and the ending, is typical of Chekhov. He ends with a moment's emotion, a dream of an open, bright future. He did not end his stories as writers typically do. His tales were consciously fragmented. Tidy endings just didn't seem honest. An artist's job, he felt, wasn't to "solve such problems as God, pessimism, etc.," but merely to select significant moments from insignificant ones, and to pose the right questions.

Virginia Woolf noted how Chekhov knew that in life, "an inconclusive ending" is "much more usual than anything extreme." The beginnings and ends of stories, he felt, was where "we authors do most of our lying." This idea, that we shouldn't treat the unresolved as resolved, was Chekhov's wisdom. He had what Keats called negative capability. His legacy was his worldview, and it was one of gorgeous restraint. His first "serious" story, as it turns out, written around his twenty-eighth birthday, explores similar themes as "The Betrothed." Days before beginning it, Chekhov wrote to his old editor, Nikolai Leikin, excusing himself for failing to deliver a story he requested. Leikin had asked for a Christmas tale, but Chekhov, at a turning point, simply couldn't deliver a normal Christmas story. "You say that it is all the same to you how the story turns out," he wrote, on December 27, "but I do not share this view."

On January 1, 1888, Chekhov began "The Steppe" in earnest.

A young boy of nine, Egor, or Egorushka, is traveling on a battered carriage through the countryside with two men who are going to sell wool. They're taking Egor, on behalf of his mother, to enroll him in school. There are wonderful descriptions of the countryside, storms, and random characters. A windmill waves its arms in the distance, in Egor's mind, like a man. The story ends as the two men leave him with a woman who promises to put him in school. Tears cloud the boy's eyes as the two men leave. Egor is gripped by the feeling that a new life is just beginning, that everything is changing.

He wonders what his new life will be like.

ACKNOWLEDGMENTS

THIS BOOK WOULDN'T have been possible without my agent Eric Lupfer. Early in the process, Eric offered me the ear, sage advice, and steady hand that I needed. He shepherded the project with great skill, attention, and good humor. Just as much is owed to my brilliant and generous editor Amanda Cook, whose conceptual eye and analytical acuity continue to humble me. Amanda went far beyond the call of duty in helping develop a young and stubborn writer. Crown's Emma Berry and Domenica Alioto also have my gratitude for many improvements and conceptual fixes. Patricia Boyd, my copy editor, was as discerning as she was discreet.

New America—where I'm privileged to be a Future Tense Fellow—has been the best experience of my professional life. No other think tank does so much to empower junior staff to contribute to the public dialogue. I'm thankful to Andrés Martinez for first hiring me and to Torie Bosch, my editor at *Slate*, for allowing me the latitude to finish the manuscript. Rachel White, Faith Smith, and many others deserve credit for helping steward the remarkable intellectual culture at New America. My year assisting Peter Beinart was a sure highlight. Peter was as liberal with his time and editorial wisdom as he was encouraging and rightly demanding. Watching him work and learning from him was an inspiration. I'm also indebted to Jamie Zimmerman, whose entrepreneurial spirit and dedication to international development are worthy of admiration. Reid Cramer, Rachel Black, and Justin King made every day in the office a pleasure.

Without help from the scientists and practitioners whose work I've covered and who have dedicated their lives to understanding human behavior, I would have quickly lost my way. I would like to single out Travis Proulx, Arie Kruglanski, Gary Noesner, and Tony McCaffrey. Each man's achievements and insights demanded, on the strength of great merit and interest, more and more space in the book. I'm grateful for their time and for correcting my misconceptions. While any mistakes in the book are mine alone, any strengths are due to people like them, their work, and their ideas.

Three others who have been integral to my general good fortune are Sendhil Mullainathan, Gary King, and John Sexton. Each of them opened up new intellectual worlds to me and supported me throughout the years. My dear friends Kate, Emad, Divya, Sanjay, Colman, Max, Stephanie, Lee, and Amy enlivened the weekends with their adventurous spirits. Many of them read parts of the book and helped me clear up confusing tidbits. Jeff Peters, Alexa Holmes, Alice Haller, Robert Anderson, Evan Carr, and Herbert Chase also helped significantly improve the book. It is appreciated.

Throughout, my family was enormously supportive. My parents know how much I valued their help during the process, in revising early drafts and in innumerable other ways. Francesco, see you in Hollywood. Lapo, keep on drawing!

vii   **"I don't trust ambiguity":** Scott Eyman, *John Wayne: The Life and Legend* (New York: Simon & Schuster, 2014), 221.

PROLOGUE

1   **In 1996, London's City and Islington:** Thomas's demonstration at City and Islington marked the first time that he publicly demonstrated his methods. Nigel Levy, "The Language Master," *The Knowledge*, BBC2, first aired on March 23, 1997. Notice that Thomas's methods here were poorly suited for evaluation by randomized control trial, in part because he was teaching grammar constructs "out of order." On July 2, 2014, Levy was kind enough to spare a few minutes to talk about the documentary and Thomas's legacy. To first gauge Thomas's techniques, Levy learned two languages with Thomas, as he recounted: "I went to Tel Aviv and met him there. He was living between Tel Aviv and New York, and I spent a couple of days with him learning French. Later on, to start afresh, because I'd already learned French badly at school, I learned Spanish. I learned Spanish with him in New York for three days. And then I went to the Cervantes Institute a week later, which is a Spanish language institute in London, and I talked to a couple of instructors there. They told me that the kind of language that I

was using—and I wasn't great because my vocabulary was poor—but
the complexity of language I was using when I did find the words to
say what I wanted was far beyond a week's work. It was years' work."
Levy also described learning with Thomas and emphasized that students' hold on the language fades over time depending on how regularly they use it: "Studying with Thomas was very intense. It could go
nine or ten hours. Essentially, it's you sitting with him face-to-face,
and he explains the language to you. He's broken down the language
in a way that's particularly comprehensible and logical. He doesn't usually break it down into standard grammatical structures. His idea was
to explain almost how the language came to be, as well as how the
language works. At the end of three days, you feel that you have a
three-dimensional structure of the language in your mind, an understanding of the architecture of the language: how the language works,
including the grammar. There's not much emphasis on vocabulary. It's
really about grasping the construction of the language. So in all tenses,
your hold on the language feels truly three-dimensional. It's complete;
there is nothing left to learn. You have covered every possible way of
saying things, and he will say at the end of the day that there is no
more to the language than this. It's an amazing feeling after two or
three days, to have this in your head. How long that stays there without reinforcing it is the question. That's where the individual comes
in, because some people are more or less competent in that process of
actually beginning to use it. But, you know, it was an astonishing experience." Thomas's students at the time of the demonstration were sixteen through nineteen years old. Levy also emphasized how Thomas
broke learning down into small challenges and rewards, which motivated his students by giving them a constant sense of achievement. For
more on this idea, see Dustin B. Thoman, Jessi L. Smith, and Paul J.
Silvia, "The Resource Replenishment Function of Interest," *Social Psychological and Personality Science* 2, no. 6 (2011): 592–599. For additional
background on the psychology of interest, see the endnote "a confusing idea into an interesting one," toward the end of Chapter 7's endnotes.

3   **"most alien thing"**: Jonathan Solity, *The Learning Revolution* (London: Hodder Education, 2008), 17, says that Thomas distinguished

between how difficult new information can be to digest and how unfamiliar it may feel: "I felt that the most alien thing for somebody to learn was a foreign language. Not the most difficult, but the most alien—simply because you know nothing when you begin." Solity's book is the best resource on the psychology behind Thomas's methods.

3 **Thomas was already legendary:** Biographical information and commentary came from Philip Blackmore, "Last Word in Language Teaching," *Sunday Times* (London), May 23, 1999; Anthea Lipsett, "My Message: 'Anybody Can Learn,'" *Guardian* (Manchester), September 2, 2008; Jane Warren, "War Hero Who Taught the Stars New Languages in Just Three Days," *Express* (London), January 20, 2005; Christopher Robbins, "Obituary: Michel Thomas," *Guardian* (Manchester), January 19, 2005; Anti-Defamation League, "Paid Notice: Deaths. Thomas, Michel," *New York Times*, January 11, 2005; John-Paul Flintoff, "Language Barrier: Michel, the Man Who'd Like to Teach the World to Talk," *Financial Times*, March 27, 2004; Helen Davis, "As if by Magic," *Guardian* (Manchester), May 9, 2000; Emily Moore, interview with Emma Thompson, "My Inspiration," *Guardian* (Manchester), October 26, 1999; Natasha Walter, "From Hell to Hollywood," *Independent* (London), October 21, 1999; Howard Kaplan, "The Language Master," *Jerusalem Report*, August 11, 1994; Michelle Osborn, "Learn to Speak the Language—in 10 days," *USA Today*, October 23, 1989; Adam Bernstein, "Michel Thomas Dies," *Washington Post*, January 11, 2005; Clem Richardson, "An Army of One Holocaust Survivor Helped Topple Nazi," *New York Daily News*, July 19, 2004; Jon Thurber, "Michel Thomas, 90; Linguist Received Silver Star, Taught Foreign Languages," *Los Angeles Times*, January 11, 2005; Christopher Robbins, *The Test of Courage: Michel Thomas* (London: Century, 1999). For background on the 2001 article about Thomas in the *Los Angeles Times*, see Christopher Robbins, *The Test of Courage: Michel Thomas* (London: Century, 1999; rev. digital ed. London: Apostrophe Books, 2012), afterword. In 2003, the UC Berkeley School of Law professor Robert Cole organized a mock trial on the episode (with the UC Berkeley School of Journalism). See Michael Rosen-Molina, "One More Attempt to Clear his Name," *Berkeleyan*, April 15, 2003.

4   **no mere biographical curiosities:** Another striking parallel between Thomas's exploits as an interrogator and his teaching methods arose in comments made by some of City and Islington students: "It seems he can read people's minds," "He can read everyone's mind," and "When he talks to you and asks you a question, it's like he knows what you're thinking inside." The comments amusingly mirror the words of Thomas's former boss in the CIC, Leo Marks, who served as Special Operations Executive from 1942 to 1946, and who also appeared in the BBC documentary: "It is almost technically impossible to lie to Michel Thomas. He may not detect what the truth is. But he will know when he's not being given it."

5   **In 1946, Rudolf Schelkmann:** Howard Kaplan, "The Language Master," *Jerusalem Report*, August 11, 1994, notes that three other former SS officers were present. Robbins, *The Test of Courage*, from which this scene is drawn, initially lists four SS men beyond Schelkmann, but later names only three: Gerhard Laufer, Siegfried Weber, and Johann Weber.

7   **Counterintelligence operations turn on such minutiae:** Erving Goffman, *Strategic Interaction* (Philadelphia: University of Pennsylvania Press, 1969), 21–25.

9   **the information we need to make sense:** Different research traditions favor distinct definitions of ambiguity and uncertainty. One social psychologist I interviewed told me that he attended a panel on uncertainty at a recent conference (thinking it was right in his wheelhouse), only to discover that the economists running the panel were using the terms far differently. In decision theory, ambiguity is often defined as "uncertainty about probabilities." The ambiguity-aversion literature reflects this distinction. My definition of *ambiguity* derives from Stanley Budner, "Intolerance of Ambiguity as a Personality Variable," *Journal of Personality* 30, no. 1 (1962): 29–50. My definition of uncertainty as the mind state caused by ambiguity mirrors Arie Kruglanski's. In Chapter 6, I distinguish between ambiguity and risk as two sources of uncertainty. For background on the various uses of the terms, see Sebastien Grenier, Anne-Marie Barrette, and Robert Ladouceur, "Intolerance of Uncertainty and Intolerance of Ambiguity: Similarities and Differences," *Personality and Individual Differences* 39, no. 3 (2005): 593–600; Michael Smithson, "Psychology's Ambivalent View of Un-

certainty," in *Uncertainty and Risk: Multidisciplinary Perspectives*, ed. Gabriele Bammer and Michael Smithson (London: Routledge, 2009); Colin Camerer and Martin Weber, "Recent Developments in Modeling Preferences: Uncertainty and Ambiguity," *Journal of Risk and Uncertainty* 5 (1992): 325–370. For another discussion detailing how one might break down feelings of uncertainty, see Jerome Kagan, "Categories of Novelty and States of Uncertainty," *Review of General Psychology* 13, no. 4 (2009): 290–301. I treat the plurals "uncertainties" and "ambiguities" as synonyms.

9   **an emotional amplifier:** The best work done on the upside of uncertainty in contexts not covered in depth in this book comes from Timothy Wilson and Daniel Gilbert. See, for instance, Erin R. Whitchurch, Timothy D. Wilson, and Daniel T. Gilbert, " 'He Loves Me, He Loves Me Not . . . ': Uncertainty Can Increase Romantic Attraction," *Psychological Science* 22, no. 2 (2011): 172–175; Timothy D. Wilson et al., "The Pleasures of Uncertainty: Prolonging Positive Moods in Ways People Do Not Anticipate," *Journal of Personality and Social Psychology* 88, no. 1 (2005): 5–21; Yoav Bar-Anan, Timothy D. Wilson, and Daniel T. Gilbert, "The Feeling of Uncertainty Intensifies Affective Reactions," *Emotion* 9, no. 1 (2009): 123–127; Jaime L. Kurtz, Timothy D. Wilson, and Daniel T. Gilbert, "Quantity Versus Uncertainty: When Winning One Prize Is Better Than Winning Two," *Journal of Experimental Social Psychology* 43 (2007): 979–985.

9   **"what we agree with leaves us inactive":** Johann Eckermann and Frédéric Soret, *Conversations with Goethe*, vol. 1, trans. John Oxenford (London: Smith, Elder & Co., 1850), 366.

9   **We like our uncertainty:** The psychologist Robert Solso offered a nice description of how art employs ambiguity: "Much of art has been purposely designed to generate a form of creative tension in the viewer that cries out for resolution. In many forms of classic art, the artist presented social issues that embarrassed the establishment, while many contemporary artists present visual statements about art, religion, psychoanalysis, as well as social conditions. All of these . . . demand active participation in the construction of 'reality.' " Robert L. Solso, *The Psychology of Art and the Evolution of the Conscious Brain* (Cambridge, MA: MIT Press, 2003), 237.

10   **The paradox of modern life:** Hartmut Rosa, "Social Acceleration:

Ethical and Political Consequences of a Desynchronized High-Speed Society," *Constellations* 10, no. 1 (2003): 14. Also see Hartmut Rosa, *Social Acceleration: A New Theory of Modernity* (New York: Columbia University Press, 2013); Judy Wajcman, *Pressed for Time: The Acceleration of Life in Digital Capitalism* (Chicago: University of Chicago Press, 2014).

10   **Estimates are that 90 percent:** Matthew Wall, "Big Data: Are You Ready for Blast-Off?" *BBC News*, March 3, 2014.

10   **we face the social anxieties:** Thomas B. Edsall, "Is the American Middle Class Losing Out to China and India?" *New York Times*, April 1, 2014.

10   **machines appear set to replace humans:** Derek Thompson, "What Jobs Will the Robots Take?" *Atlantic*, January 23, 2014.

10   **"disorder—a combination of the breakdown":** Noreena Hertz, *Eyes Wide Open: How to Make Smart Decisions in a Confusing World* (New York: HarperCollins, 2013), 9–10.

11   **"How well do you deal with unstructured problems":** Lawrence Katz, "Get a Liberal Arts B.A., Not a Business B.A., for the Coming Artisan Economy," *PBS NewsHour*, Making Sen$e, July 15, 2014; Lawrence Katz, interview with author, August 29, 2014.

11   **Miguel Escotet:** Gena Borrajo, interview with Miguel Ángel Escotet, *EDUGA* 59 (winter 2012). For Escotet's breakdown of emotional variables, see Miguel Ángel Escotet, "Cognitive and Affective Variables That Should Rule Education," *Miguel Ángel Escotet Scholarly Blog*, July 28, 2013, www.miguelescotet.com/2013/cognitive-and-affective-variables-that-should-rule-education/. Escotet confirmed that although this was a European interview, his views on this issue extend to the United States: "Most of the problems of US education relate to the emphasis in developing cognitive skills . . . at the expense of reducing or eliminating affective/emotional skills" (Miguel Ángel Escotet, email to author, August 2, 2014).

11   **no relationship whatsoever to IQ:** Donna M. Webster and Arie Kruglanski, "Individual Differences in Need for Cognitive Closure," *Journal of Personality and Social Psychology* 67, no. 6 (1994): 1049–1062.

11   **a concept called the *need for closure*:** Kruglanski provided a history of the concept and its antecedents in Arie W. Kruglanski, *The Psychology of Closed Mindedness* (New York: Psychology Press, 2004). Three reviews of the relevant literature are Arne Roets et al., "The Motivated

Gatekeeper of Our Minds: New Directions in Need for Closure Theory and Research," *Advances in Experimental Social Psychology*, in press; Arie W. Kruglanski and Shira Fishman, "The Need for Cognitive Closure," in *Handbook of Individual Differences in Social Behavior*, ed. Mark R. Leary and Rick H. Hoyle (New York: Guilford, 2009), 343–353; Arie W. Kruglanski et al., "Three Decades of Lay Epistemics: The Why, How, and Who of Knowledge Formation," *European Review of Social Psychology* 20, no. 1 (2009): 146–191. The definition here can be found in Arie W. Kruglanski, Donna M. Webster, and Adena Klem, "Motivated Resistance and Openness to Persuasion in the Presence or Absence of Prior Information," *Journal of Personality and Social Psychology* 65, no. 5 (1993): 861.

12 **After the war, Else Frenkel-Brunswik:** See Else Frenkel-Brunswik, "A Study of Prejudice in Children," *Human Relations* 1 (1948); Else Frenkel-Brunswik, "Intolerance of Ambiguity as an Emotional and Perceptual Personality Variable," *Journal of Personality* 18, no. 1 (1949): 108–143. Ibid., 128, describes the dog-cat experiment. To get a sense of the visuals of the dog and cat drawings, see Sheldon J. Krochin and Harold Basowitz, "The Judgment of Ambiguous Stimuli as an Index of Cognitive Functioning in Aging," *Journal of Personality* 25, no. 1 (1956): 84. I also drew from Donald L. Levine, *The Flight from Ambiguity: Essays in Social and Cultural Theory* (Chicago: University of Chicago Press, 1985), 12. Also see Theodor W. Adorno et al., *The Authoritarian Personality* (New York: Harper & Brothers, 1959). The tolerance-of-ambiguity concept is very much alive and distinct from the need for closure. See Adrian Furnham and Joseph Mars, "Tolerance of Ambiguity: A Review of the Recent Literature," *Psychology* 4, no. 9 (2013): 717–728. The need for closure includes aversion to ambiguity within its conceptualization, but as covered in Chapters 3 and 4, extends beyond it. Kruglanski's broader concept is particularly useful because of its emphasis on situational factors. Many of the related conceptualizations, including dogmatism, authoritarianism, intolerance for incongruity, need for structure, sense of coherence, intolerance of uncertainty, uncertainty avoidance, and openness to experience are covered in Kruglanski, *Psychology of Closed Mindedness*. Note that my use of synonyms and the abundance of these terms make some overlap in language inevitable. Also see Jerome Kagan, "Motives and Devel-

opment," *Journal of Personality and Social Psychology* 22, no. 1 (1972): 51–66; Kees van den Bos, "Making Sense of Life: The Existential Self Trying to Deal with Personal Uncertainty," *Psychological Inquiry* 20, no. 4 (2009): 197–217; Richard M. Sorrentino and Christopher J.R. Roney, *The Uncertain Mind: Individual Differences in Facing the Unknown* (Philadelphia: Psychology Press, 2000); Danielle A. Einstein, "Extension of the Transdiagnostic Model to Focus on Intolerance of Uncertainty: A Review of the Literature and Implications for Treatment," *Clinical Psychology: Science and Practice* 21, no. 3 (2014): 280–300; Amos Tversky and Daniel Kahneman, "Advances in Prospect Theory: Cumulative Representation of Uncertainty," *Journal of Risk and Uncertainty* 5 (1992): 297-323.

13   **"the situation you're in, your culture":** Kruglanski was very generous with his time, granting me extensive interviews and graciously responding to numerous pesky questions via email. This quote came from our first interview on August 21, 2012. Three other situations that can heighten the need for closure are an obligation to respond to a confusing event rather than simply observe it, alcohol intoxication, and the dullness of the cognitive task subjects are engaged in.

13   **we trust people in our social groups more:** This newer finding fits perfectly into Kruglanski's conceptualization in light of the longtime emphasis on how a high need for closure increases outgroup derogation. Sinem Acar-Burkay, Bob M. Fennis, and Luk Warlop, "Trusting Others: The Polarizing Effect of Need for Closure," *Journal of Personality and Social Psychology* 107, no. 4 (2014): 719-735.

13   **Thomas turned the Nazis' own doubt-repressing:** Erich Fromm, *Escape from Freedom* (New York: Farrar & Rinehart, 1941), discussed the flight from the "ambiguity of freedom" in the context of Nazism and authoritarianism. George Johnson hit on the same point when discussing Einstein's theory of relativity: "It's no wonder Nazis hated relativity. They lived in a world of absolutes. There was a master race with one true religion and one true language, with a music and literature that celebrated its glory. There was a true German empire, sliced up by the arbitrary boundaries of concoctions called nation-states. With absolute might the Fatherland would regain its proper position in space and time." George Johnson, "Quantum Leaps," review of *Einstein's*

Jewish Science, by Steven Gimbel, *New York Times*, August 3, 2012. See also Zygmunt Bauman, *Modernity and Ambivalence* (Cambridge, UK: Polity Press, 1991).

CHAPTER ONE

19   **Göran Lundqvist arrived home:** Simon Garfield, "Absolute Hype: Absolut Vodka Is the Flavour of the Month," *Mail on Sunday* (London), July 25, 1999.

19   **the company was in the midst:** The background on Absolut came from Richard W. Lewis, *Absolut Book: The Absolut Vodka Advertising Story* (Rutland, VT: Journey Editions, 1996); Richard W. Lewis, *Absolut Sequel: The Absolut Advertising Story Continues* (North Clarendon, VT: Periplus, 2005); Mark Tungate, *Adland: A Global History of Advertising* (Philadelphia: Koran Page, 2007); James B. Twitchell, *20 Ads That Shook the World: The Century's Most Groundbreaking Advertising and How It Changed Us All* (New York: Three Rivers Press, 2000). For an alternative bottle origin story, see Carl Hamilton, *Absolut: Biography of a Bottle* (New York: Texere, 1994), 62. I also drew on Stuart Elliott, "Absolut Marketing: Vodka Sales Toast Ads' Success," *USA Today*, November 22, 1989; Kathleen Day, "Collecting, or Being Collected?" *Washington Post*, August 2, 1997; Andrea Adelson, "Unusual Ads Help a Foreign Vodka to the Top," *New York Times*, November 28, 1988.

22   **Richard Lewis:** Richard Lewis, interview with author, February 6, 2013.

23   **In 1949, two Harvard psychologists:** Jerome S. Bruner and Leo Postman, "On the Perception of Incongruity: A Paradigm," *Journal of Personality* 18, no. 2 (1949): 206–223. Note that subjects showed similar compromise reactions when describing the colors of black trick cards: "Graying tinged with red"; "Black with reddish gray background"; The reference to T. S. Eliot's sister and the art store comes from Bradd Shore, "Keeping the Conversation Going: An Interview with Jerome Bruner," *Ethos* 25, no. 1 (1997): 7–62.

25   **And when the subjects were stuck and yet still:** Bruner and Postman don't address this speculation, but as Arie W. Kruglanski and Shira Fishman, "The Need for Cognitive Closure," in *Handbook of Individual Differences in Social Behavior*, ed. Mark R. Leary and Rick H.

Hoyle (New York: Guilford, 2009), 343–353, note, the need for closure "may be heightened in situations in which a decision is required immediately, as for example, under time pressure . . . or in situations in which a judgment is required, as opposed to those in which the individual is at liberty to abstain from forming a definite opinion."

26 **Our preconceptions are vital:** Travis Proulx has written extensively about preconceptions, or "expected relationships" (see Chapter 2 endnotes). I'm also indebted to Jamie Arndt et al., "Value: A Terror Management Perspective on the Human Question for Multilevel Meaning," in *The Psychology of Meaning*, ed. Keith D. Markman, Travis Proulx, and Matthew J. Lindberg (Washington, DC: American Psychological Association, 2013). The stoplight example is drawn from this article. Also see Maria Miceli and Cristiano Castelfranchi, *Expectancy and Emotion* (Oxford: Oxford University Press, 2015).

26 **the so-called McGurk effect:** I've used a variant of the original for simplicity; see Lawrence D. Rosenblum, *See What I'm Saying: The Extraordinary Powers of Our Five Senses* (New York: W. W. Norton, 2010). The original paper is Harry McGurk and John MacDonald, "Hearing Lips and Seeing Voices," *Nature* 264 (1976): 746–748. Researchers dispute the explanation for the McGurk effect. See Sabine Windmann, "Effects of Sentence Context and Expectation on the McGurk Illusion," *Journal of Memory and Language* 50, no. 2 (2004): 212–230. The interview with MacDonald was on October 30, 2012. He recalled when he first discovered the effect: "I thought, goodness, have I made a mistake? Have I written the wrong combinations down for them?" It wasn't until he and McGurk turned their backs to the video screen that they began to grasp what they'd discovered.

27 **"Aoccdrnig to rseearch":** Keith Rayner et al., "Raeding Wrods With Jubmled Lettres," *Psychological Science* 17, no. 3 (2006): 192–193; Hadas Velan and Ram Frost, "Cambridge University Versus Hebrew University: The Impact of Letter Transposition on Reading English and Hebrew," *Psychonomic Bulletin & Review* 14, no. 5 (2007): 913–918; Kiel Christianson, Rebecca L. Johnson, and Keith Rayner, "Letter Transpositions Within and Across Morphemes," *Journal of Experimental Psychology* 31, no. 6 (2005): 1327–1339; Jonathan Grainger and Carol Whitney, "Does the Huamn Mind Raed Wrods as a Wlohe?" *TRENDS in Cognitive Sciences* 8, no. 2 (2004): 58–59.

27   **"fundamental problem of life"**: Jordan Peterson, "Three Forms of Meaning and the Management of Complexity," in *The Psychology of Meaning*, ed. Keith D. Markman, Travis Proulx, and Matthew J. Lindberg (Washington, DC: American Psychological Association, 2013), wrote that "we live in a sea of complexity. . . . This profound problem—the infinite search space for perceptual representation—looms over all other current psychological concerns."

27   **"Belief," Flannery O'Connor once wrote**: The full quote is "Belief, in my own case anyway, is the engine that makes perception operate." O'Connor was deeply religious, so I'm taking liberties by cutting out her qualifier. Flannery O'Connor, *A Good Man Is Hard to Find*, ed. Frederick Asals (New Brunswick, NJ: Rutgers University Press, 1993), 57.

27   **"great blooming, buzzing confusion"**: William James, *The Principles of Psychology* (New York: Henry Holt and Company, 1890), 488.

28   **In 1953, a writer**: The origin story of Mad Libs comes from Leonard Stern, "As Mad Libs Turn 50, Play an Exclusive Game," *Today*, April 16, 2008. Also see Margalit Fox, "Leonard B. Stern, Creator of Mad Libs, Dies at 88," *New York Times*, June 9, 2011.

29   **The children's game is absurdly simple**: The instructions for Mad Libs are in fact advertised as "ridiculously simple."

29   **Here's a Mad Libs snippet**: Roger Price and Leonard Stern, "How to Serve Wine," in *Mad Libs: #1 Original Mad Libs* (New York: Price Stern Sloan, 2001).

29   **Mad Libs is such a cultural phenomenon**: I've cobbled the data together from several sources: David Mitchell, "David Mitchell on Historical Fiction," *Telegraph* (London), May 8, 2010; Vit Wagner, "Tolkien Proves He's Still the King," *Toronto Star*, April 16, 2007; Lisa Suennen, "Mad Libs, VC Edition," *Fortune*, June 13, 2011.

30   **In 1970, the Swedish**: Göran Nerhardt's weight experiment and the failed version at a train station is detailed in Rod A. Martin, *The Psychology of Humor: An Integrative Approach* (London: Elsevier Academic Press, 2007). The "successful" version of the experiment was published as Göran Nerhardt, "Humor and Inclination to Laugh: Emotional Reactions to Stimuli of Different Divergence from a Range of Expectancy," *Scandinavian Journal of Psychology* 11, no. 1 (1970): 185–195. Nerhardt details his own explanation for the failed version in Göran Nerhardt, "Incongruity and Funniness: Toward a New Descriptive

Model," in *Humor and Laughter: Theory, Research, and Applications*, ed. Antony J. Chapman and Hugh C. Foot (New Brunswick, NJ: Transaction Publishers, 2007), 57. Two researchers who similarly questioned why Nerhardt's subjects were laughing in the lab experiment published their speculation in Robert S. Wyer Jr. and James E. Collins II, "A Theory of Humor Elicitation," *Psychological Review* 99, no. 4 (1992): 667. Wyer and Collins also provide a nice review of relevant predecessors like Berlyne and Koestler. For background on the theory laid out in this chapter, see Jerry M. Suls, "A Two-Stage Model for the Appreciation of Jokes and Cartoons: An Information-Processing Analysis," in *The Psychology of Humor*, ed. Jeffrey Goldstein and Paul McGhee (New York: Academic Press, 1972). Suls emphasized two steps: incongruity and its resolution. I've simply placed more emphasis on setting up the surprise by firmly establishing the expectation that is violated. Also see Thomas R. Shultz and Robert Pilon, "Development of the Ability to Detect Linguistic Ambiguity," *Child Development* 44, no. 4 (1973): 728–733; Thomas R. Schultz, "The Role of Incongruity and Resolution in Children's Appreciation of Humor," *Journal of Experimental Child Psychology* 13 (1972): 456–477; Thomas R. Schulz, "Development and Appreciation of Riddles," *Child Development* 45, no. 1 (1974): 100–105; and Graeme Ritchie, "Incongruity and Its Resolution," in *The Linguistic Analysis of Jokes* (Florence, KY: Routledge, 2003).

31   **Michael Godkewitsch, another:** Michael Godkewitsch, "Correlates of Humor: Verbal and Nonverbal Aesthetic Reactions as Functions of Semantic Distance Within Adjective-Noun Pairs," in *Studies in the New Experimental Aesthetics*, ed. Daniel E. Berlyne (Washington, DC: Hemisphere, 1974), 279–304.

31   **"At the train station":** Rod Martin, interview with author, February 7, 2013.

32   *On a Swiss menu:* Are these actual signs? Some of them probably are. They appear in online sources like Johanna Sundberg, "English Confusion," webpage of University of Washington, accessed March 3, 2015, www.faculty.washington.edu/jmiyamot/zmisc/eng_cnfu.htm. For our purposes, it doesn't really matter. It should be noted that funny (and certainly real) English signs found abroad are something of a comedic genre. See, for example, "Strange Signs from Abroad," *New York Times*, May 11, 2010.

33   **Call me a cab:** Thomas R. Shultz and Frances Horibe, "Development of the Appreciation of Verbal Jokes," *Developmental Psychology* 10, no. 1 (1974): 13–20.

34   **Howard Pollio and Rodney Mers:** Thanks go to Peter McGraw for helping me track this down. Howard R. Pollio and Rodney Mers, "Predictability and the Appreciation of Comedy," *Bulletin of the Psychonomic Society* 4, no. 4A (1984): 229–232. For McGraw's theory of humor, see Peter A. McGraw and Caleb Warren, "Benign Violations: Making Immoral Behavior Funny," *Psychological Science* 21, no. 8 (2010): 1141–1149.

34   **Not all humor, of course:** Rod Martin took special care to emphasize this when we spoke on February 7, 2013. "In most humor in everyday life," he told me, "there isn't quite an 'I get it' aspect to it. I have a book of the jokes of standup comedians, of all famous standup comedians. When you read it, you see that none of what they're doing are incongruity-resolution jokes. It's more that they're just telling a funny story, or they're kind of exaggerating things. So there's no resolution. They're playing with ideas. I would say that probably the prevailing theory among researchers is that humor involves a shift, as when two opposite scripts are activated at the same time. Of course, some would argue that a grand unifying theory of humor may be impossible."

35   **In 1998, Bill Cosby:** Associated Press, "Cosby to Do 'Kids Say the Darndest Things' Series," *Ottawa Citizen*, October 23, 1997; Ron Miller, "A Link to Kids, Past and Present: On CBS They're Still Saying the Darndest Things to Linkletter, Now 85," *San Jose Mercury News*, March 5, 1998; Tom Bierbaum, " 'Kids' Gets Darndest Ratings," *Daily Variety*, January 13, 1998; Bonnie Malleck, "Networks Rethink Freak Friday," *Hamilton (Ontario) Spectator*, June 2, 2000; Jonathan Storm, "On CBS, It's Out with the New, in with the Old—and Vice Versa," *Philadelphia Inquirer*, May 18, 2000. Search "Kemett Hayes Cosby" on YouTube for the interview. For more, see Bill Cosby, *Kids Say the Darndest Things* (New York: Bantam Books, 1998).

36   **What makes the wind?:** The background on Piaget comes from Seymour Papert, "Child Psychologist Jean Piaget," *Time*, May 29, 1999; Jean Piaget and Bärbel Inhelder, *The Psychology of the Child*, trans. Helen Weaver, introduction by Jerome Kagan (New York: Basic Books, 1969); Jean Piaget, *The Equilibration of Cognitive Structures*, trans. Terrance Brown and Kishore Julian Thampy (Chicago: University of Chicago

Press, 1985); Jean Piaget, *The Origins of Intelligence in Children*, trans. Margaret Cook (New York: International Universities Press, 1952). For the interviews with children on movement and life, see in particular the chapters Jean Piaget, "The Concept of 'Life'" and "Origins of Child Animism, Moral Necessity and Physical Determinism," in Jean Piaget, *The Child's Conception of the World*, trans. Joan and Andrew Tomlinson (London: Routledge & Kegan Paul, 1929). The tendency to revert to preconceptions is also supported by a confirmation bias framework.

37 **The sun and moon even follow us:** Piaget, *Child's Conception of the World*, 215. For a more detailed explanation, see Rhett Allain, "Why Does the Moon Follow Me?" *Wired Science Blogs: Dot Physics*, September 27, 2010.

38 **Our appetite for consistency is a means to an end:** Arie W. Kruglanski and Garriy Shteynberg, "Cognitive Consistency as a Means to an End: How Subjective Logic Affords Knowledge," in *Cognitive Consistency: A Fundamental Principle in Social Cognition*, ed. Bertram Gawronski and Fritz Strack (New York: Guilford Press, 2012), 245–264; note that "our story begins with cognitive consistency theories, whose major interest, ironically, was in cognitive *inconsistency*."

39 **Stolichnaya, had some image problems:** For background on Korean Air Lines 007, see Phillip Taubman, "Theories and Conspiracy Theories," review of *Black Box KAL 007 and the Superpowers*, by Alexander Dallin, and *KAL Flight 007: The Hidden Story*, by Oliver Clubb, *New York Times*, April 21, 1985; Michael Gordon, "Ex-Soviet Pilot Still Insists KAL 007 was Spying," *New York Times*, December 9, 1996. For the Soviet boycott of the Olympics, see John F. Burns, "Moscow Will Keep Its Team from Los Angeles Olympics," *New York Times*, May 9, 1984.

40 **the ad had to be pulled:** Lewis marks the transition from the realistic bottle to the represented bottle as starting with "Absolut Stardom." Richard W. Lewis, *Absolut Book: The Absolut Vodka Advertising Story* (Rutland, VT: Journey Editions, 1996), 31. The "Asbolut Rarity" ad is from ibid., 23.

CHAPTER TWO

41 **As a boy, Van Gogh took:** Van Gogh's mother, an amateur artist, gave him his first lessons. Charles Davidson, *Bone Dead, and Rising:*

Vincent Van Gogh and the Self Before God (Eugene, OR: Cascade Books, 2011), 64.

41   **Trappist monks produce:** The brewery is located within the municipality of Tilburg, in Berkel-Enschot, on the outskirts of the city of Tilburg.

41   **The Netherlands is a hotbed:** Lutz Bornmann, Loet Leydesdorff, and Günter Krampen, "Which Are the 'Best' Cities for Psychology Research Worldwide?" *Europe's Journal of Psychology* 8, no. 4 (2012): 535–546.

41   **the reason for my trip:** For first bringing Proulx's research to my attention, I thank Alison Flood, "Reading Kafka 'Enhances Cognitive Mechanisms,' Claims Study," *Guardian* (Manchester), September 17, 2009; Benedict Carey, "How Nonsense Sharpens the Intellect," *New York Times*, October 5, 2009.

42   **Over the last few years, Proulx:** The information on Proulx comes from numerous interviews, including those during my visit to Tilburg, October 11–14, 2012. Key papers drawn on in this chapter include Travis Proulx, Steven J. Heine, and Kathleen D. Vohs, "When Is the Unfamiliar the Uncanny?" *Personality and Social Psychology Bulletin* 36, no. 6 (2010): 817–829; Travis Proulx and Michael Inzlicht, "The Five 'A's of Meaning Maintenance: Finding Meaning in the Theories of Sense-Making," *Psychological Inquiry* 23, no. 4 (2012): 317–335; Travis Proulx and Michael Inzlicht, "Moderated Disanxiousuncertilibrium: Specifying the Moderating and Neuroaffective Determinants of Violation-Compensation Effects," *Psychological Inquiry* 23, no. 4 (2012): 386–396. See this same special issue of *Psychological Inquiry* for advice on, praise of, and criticism of Proulx and Inzlicht's "Five 'A's" paper, which was the target article. The paper "Moderated Disanxiousuncertilibrium" was their reply. Also note that in this chapter, I've used Proulx's later iteration of his theory as described in Eva Jonas et al., "Threat and Defense: From Anxiety to Approach," in *Advances in Experimental Social Psychology*, vol. 49, ed. James M. Olson and Mark P. Zanna (Burlington, VT: Academic Press, 2014). For another special issue on Proulx's work, see Travis Proulx, "Threat-Compensation in Social Psychology: Is There a Core Motivation?" *Social Cognition* 30, no. 6 (2012): 643–651. Other papers drawn on include Travis Proulx and Steven J.

Heine, "Death and Black Diamonds: Meaning, Mortality, and the Meaning Maintenance Model," *Psychological Inquiry* 17, no. 4 (2006): 309–318; Travis Proulx, Michael Inzlicht, and Eddie Harmon-Jones, "Understanding All Inconsistency Compensation as a Palliative Response to Violated Expectations," *Trends in Cognitive Science* 16, no. 5 (2012): 285–291; Travis Proulx and Steven J. Heine, "The Frog in Kierkegaard's Beer: Finding Meaning in the Threat-Compensation Literature," *Social and Personality Psychology Compass* 4, no. 10 (2010): 889–905; Steven J. Heine, Travis Proulx, and Kathleen Vohs, "The Meaning Maintenance Model," *Personality and Social Psychology Review* 10, no. 2 (2006): 88–110; Daniel Randles, Travis Proulx, and Steven J. Heine, "Turn-Frogs and Careful-Sweaters: Non-Conscious Perception of Incongruous Word Pairings Provokes Fluid Compensation," *Journal of Experimental Social Psychology* 47 (2011): 246–249; Travis Proulx and Steven J. Heine, "Connections from Kafka: Exposure to Meaning Threats Improves Implicit Learning of an Artificial Grammar," *Psychological Science* 20, no. 9 (2009): 1125–1131; Travis Proulx and Steven J. Heine, "The Case of the Transmogrifying Experimenter: Affirmation of a Moral Schema Following Implicit Change Detection," *Psychological Science* 19, no. 12 (2008): 1294–1300. See also these important, related sources: Ian McGregor et al., "Compensatory Conviction in the Face of Personal Uncertainty: Going to Extremes and Being Oneself," *Journal of Personality and Social Psychology* 80, no. 3 (2001): 472–488; Ian McGregor and Denise C. Marigold, "Defensive Zeal and the Uncertain Self: What Makes You So Sure?" *Journal of Personality and Social Psychology* 85, no. 1 (2003): 838–852; Ian McGregor, "Offensive Defensiveness: Toward an Integrative Neuroscience of Compensatory Zeal After Mortality Salience, Personal Uncertainty, and Other Poignant Self-Threats," *Psychological Inquiry* 17, no. 4 (2006): 299–308; Ian McGregor et al., "Anxious Uncertainty and Reactive Approach Motivation," *Personality Processes and Individual Differences* 99, no. 1 (2010); Eddie Harmon-Jones, David M. Amodio, and Cindy Harmon-Jones, "Action-Based Model of Dissonance: A Review, Integration, and Expansion of Conceptions of Cognitive Conflict," *Advances in Experimental Social Psychology* 41 (2009): 119–166.

42 **Literary critic Henry Sussman:** Henry Sussman, "The Text That

Was Never a Story: Symmetry and Disaster in 'A Country Doctor,'" in *Approaches to Teaching Kafka's Short Fiction*, ed. Richard T. Gray (New York: Modern Language Association of America, 1995).

43   **The Kafka subjects saw more patterns:** Travis Proulx, email to author on July 8, 2014, clarified that the most robust example of improvements in accuracy after experiencing incoherence is found in Randles, Proulx, and Heine, "Turn-Frogs and Careful-Sweaters," in which increases in accuracy were calculated in multiple ways. Note that checking off 33 percent more letter strings than the control group is distinct from checking off 33 percent more of the letter strings as a percentage of the total. The control group identified 16.5 letter strings as Grammar A, while the ambiguous-story group identified 21.95, so the 33 percent figure comes from dividing 5.45 by 16.5. As percentages of the total (60 letter strings), the control is at 27.5 percent and the surreal Kafka group is at 36.6 percent, a difference of 9.1 percent. Also see the notes for "galvanized to collect clues."

45   **psychologist Brenda Major had adapted:** Travis Proulx and Brenda Major, "A Raw Deal: Heightened Liberalism Following Exposure to Anomalous Playing Cards," *Journal of Social Issues* 69, no. 3 (2013): 455–472. In this experiment, subjects were exposed to the trick cards by playing Blackjack with the experimenter. Also see Willem W. A. Sleegers, Travis Proulx, and Ilja van Beest, "Extremism Reduces Conflict Arousal and Increases Values Affirmation in Response to Meaning Violations," *Biological Psychology*, in press.

47   **On December 16, 1954:** The well-known source is Leon Festinger, Henry W. Riecken, and Stanley Schachter, *When Prophecy Fails: A Social and Psychological Study of a Modern Group That Predicted the Destruction of the World* (Minneapolis: University of Minnesota Press, 1956). I've supplemented this information with various news reports, including "He Quits Job to Wait End of World Dec. 21," *Chicago Daily Tribune*, December 16, 1954; Associated Press, "Doctor Leaves College Job, Predicts Cataclysm," *Los Angeles Times*, December 17, 1954; "Doctor Warns of Disasters in World Tuesday," *Chicago Daily Tribune*, December 17, 1954; Reuters, "Denies Predicting End of the World," *Irish Times* (Dublin), December 18, 1954; "Space Seer's 'Tidal Wave' Due Today," *Washington Post*, December 21, 1954; Associated Press, "Doom

Prophet Calls of Cataclysm—for Today," *Newsday*, December 21, 1954; Associated Press, "Earth 'Disaster' Stayed, Woman Prophet Says," *Hartford Courant*, December 22, 1954; Associated Press, "Quakes Back Predictions, Woman Says," *Los Angeles Times*, December 22, 1954; "World Spared for Time, Say Doom Prophets," *Chicago Daily Tribune*, December 22, 1954; Associated Press, "Sister Asks Commitment for Cataclysm Forecaster," *Hartford Courant*, December 23, 1954; "Petitions Court to Declare Dr. Laughead Mentally Ill," *Chicago Daily Tribune*, December 23, 1954; "Sect Expects to Depart This Earth Tonight," *Chicago Daily Tribune*, December 24, 1954; Associated Press, "Seer Awaiting 'Space Ship' Misses Boat," *Washington Post*, December 25, 1954; "Dr. Laughead Expects Some News Today," *Chicago Daily Tribune*, December 21, 1954; United Press, "Prophecies Seen Borne Out," *New York Times*, December 22, 1954; Associated Press, "Prophet of Doom Sticks to 'Cataclysm' Forecast," *Hartford Courant*, December 21, 1954; "End of the World Prophet Found in Error, Not Insane," *Chicago Daily Tribune*, January 1, 1955. For more on the psychology of end-of-world predictions, see Vaughan Bell, "Apocalypse 2011: What Happens to a Doomsday Cult When the World Doesn't End?" *Slate*, May 20, 2011; Jon R. Stone, ed., *Expecting Armageddon: Essential Readings in Failed Prophecy* (New York: Routledge, 2000).

54 **develop his theory of *cognitive dissonance*:** Beyond the summary in Riecken and Schachter, *When Prophecy Fails*, 25, see Leon Festinger, *A Theory of Cognitive Dissonance* (Stanford, CA: Stanford University Press, 1957). For evidence of cognitive dissonance in monkeys, see John Tierney, "Go Ahead, Rationalize. Monkeys Do It, Too," *New York Times*, November 6, 2007; Louisa C. Egan, Paul Bloom, and Laurie R. Santos, "Choice-Induced Preferences in the Absence of Choice: Evidence from a Blind Two Choice Paradigm with Young Children and Capuchin Monkeys," *Journal of Experimental Social Psychology* 46 (2010): 204–207; Louisa C. Egan, Laurie R. Santos, and Paul Bloom, "The Origins of Cognitive Dissonance," *Psychological Science* 18, no. 11 (2007): 978–983.

54 **Over a thousand published studies:** Jeff Stone, "Consistency as a Basis for Behavioral Interventions: Using Hypocrisy and Cognitive Dissonance to Motivate Behavior Change," in *Cognitive Consistency: A*

Fundamental Principle in Social Cognition, ed. Bertram Gawronski and Fritz Strack (New York: Guilford Press, 2012).

54 **In 1974, psychologists Mark Zanna:** Mark P. Zanna and Joel Cooper, "Dissonance and the Pill: An Attribution Approach to Studying the Arousal Properties of Dissonance," *Journal of Personality and Social Psychology* 29, no. 5 (1974): 703–709; Joel Cooper, *Cognitive Dissonance: Fifty Years of a Classic Theory* (London: Sage, 2007), 47–49. (In *Cognitive Dissonance,* Cooper seems to have misremembered the nature of the essay that students were asked to write.) On a fascinating side note, Cooper recounts: "In 1983, I had a chance to ask Leon Festinger what he thought about the motivational properties of dissonance when he was writing the theory. Did he believe that there was actually a drive and that people would feel discomfort, or was it a metaphor for how the system would work? He explained that that was not a question that would have arisen in the 1950s. Scientists built 'black box' models— models of how a system should work if it were to account for the data. As long as it accounted for the data, a scientist could continue to be proud of what he had put in the 'black box.' "

55 **Since Zanna and Cooper's study:** Beyond Cooper, *Cognitive Dissonance,* see Gawronski and Strack, *Cognitive Consistency;* Eddie Harmon-Jones and Judson Mills, eds., *Cognitive Dissonance: Progress on a Pivotal Theory in Social Psychology* (Washington, DC: American Psychological Association, 1999). I've also drawn on Bertram Gawronski, "Meaning, Violation of Meaning, and Meaninglessness in Meaning Maintenance," *Psychological Inquiry* 23, no. 4 (2012): 346–349; Bertram Gawronski, "Back to the Future of Dissonance Theory: Cognitive Consistency as a Core Motive," *Social Cognition* 30, no. 6 (2012): 652– 668. Cooper, *Cognitive Dissonance,* emphasized that "dissonance . . . is driven by the perception of unwanted consequences." Also see Anthony G. Greenwald and David L. Ronis, "Twenty Years of Cognitive Dissonance: Case Study of the Evolution of a Theory," *Psychological Review* 85, no. 1 (1978): 53–57. As Gawronski, "Back to the Future," points out, challenges to Festinger had already begun before Zanna and Cooper's "Dissonance and the Pill" study.

55 **Part of the problem:** Details of this are spelled out, as is most of the information in the following pages of this chapter, in the 2014 paper

mentioned at the end of this section. I'm indebted to each of its authors: Eva Jonas, Ian McGregor, Johannes Klackl, Dmitrij Agroskin, Immo Fritsche, Colin Holbrook, Kyle Nash, Travis Proulx, and Markus Quirin, "Threat and Defense: From Anxiety to Approach," *Advances in Experimental Social Psychology* 49 (2014): 219–286. Jeffrey A. Gray and Neil McNaughton, *The Neuropsychology of Anxiety: An Enquiry into the Functions of the Septo-Hippocampal System*, 2nd ed. (Oxford: Oxford University Press, 2000), contribute important insight in the previous paper's formulation of meaning making.

56   **psychology . . . is fragmented:** For a nice recent and relevant discussion, see Anthony G. Greenwald, "There Is Nothing So Theoretical as a Good Method," *Perspectives on Psychological Science* 7, no. 2 (2012). Also see Stephen C. Yanchar and Brent D. Slife, "Pursuing Unity in a Fragmented Psychology: Problems and Prospects," *Review of General Psychology* 1, no. 3 (1997): 235–255.

56   **We've seen the unhealthy outcomes:** For background on the Bone Wars, I drew on Keith Thomson, *The Legacy of the Mastodon* (New Haven, CT: Yale University Press, 2008); Mark Jaffe, *The Gilded Dinosaur: The Fossil War Between E.D. Cope and O.C. Marsh and the Rise of American Science* (New York: Crown Books, 2000); David Rains Wallace, *The Bonehunters' Revenge: Dinosaurs, Greed, and the Greatest Scientific Feud of the Gilded Age* (New York: Houghton Mifflin Harcourt, 1999); Bill Bryson, *A Short History of Nearly Everything* (New York: Broadway Books, 2004); Paul D. Brinkman, *The Second Jurassic Dinosaur Rush: Museums and Paleontology in America at the Turn of the Twentieth Century* (Chicago: University of Chicago Press, 2010), 9.

57   **Eddie and Cindy Harmon-Jones:** Eddie Harmon-Jones and Cindy Harmon-Jones, "Feeling Better or Doing Better? On the Functions of Inconsistency Reduction (and Other Matters)," *Psychological Inquiry* 23, no. 4 (2012): 350–353

57   **Proulx, in a 2012 article with:** Proulx and Inzlicht, "Five 'A's of Meaning Maintenance."

57   **"Newton had replaced":** Proulx, Inzlicht, and Harmon-Jones, "Understanding All Inconsistency Compensation." I've also borrowed the helpful albino crow example from this article.

58   **This human alarm system:** For an interesting application of the

"human alarm system," see Van den Bos et al., "Justice and the Human Alarm System: The Impact of Exclamation Points and Flashing Lights on the Justice Judgment Process," *Journal of Experimental Social Psychology* 44 (2008): 201–219. For evidence that this system is activated after both positive and negative events, see Tobia Egner, "Surprise! A Unifying Model of Dorsal Anterior Cingulate Function?" *Nature Neuroscience* 14, no. 10 (2010): 1219–1220; Flavio T. P. Oliveira, John J. McDonald, and David Goodman, "Performance Monitoring in the Anterior Cingulate Is Not All Error Related: Expectancy Deviation and the Representation of Action-Outcome Associations," *Journal of Cognitive Neuroscience* 19, no. 12 (2007): 1994–2004; William H. Alexander and Joshua W. Brown, "Medial Prefrontal Cortex as an Action-Outcome Predictor," *Nature Neuroscience* 14, no. 10 (2011): 1338–1346. Also see Marret K. Noordewier and Seger M. Breugelmans, "On the Valence of Surprise," *Cognition and Emotion* 27, no. 7 (2013): 1325–1334. "If you could freeze people in the first moment after something unpredicted happens," Noordewier told me in an interview, "you are likely to see this initial negative reaction."

58   **Latinas, who expected to:** Sarah S. M. Townsend et al., "Can the Absence of Prejudice Be More Threatening Than Its Presence? It Depends on One's Worldview," *Journal of Personality and Social Psychology* 99, no. 6 (2010): 933–947; Wendy Berry Mendes et al., "Threatened by the Unexpected: Physiological Responses During Social Interactions with Expectancy-Violating Partners," *Journal of Personality and Social Psychology* 92, no. 4 (2007): 698–716; Özlem Ayduk et al., "Consistency Over Flattery: Self-Verification Processes Revealed in Implicit and Behavioral Responses to Feedback," *Social Psychological and Personality Science* 4, no. 5 (2013): 538–554; William B. Swann, "Allure of Negative Feedback: Self-Verification Strivings Among Depressed Persons," *Journal of Abnormal Psychology* 101, no. 2 (1992): 293–306; William B. Swann Jr., "To Be Adored or to Be Known? The Interplay of Self-Enhancement and Self-Verification," in *Foundations of Social Behavior*, vol. 2, ed. R. M. Sorrentino and E. T. Higgins (New York: Guilford, 1990), 408–448; Elliot Aronson and J. Merrill Carlsmith, "Performance Expectancy as a Determinant of Actual Performance," *Journal of Abnormal and Social Psychology* 65, no. 3 (1962): 178–182; Jason E.

Plaks and Kristin Stecher, "Unexpected Improvement, Decline, and Stasis: A Prediction Confidence Perspective on Achievement Success and Failure," *Journal of Personality and Social Psychology* 93, no. 4 (2007): 667–684. For a fascinating look at other surprising contexts where we prefer consistency, see E. Tory Higgins, *Beyond Pleasure and Pain: How Motivation Works* (Oxford: Oxford University Press, 2011).

58 **galvanized to collect clues:** This pattern hunger can be problematic and lead us to envision connections where they don't exist: in random images or in fluctuations of the stock market, for instance. The most well-known study of increases in illusory pattern perception is Jennifer A. Whitson and Adam D. Galinsky, "Lacking Control Increases Illusory Pattern Perception," *Science* 322 (2008): 115–117. Also see Jennifer A. Whitson, Adam D. Galinsky, and Aaron Kay, "The Emotional Roots of Conspiratorial Perceptions, System Justification, and Belief in the Paranormal," *Journal of Experimental Social Psychology* 56 (2015): 89–95. The position I've adopted is from Jonas et al., "Threat and Defense: From Anxiety to Approach," which addresses a construct related to the need for closure: "Need for structure can be satisfied by orienting toward familiar structure but may also be met by heightened detection of novel structure, either real . . . or imagined." Adam Galinsky's well-respected work on social power, I should note, is relevant to many ideas in the book.

59 **It soothes our angst by pushing us toward:** Also see Willem Sleegers and Travis Proulx, "The Comfort of Approach: Self-Soothing Effects of Behavioral Approach in Response to Meaning Violations," *Frontiers in Psychology*, January 9, 2015.

59 **satisfies the need for closure:** Małgorzata Kossowska, email to author, April 16, 2015. See Aneta Czernatowicz-Kukuczka, Katarzyna Jaśko, and Małgorzata Kossowska, "Need for Closure and Dealing with Uncertainty in Decision Making Context: The Role of the Behavioral Inhibition System and Working Memory Capacity," *Personality and Individual Differences* 70 (2014): 126–130; Roets and Alain van Hiel, "Why Some Hate to Dilly-Dally and Others Do Not: The Arousal-Invoking Capacity of Decision-Making for Low- and High-Scoring Need for Closure Individuals," *Social Cognition* 26, no. 3 (2008): 333–346.

59 **"assimilation is so often incomplete":** Steven Heine, interview with

the author, February 15, 2013. This, by the way, is the reason psychologists are using subliminally presented anomalies. They don't want the stimuli to be correctly accommodated.

59   **respond to these lingering anxieties:** Jonas et al., "Threat and Defense: From Anxiety to Approach," lists additional ways of coping with behavioral inhibition system anxiety such as buying things. I focus exclusively on affirmation and abstraction, according to Proulx and Inzlicht, "The Five 'A's of Meaning Maintenance." On the mental state of people who are constantly noticing oddities and anomalies, see Gordon Marino, "The Danish Doctor of Dread," *New York Times*, March 17, 2012.

60   **authoritarian-leaning participants:** David R. Weise et al., "Terror Management and Attitudes Toward Immigrants: Differential Effects of Mortality Salience for Low and High Right-Wing Authoritarians," *European Psychologist*, 17, no. 1 (2012): 63–72.

60   **faith in God *or* Darwin's theory of evolution:** Bastiaan T. Rutjens, Joop van der Pligt, and Frenk van Harreveld, "Deus or Darwin: Randomness and Belief in Theories About the Origin of Life," *Journal of Experimental Social Psychology* 46 (2010): 1078–1080. For more evidence to the point that scientific theories can serve the same stabilizing function as religious beliefs, see Rutjens et al., "Steps, Stages, and Structure: Finding Compensatory Order in Scientific Theories," *Journal of Experimental Psychology, General* 142, no. 2 (2013): 313–318. Also see C. K. Aaron, David A. Moscovitch, and Kristin Laurin, "Randomness Attributions of Arousal, and Belief in God," *Psychological Science* 21, no. 2 (2010): 216–218.

60   **The so-called depletion:** Jonas et al., "Threat and Defense: From Anxiety to Approach."

60   **Similarly, different theories:** Critics of Proulx's theory point to Steven Shepherd et al., "Evidence for the Specificity of Control Motivations in Worldview Defense: Distinguishing Compensatory Control from Uncertainty Management and Terror Management Processes," *Journal of Experimental Social Psychology* 47 (2011): 949–958. Proulx counters that he and his colleagues agree that people prefer to affirm content similar to that which was threatened; that one study isn't sufficient; and that researchers need to conduct precisely this kind of study to discover when and how content moderates affirmation effects.

61   **Our search for patterns:** Also see Daniel Randles et al., "Is Dissonance Reduction a Special Case of Fluid Compensation?" *Journal of
Personality and Social Psychology* (accepted January 2015).

61   **Just holding a loved one's hand:** James A. Coan, Hillary S. Schae-
fer, and Richard J. Davidson, "Lending a Hand: Social Regulation of
the Neural Response to Threat," *Psychological Science* 17, no. 12 (2006):
1032–1039. Also relevant here are the studies showing how acetaminophen eliminates compensatory effects. See Nathan C. DeWall, David
S. Chester, and Dylan White, "Can Acetaminophen Reduce the Pain
of Decision-Making?" *Journal of Experimental Social Psychology* 56
(2015): 117–120.

CHAPTER THREE

65   **In the days after the April 18, 1906, San Francisco earthquake:**
Background on the earthquake comes from a variety of sources, in-
cluding Simon Winchester, *A Crack in the Edge of the World: America
and the Great California Earthquake of 1906* (New York: Harper Peren-
nial, 2005); Malcolm E. Barker, ed., *Three Fearful Days: San Francisco
Memoirs of the 1906 Earthquake & Fire* (San Francisco: Londonborn
Publications, 1998); E. J. Helley, "Flatland Deposits: Their Geology
and Engineering Properties and Their Importance to Comprehensive
Planning," Geological Survey Professional Paper 943 (Washington,
DC: US Department of the Interior, 1979), 55–56. For the love stories after the San Francisco earthquake, I am enormously indebted to
Ron Filion and Pamela Storm for compiling news clippings as part of
their San Francisco 1906 Earthquake Marriage Project (see their "San
Francisco 1906 Earthquake Marriage Project: In the News . . . ," accessed March 3, 2015, www.sfgenealogy.com/1906/06inthenews.htm).
San Francisco City Hall held an exhibit based on their research in
2006. I'm even more grateful to Ron Filion for helping me track down
three of the original stories that I had trouble independently confirm-
ing. Specifically, I drew on "Oakland Man Would Keep Pretty Girls
at Home: Calls at Harbor Hospital in Search of the Supposed Matrimonial Bureau," *San Francisco Call*, May 7, 1906; "Marriage License
Office Busy Despite the Fire," *San Francisco Call*, May 1, 1906; "Young
Couple in the Ruins," *Oakland Tribune*, May 19, 1906; "Earthquakes as

Matrimonial Agents," *Oakland Tribune*, May 5, 1906; "Two Refugees Married: Romance of the San Francisco Disaster Ends in Wedding at San Diego," *Los Angeles Times*, December 7, 1906; "Earthquake Ripened Love: Calamity Makes New Record for Marriages," *Los Angeles Times*, May 20, 1906; "Willing to Become Martyr in Cause of Matrimony," *San Francisco Bulletin*, May 7, 1906; "More Applications for Refugee Wives," *Oakland Enquirer*, May 7, 1906; "Quake Bride Recalls Honeymoon in Ruins," *San Francisco Examiner*, April 15, 1906; "Girls Coming From Camps: Homeless Refugees Saved from Hardships," *Los Angeles Times*, May 9, 1906; "Marriage License Office Has Its Banner Month: Number of Permits Granted Exceed That of Any Similar Period in History of City," *San Francisco Call*, May 19, 1906; "Knows Not the Name of His Lady Love," *Oakland Tribune*, May 11, 1905; "Love Smites Fleeing Pair," *Oakland Tribune*, May 2, 1906. For another realm in which we seek out meaning after traumatic events, see Maria Konnikova, "Why We Need Answers," *New Yorker*, April 30, 2013. Also interesting and relevant is Jamuna Prasad, "A Comparative Study of Rumours and Reports in Earthquakes," *British Journal of Psychology* 41, no. 3–4 (1950): 128–144.

68 **Roughly 15 percent of Americans:** Sandro Galea, Arijit Nandi, and David Vlahov, "The Epidemiology of Post-Traumatic Stress Disorder After Disaster," *American Journal of Epidemiology* 27, no. 1 (2005): 78–91.

68 **psychologist Ronnie Janoff-Bulman:** Ronnie Janoff-Bulman, *Shattered Assumptions: Towards a New Psychology of Trauma* (New York: Free Press, 1992). For more background, see Crystal L. Park, "Making Sense of the Meaning Literature: An Integrative Review of Meaning Making and Its Effects on Adjustment to Stressful Life Events," *Psychological Bulletin* 136, no. 2 (2010): 257–301; Kees van den Bos and Marjolein Maas, "Adhering to Consistency Principles in an Unjust World: Implications for Sense Making, Victim Blaming, and Justice Judgments," in *Cognitive Consistency: A Fundamental Principle in Social Cognition*, ed. Bertram Gawronski and Fritz Strack (New York: Guilford Press, 2012).

69 **reminding Americans of 9/11 increased:** Edward Orehek et al., "Need for Closure and the Social Response to Terrorism," *Basic and Applied Social Psychology* 32 (2010): 279–290.

69 **to focus on mortality:** Eva Jonas et al., "Threat and Defense: From

Anxiety to Approach," in *Advances in Experimental Social Psychology*, vol. 49, ed. James M. Olson and Mark P. Zanna (Burlington, VT: Academic Press, 2014).

69   **Journalist Frank White:** Frank White, *The Overview Effect: Space Exploration and Human Evolution*, 2nd edition (Reston, VA: American Institute of Aeronautics and Astronautics, 1988.) Also see James Gorman, "Righteous Stuff: How Astronauts Find God," *Omni* 6, no. 8 (May 1984).

70   **Piercarlo Valdesolo and Jesse Graham:** Piercarlo Valdesolo and Jesse Graham, "Awe, Uncertainty, and Agency Detection," *Psychological Science* 25, no. 1 (2014): 170–178. For bringing the study to my attention, I thank Jeffrey Kluger, "Why There Are No Atheists at the Grand Canyon," *Time*, November 27, 2013. For background on the relationship between awe and the need for closure, see Michelle N. Shiota, Dacher Keltner, and Amanda Mossman, "The Nature of Awe: Elicitors, Appraisals, and Effects on Self-Concept," *Cognition and Emotion* 21, no. 5 (2007): 944–963. For more on awe, see Dacher Keltner and Jonathan Haidt, "Approaching Awe, a Moral, Spiritual, and Aesthetic Emotion," *Cognition and Emotion* 17, no. 2 (2003): 297–314; Melanie Rudd, Kathleen D. Vohs, and Jennifer Aker, "Awe Expands People's Perception of Time, Alters Decision Making, and Enhances Well-Being," *Psychological Science* 23, no. 10 (2012): 1130–1136.

71   **On September 10, 1989:** US Department of Commerce, "Natural Disaster Survey Report: Hurricane Hugo, September 10–22, 1989" (Silver Spring, MD: National Oceanic and Atmospheric Administration, May 1990); Peter Applebome, "Hugo's 3-Year Wake: Lessons of a Hurricane," *New York Times*, September 18, 1992.

71   **Pennsylvania State University's Catherine Cohan:** Catherine L. Cohan and Steve W. Cole, "Life Course Transitions and Natural Disaster: Marriage, Birth, and Divorce Following Hurricane Hugo," *Journal of Family Psychology* 16, no. 1 (2002): 14–25; Catherine L. Cohan, "Family Transitions Following Natural and Terrorist Disaster: Hurricane Hugo and the September 11 Terrorist Attack," in *Handbook of Stressful Transitions Across the Lifespan*, ed. Thomas W. Miller (New York: Springer, 2010), 149–164. What happened to divorces in San Francisco after the 1906 quake? To my knowledge, no one has

looked at this question. As Ron Filion of the San Francisco Marriage Project told me via email, he and colleague Pamela Storm did not examine records of divorces. Divorces were also harder to get, of course. He added: "Some may have even used the disaster as a method to disappear. I'm sure the court process was severely interrupted and may have delayed some that were in progress. Whether or not any couples reconciled (temporarily or permanently) because of the disaster would be hard to know."

72   **recent natural disasters:** Nicole LaPorte, "The Katrina Divorces," *Daily Beast*, August 22, 2010; Reuters, "Divorce Ceremonies Pick Up in Japan After Disaster," July 4, 2011. Michael Fitzpatrick, "Japan: How a Quake Changed a Culture," *Global Post* (Boston), October 9, 2011, notes: "Marriages are up, too. Match-making agency Marry Me reported that inquiries about joining had risen 30 percent since the end of April. Other local match-making agencies reported a surge in members. . . . [O]ne wedding service told the Asahi Newspaper that it had seen a 50 percent increase at its Fukushima branch."

72   **"Whoever is standing next to you":** Catherine Cohan, interview with author, March 28, 2012. As Cohan was quick to rightly point out, whatever guesses we make about individual motives after natural disasters are just that: "These are population-level data. So it's very speculative what is going on at the individual level."

73   **They slam shut, and then they lock:** In cases, depending on one's ability to achieve closure (ACC), high need for closure individuals will search for longer periods of time than those low in need for closure will. See Roets et al., "The Motivated Gatekeepers of Our Minds."

73   **a simulation of how juries work:** Arie W. Kruglanski, Donna M. Webster, and Adena Klem, "Motivated Resistance and Openness to Persuasion in the Presence or Absence of Prior Information," *Journal of Personality and Social Psych*ology 65, no. 5 (1993): 861. Also see Arie W. Kruglanski and Donna M. Webster, "Motivated Closing of the Mind: 'Seizing' and 'Freezing,'" *Psychological Review* 103, no 2 (1992): 263–283. For an investigation of the interaction between need for closure as stimulated by noise and time pressures and reduced cognitive capacity, see Arne Roets et al., "Determinants of Task Performance and Invested Effort: A Need for Closure by Relative Cognitive Capac-

ity Interaction Analysis," *Personality and Social Psychology Bulletin* 34, no. 6 (2008): 779-792.

75 **when conducting job interviews:** The primacy studies include Thomas E. Ford and Arie W. Kruglanski, "Effects of Epistemic Motivations on the Use of Accessible Constructs in Social Judgment," *Personality and Social Psychology Bulletin* 21, no. 9 (1995): 950–962; Tallie Freund, Arie W. Kruglanski, and Avivit Shpitzajzen, "The Freezing and Unfreezing of Impressional Primacy: Effects of the Need for Structure and the Fear of Invalidity," *Personality and Social Psychology Bulletin* 11, no. 4 (1985): 479–487; Donna M. Webster, Linda Richter, and Arie W. Kruglanski, "On Leaping to Conclusions When Feeling Tired: Mental Fatigue Effects on Impressional Primacy," *Journal of Experimental Social Psychology* 32 (1996): 181–195; Alan W. Heaton and Arie W. Kruglanski, "Person Perception by Introverts and Extraverts Under Time Pressure: Effects of Need for Closure," *Personality and Social Psychology Bulletin* 17 (1991): 161–165. The Jane example comes from Webster and Kruglanski, "Individual Differences in Need for Cognitive Closure," *Journal of Personality and Social Psychology* 67, no. 6 (1994): 1057.

75 **asked to rate how effective a job candidate:** Arie W. Kruglanski and Tallie Freund, "The Freezing and Unfreezing of Lay-Inferences: Effects on Impressional Primacy, Ethnic Stereotyping, and Numerical Anchoring," *Journal of Experimental Social Psychology* 19, no. 5 (1983): 454.

75 **the usual emphasis on finishing strong:** As Kruglanski points out, you can get "recency" effects, in which the interviewer remembers the latter half of the interview more, if you ask the person to form an opinion of the candidate *after* the interview. Obviously, in the real world, job interviewers are aware before the interviews that the point of screening candidates is to form opinions of them. See Linda Richter and Arie W. Kruglanski, "Seizing on the Latest: Motivationally Driven Recency Effects in Impression Formation," *Journal of Experimental Social Psychology* 34 (1998): 313–329.

75 **Other studies showed:** Kruglanski and Freund, "Freezing and Unfreezing of Lay-Inferences." Also see Arie W. Kruglanski, *The Psychology of Closed Mindedness* (New York: Psychology Press, 2004), 84.

76 **Think of trust as the oil:** David DeSteno, *The Truth About Trust:*

How It Determines Success in Life, Love, Learning, and More (New York: Hudson Street Press, 2014).

76 **In 2014, researchers at BI Norwegian:** Sinem Acar-Burkay, Bob M. Fennis, and Luk Warlop, "Trusting Others: The Polarizing Effect of Need for Closure," *Journal of Personality and Social Psychology* 107, no. 4 (2014): 719-735.

77 **at play in romantic relationships:** Richard M. Sorrentino et al., "Uncertainty Orientation and Trust in Close Relationships: Individual Differences in Cognitive Styles," *Personality Processes and Individual Differences* 68, no. 2 (1995): 314-327.

77 **"We're going to exhibit these tendencies":** Ariely was discussing illusory pattern perception. Greg Miller, "This Is Getting Out of Control," *Science*, October 2, 2008.

77 **others fall back on their groups' core beliefs:** I'm speculating. For evidence of polarization in the United States, see Jeffrey M. Jones, "Obama's Fifth Year Job Approval Ratings Among Most Polarized," *Gallup Politics*, January 23, 2014; Jeffrey M. Jones, "Obama's Fourth Year in Office Ties as Most Polarized Ever," *Gallup Politics*, January 24, 2013; Carroll Doherty, "7 Things to Know About Polarization in America," *Pew Research Center*, June 12, 2014; "Political Polarization in the American Public: How Increasing Ideological Uniformity and Partisan Antipathy Affect Politics, Compromise and Everyday Life," *Pew Research Center*, June 12, 2014. Also see Dylan Matthews, "It's Official: The 112th Congress Was the Most Polarizing Ever," *Washington Post*, January 17, 2013.

77 **Under time pressure, one study:** Arie W. Kruglanski and Donna M. Webster, "Group Members' Reactions to Opinion Deviates and Conformists at Varying Degrees of Proximity to Decision Deadline and Environmental Noise," *Journal of Personality and Social Psychology* 61, no. 2 (1991): 212-225.

78 **A 2003 experiment:** Antonio Pierro et al., "Autocracy Bias in Informal Groups under Need for Closure," *Personality and Social Psychology Bulletin* 29, no. 3 (2003): 405-417. Also see James Y. Shah et al., "Membership Has Its (Epistemic) Rewards: Need for Closure Effects on In-Group Bias," *Journal of Personality and Social Psychology* 75, no. 2 (1998): 383-393; Donna M. Webster and Arie W. Kruglanski, "Cog-

nitive and Social Consequences of the Need for Cognitive Closure," *European Review of Social Psychology* 8, no. 1 (1997): 133–173. For more background on the social effects of the need for closure, see Kruglanski, *The Psychology of Closed Mindedness.*

78 **famously bragged, "I don't do nuance":** Joe Klein, "Why the 'War President' Is Under Fire," *Time*, February 15, 2004.

78 **Bush's popularity tracked:** Arie W. Kruglanski and Edward Orehek, "The Need for Certainty as a Psychological Nexus for Individuals and Society," in *Extremism and the Psychology of Uncertainty*, ed. Michael A. Hogg and Danielle L. Blaylock (Hoboken, NJ: Wile-Blackwell, 2012); Robb Willer, "The Effects of Government-Issued Terror Warnings on President Approval Ratings," *Current Research in Social Psychology* 10, no. 1 (2004): 1–12. Also of interest is Chris Mooney, "The Science of Why We Don't Believe Science," *Mother Jones*, April 18, 2011. For more general background on trust in government as an escape from uncertainty beyond the context of terrorism, see Steven Shepherd and Aaron C. Kay, "When Government Confidence Undermines Public Involvement in Modern Disasters," *Social Cognition* 32, no. 3 (2014): 206–216. Incidentally, faith in scientific progress might have a similar effect: Marijn H.C. Meijers and Bastiaan T. Rutjens, "Affirming Belief in Scientific Progress Reduces Environmentally Friendly Behavior," *European Journal of Social Psychology*, 44, no. 5 (2014): 487–495.

78 **"support for militancy, torture":** Kruglanski and Orehek, "The Need for Certainty." For background on reactions to terrorism as well as its roots, see Michael A. Hogg and Danielle L. Blaylock, eds., *Extremism and the Psychology of Uncertainty* (Hoboken, NJ: Wiley-Blackwell, 2012); Arie W. Kruglanski et al., "The Psychology of Radicalization and De-radicalization: How Significance Quest Impacts Violent Extremism," *Advances in Political Psychology* 35, supplement S1 (2014): 69–93. Also see Dmitrij Agroskin and Eva Jonas, "Out of Control: How and Why Does Perceived Lack of Control Lead to Ethnocentrism?" *Review of Psychology* 17, no. 2 (2010): 79–90; Patrick J. Leman and Marco Cinnirella, "Beliefs in Conspiracy Theories and the Need for Cognitive Closure," *Frontiers in Psychology* 4, article 378 (2013).

79 **over 50 percent of *Fortune* 500 companies:** Dane Stangler, "The Economic Future Just Happened," Ewing Marion Kauffman Foundation, Kansas City, MO, June 9, 2009.

79   **economist Frank Knight:** Michael E. Raynor, *The Strategy Paradox: Why Committing to Success Leads to Failure (And What to Do About It)* (New York: Random House, 2007); Paul J. H. Schoemaker, *Profiting from Uncertainty: Strategies for Succeeding No Matter What the Future Brings* (New York: Free Press, 2002); Frank H. Knight, *Risk, Uncertainty and Profits* (New York: Houghton Mifflin Company, 1921), 311.

79   **In 1929, John Dewey:** John Dewey, *The Quest for Certainty: A Study of the Relation of Knowledge and Action* (New York: Minton, Balch & Company, 1929).

79   **An awareness of these psychological insights:** The interventions designed to lower the subjects' need for closure are included in the studies cited earlier in this chapter on primacy. The study on medical decisions is Lauren G. Block and Patti Williams, "Undoing The Effects of Seizing and Freezing: Decreasing Defensive Processing of Personally Relevant Messages," *Journal of Applied Social Psychology* 32, no. 4 (2002): 803–830. The importance of making the consequences of actions salient at the right time also comes up Uri Bar-Joseph and Arie W. Kruglanski, "Intelligence Failure and Need for Cognitive Closure: On the Psychology of the Yom Kippur Surprise," *Political Psychology* 24, no. 1 (2003): 75–99; Uri Ba-Joseph, *The Watchman Fell Asleep: The Surprise of Yom Kippur and Its Sources* (Albany, NY: State University of New York Press, 2005).

79   **coping with organizational change:** Arie W. Kruglanski et al., " 'On the Move' or 'Staying Put': Locomotion, Need for Closure, and Reactions to Organizational Change," *Journal of Applied Social Psychology* 37, no. 6 (2007): 1305–1340.

79   **soldiers evaluated military recruits:** Freund, Kruglanski, and Shpitzajzen, "The Freezing and Unfreezing of Impressional Primacy."

80   **Adding these kinds of questions:** There have been cross-national measures of need for closure and similar concepts. See, for instance, Geert Hofstede, *Culture's Consequence: Comparing Values, Behaviors, Institutes, and Organizations Across Nations*, 2nd ed. (Thousand Oaks, CA: Sage, 2001). Also see Kruglanski, *The Psychology of Closed Mindedness.*

80   **Yet few firms have in place formal systems:** See John, Sullivan, "Developing Bonus Systems for Rewarding Corporate Recruiters," *ERE.com*, April 23, 2007, www.ere.net/2007/04/23/developing-bonus-systems-for-rewarding-corporate-recruiters.

81   **urgency can sometimes be a good thing:** As Kruglanski put it, "need for closure makes for commitment and perseverance, but also for stereotyping and prejudice as well as closed-mindedness. . . . [I]ts evaluation depends on the value that you are considering."

81   **On April 18, 1969, Joseph Alioto:** "S.F. Mayor Planning Big Anti-Quake Party," *Los Angeles Times*, April 4, 1969; "Thousands Scorn Quake Prophets," *Chicago Tribune*, April 19, 1969; David S. Broder, "A Survival Celebration in San Francisco," *Washington Post*, April 19, 1969; Martin F. Nolan, "San Francisco: Just Happy to Be Alive," *Boston Globe*, April 19, 1969; Martin F. Nolan, "Life Goes On As Usual in San Francisco," *Boston Globe*, April 20, 1969; "No Cause To Quake," *Guardian* (Manchester), April 19, 1969; Daryl Lembke, "63 Years Later They Laugh It Off in San Francisco," *Los Angeles Times*, April 19, 1969. See Ron Filion and Pamela Storm, "Giuseppe Alioto (22 Dec 1886–13 Oct 1961) and Domenica Mae Lazio (3 Jan 1893–28 Apr 1971)," San Francisco 1906 Earthquake Marriage Project, accessed March 3, 2015, www.sfgenealogy.com/1906/06alioto.htm. Filion was told the story in a 2005 interview with Antonina Scarpulla, the daughter of Giuseppe and Domenica Alioto. The couple were married on April 16, 1914.

CHAPTER FOUR

83   **The 1993 standoff outside of Waco:** For details of Waco, Ruby Ridge, the Mario Villabona crisis, and the Joel Souza tragedy, I am indebted to Gary Noesner, *Stalling for Time: My Life as an FBI Hostage Negotiator* (New York: Random House, 2010). I also drew on Ronald Kessler, *The Bureau: The Secret History of the FBI* (New York: St. Martin's Press, 2002); Dick J. Reavis, *The Ashes of Waco: An Investigation* (Syracuse, NY: Syracuse University Press, 1998); Daniel Klaidman and Michael Isikoff, "A Fire That Won't Die," *Newsweek*, September 20, 1999. Additional details on Noesner's experiences and the related background came from Judith Miller, "A Nation Challenged: Hostages; F.B.I. Veteran of Hostage Negotiations Helped in Reshaping U.S. Policy," *New York Times*, February 19, 2002; Associated Press, "Documents Show F.B.I. Rift at Texas Siege," *New York Times*, December 31, 1999; Sue Anne Pressley, "Experts Debate Effects of CS Gas: Children May Have Suffocated, Chemistry Professor Tells Waco Panel," *Washing-*

ton Post, July 27, 1995; Laurie Kellman, "ATF Agent Calls Waco Superiors Liars: They Knew Surprise Was Lost, He Says," Washington Times, July 25, 1999; United Press International, "Colombia, 31, Gets Life in Amtrak Siege Case," New York Times, February 28, 1984; Phil McCombs, "The Siege, the Gunman and the FBI Negotiator," Washington Post, October 16, 1982; "Questions Remain on Amtrak Siege," New York Times, October 12, 1982; Associated Press, "Train Gunman Yields Child, Then Gives Up, with 2 Dead," New York Times, October 12, 1982; Sierra Bellows, "The Voice of Reason," University of Virginia Magazine (winter 2010); Frances Romero, "A Former FBI Negotiator on Waco and 30 Years of Standoffs," Time, October 8, 2010; Nicholas Schmidle, "Talking to Bastards," review of Stalling for Time, by Gary Noesner, New Republic, September 21, 2010; David A. Vise, "Some Actions at Waco Were Not Authorized, Reno Testifies," Washington Post, April 6, 2000; "Death in Waco," ABC News: The Day It Happened, DVD released May 24, 2007.

83 **The Bureau of Alcohol, Tobacco and Firearms (ATF):** Now the Bureau of Alcohol, Tobacco, Firearms, and Explosives.

86 **Donna Webster and Arie Kruglanski's 1994:** Donna M. Webster and Arie Kruglanski, "Individual Differences in Need for Cognitive Closure," Journal of Personality and Social Psychology 67, no. 6 (1994): 1049–1062. Note that while this is how Kruglanski himself cites it (see Arie W. Kruglanski, The Psychology of Closed Mindedness [New York: Psychology Press, 2004], 11), the scale appears in 1993: Arie W. Kruglanski, Donna M. Webster, and Adena Klem, "Motivated Resistance and Openness to Persuasion in the Presence or Absence of Prior Information," Journal of Personality and Social Psychology 65, no. 5 (1993).

86 **psychologists Arne Roets and Alain Van Hiel:** Arne Roets and Alain Van Hiel, "Item Selection and Validation of a Brief, 15-Item Version of the Need for Closure Scale," Personality and Individual Differences 50 (2011): 90–94.

88 **if you scored 57 or above:** Miles Hewstone, Wolfgang Stroebe, and Klaus Jonas, eds., An Introduction to Social Psychology, 5th ed. (Chichester, UK: John Wiley & Sons, 2012), 213.

88 **led by Northwestern University's Bobby Cheon:** Bobby K. Cheon,

interview with author, June 19, 2014; Bobby K. Cheon et al., "Contribution of Serotonin Transporter Polymorphism (5-HTTLPR) to Automatic Racial Bias," *Personality and Individual Differences* 79 (June 2015): 35-38; Bobby K. Cheon et al., "Genetic Contributions to Need for Closure, Implicit Racial Bias, and Social Ideologies: The roles of HTTLPR and COMT Val158Met," Nanyang Technological University, submitted for publication. The latter paper was summarized in Roets et al., "The Motivated Gatekeeper of Our Minds." Cheon also found that people with two Met-alleles (compared to two Val-alleles) of COMT polymorphism showed a higher need for closure, and that this effect was additive to that stemming from 5-HTTLPR attributes. Also see Bobby K. Cheon et al., "Gene x Environment Interaction on Intergroup Bias: the Role of 5-HTTLPR and Perceived Outgroup Threat," *Social Cognitive and Affective Neuroscience*, 9, no. 9 (2014): 1268–1275.

88   **In 2015, psychologists in Poland:** Malgorzata Kossowska et al., "Electrocortical Indices of Attention Correlate with the Need for Closure," *NeuroReport* 26, no. 5 (2015): 285–290. Also see Malgorzata Kossowska et al., "Individual Differences in Epistemic Motivation and Brain Conflict," *Neuroscience Letters* 570 (2014): 38–41; Vanda Viola et al., "Routes of Motivation: Stable Psychological Dispositions Are Associated with Dynamic Changes in Cortico-Cortical Functional Connectivity," *PLoS ONE* 9, no. 6 (2014): e98010.

89   **One of the best examples:** Uri Bar-Joseph and Arie W. Kruglanski, "Intelligence Failure and Need for Cognitive Closure: On the Psychology of the Yom Kippur Surprise," *Political Psychology* 24, no. 1 (2003): 75–99; Uri Bar-Joseph, *The Watchman Fell Asleep: The Surprise of Yom Kippur and Its Sources* (Albany, NY: State University of New York Press, 2005).

92   **A wide range of studies shows that negotiating:** For a summary, see Kruglanski, *Psychology of Closed Mindedness*, 100–102. Also see Gülcimen Yurtsever, "Tolerance of Ambiguity, Information, and Negotiation," *Psychological Reports* 89 (2001): 57–64; Dipankar Ghosh, "Tolerance for Ambiguity, Risk Preference, and Negotiator Effectiveness," *Decision Sciences* 25, no. 2 (1994): 263–280. Note that in certain cases, increased ambiguity can raise the likelihood of a settlement. See Cynthia S. Fobian and Jay J. J. Christensen-Szalanski, "Ambiguity and

Liability Negotiations: The Effects of the Negotiators' Role and the Sensitivity Zone," *Organizational Behavior and Human Decision Processes* 54, no. 2 (1993): 277–298.

92 **"When most people hear a gunshot":** Gary Noesner, interview with author, October 1, 2012.

95 **he reformed the way FBI negotiators are trained:** See Vincent B. Van Hasselt et al., "Development and Validation of a Role-Play Test for Assessing Crisis (Hostage) Negotiation Skills," *Criminal Justice and Behavior* 32, no. 3 (2005): 345–361; G. Dwayne Fuselier and Gary W. Noesner, "Confronting the Terrorist Hostage Taker," *FBI Law Enforcement Bulletin* 59, no. 7 (1990): 6–11; Gary W. Noesner, "Negotiation Concepts for Commanders," *FBI Law Enforcement Bulletin* 68, no. 1 (1999): 6–14; Gary W. Noesner and Mike Webster, "Crisis Intervention: Using Active Listening Skills in Negotiations," *FBI Law Enforcement Bulletin* 66, no. 8 (1997): 13–19.

95 **an indecisive or squeamish man:** On the relationship between a low need for closure and indecision, as Arie Kruglanski clarified: a low need for closure also reflects a lack of strong desire for order and predictability, a high tolerance of ambiguity, and an openness to information. Decisiveness is merely one facet of the need for closure.

97 **the deadly standoff on Ruby Ridge:** Kessler, *The Bureau*; George Lardner Jr. and Richard Leiby, "Standoff at Ruby Ridge: Botched 'Anti-Terrorist' Operation Began with Series of Overreactions," *Washington Post*, September 3, 1995.

99 **The FBI transcripts show Noesner:** See Federal Bureau of Investigation, "Waco FBI Transcript Tapes 004-006," FBI Freedom of Information Act Library, accessed March 3, 2015, http://vault.fbi.gov. For the exchange about the Weaver case, see ibid., 69. For the exchange with Koresh about children, see ibid., 150.

104 **F. Scott Fitzgerald once wrote:** F. Scott Fitzgerald, "The Crack-Up," *Esquire*, February 1936.

105 **The negotiator didn't presume to have a fix on Koresh's:** See Federal Bureau of Investigation, "Waco FBI Transcript Tapes 004-006," 145. For more on why unpredictable behavior may be misinterpreted, see Jason E. Plaks, Carol S. Dweck, and Heidi Grant, "Violations of Implicit Theories and the Sense of Prediction and Control: Implica-

tions for Motivated Person Perception," *Journal of Personality and Social Psychology* 88, no. 2 (2005): 245–262.

106 **causes a form of cognitive dissonance:** See Ian Leslie, "Ambivalence Is Awesome: Or Is It Awful? Sometimes It's Best to Have Conflicted Feelings," *Slate*, June 13, 2013. We'll discuss creativity, too, later in the book. For more background, see Frenk van Harreveld et al., "Ambivalence and Decisional Conflict as a Cause of Psychological Discomfort: Feeling Tense Before Jumping Off the Fence," *Journal of Experimental Social Psychology* 45 (2009): 167–173; Frenk van Harreveld, Joop van der Plight, and Yael N. de Liver, "The Agony of Ambivalence and Ways to Resolve It: Introducing the MAID Model," *Personality and Social Psychology Review* 13, no. 1 (2009): 45–61; Frenk van Harreveld et al., "The Dynamics of Ambivalence: Evaluative Conflict in Attitudes and Decision Making," in *Cognitive Consistency: A Fundamental Principle in Social Cognition*, ed. Bertram Gawronski and Fritz Strack (New York: Guilford Press, 2012).

106 **the poet John Keats:** John Keats, *Complete Poems and Selected Letters of John Keats* (New York: Modern Library, 2009).

107 **After the fact, the US government tried:** Special Counsel John C. Danforth, "Report to the Deputy Attorney General Concerning the 1993 Confrontation at the Mt. Carmel Complex, Waco, Texas," Pursuant to Order No. 2256-99 of the Attorney General, November 8, 2000; Glenn F. Bunting and David Willman, "Reno, FBI Agent Differ in Views of Waco Talks," *Los Angeles Times*, July 28, 1995.

107 **Jordan, Montana:** James Brooke, "Behind the Siege in Montana, Bitter Trail of Broken Bonds," *New York Times*, March 31, 1996; Carey Goldberg, "Last of Freemen Surrender to F.B.I. at Montana Site," *New York Times*, June 14 1996; "Freemen, FBI Standoff Drags On: Lessons of Waco Put into Practice," CNN, March 28, 1996; Tom Kenworthy and Serge F. Kovaleski, "'Freemen' Finally Taxed the Patience of Federal Government," *Washington Post*, March 31, 1996.

108 **psychologists Christopher Armitage and Mark Conner:** Christopher J. Armitage and Mark Conner, "Attitudinal Ambivalence and Political Opinion: Review and Avenue for Further Research," in *Ambivalence, Politics, and Public Policy*, ed. Stephen C. Craig and Michael D. Martinez (New York: Palgrave Macmillan, 2005), 145–166.

109 **Remarkably, a person's innate need for closure:** Donna M. Webster

and Arie Kruglanski, "Individual Differences in Need for Cognitive Closure." Also see Kruglanski, *The Psychology of Closed Mindedness*, 66.

109   **Social psychologist Milton Rokeach:** For this quote, I'm indebted to Richard M. Sorrentino and Christopher J. R. Roney, *The Uncertain Mind: Individual Differences in Facing the Unknown* (Philadelphia: Psychology Press, 2000), 16–17.

109   **red teaming in the intelligence world:** Peter L. Bergen, *Man Hunt: The Ten-Year Search for Bin Laden from 9/11 to Abbottabad* (New York: Crown Publishers, 2012), 191–194.

110   **"Pablo, have you poured it yet?":** Kessler, *The Bureau*, 332. For additional sources on the transcripts, see Associated Press, "'Start the Fire?' a Davidian Asks on 1993 Tapes," *Los Angeles Times*, July 11, 2000; "Jury Clears US Over Waco Deaths," *BBC News*, July 15, 2000; Andrew Maykuth, Steve Goldstein, and Terrence Samuel, "Exactly Two Years Before the Blast, Koresh Site Burned Branch Davidians, Who Marked the Anniversary with a Protest, Deny Involvement in the Bombing," *Philadelphia Inquirer*, April 20, 1995; Mark Potok, "Waco Tape: 'Got Coleman Fuel?'" *USA Today*, February 15, 1994; CNN, "Waco Trial: Closing Arguments Today in Multi-Million Dollar Wrongful Death Case of More Than 80 Branch Davidians," transcripts, CNN, aired July 14, 2000; John C. Danforth, "Report to the Deputy Attorney General Concerning the 1993 Confrontation at the Mt. Carmel Complex, Waco, Texas." Some people, including Dick Reavis, are skeptical that the Davidians set the fire and question the audio expert's transcription of the tape.

CHAPTER FIVE

111   **In late June 2004, a fifty-two-year-old:** Trisha Torrey, interview with author, November 13, 2014. I'm not the first to write about Torrey's experience. See, for instance, Elizabeth S. Cohen, *The Empowered Patient: How to Get the Right Diagnosis, Buy the Cheapest Drugs, Beat Your Insurance Company, and Get the Best Medical Care Every Time* (New York: Ballantine Books, 2010). Torrey wrote for About.com on patient empowerment for over six years. Also see Trisha Torrey, *You Bet Your Life! The 10 Mistakes Every Patient Makes* (Baldwinsville, NY: Diagknowsis Media, 2010); Trisha Torrey, *The Health Advocate's Marketing Handbook* (Baldwinsville, NY: Diagknowsis Media, 2010).

114   **In one heartbreaking case:** Time Wire Reports, "Husband Wins Lawsuit in Chemotherapy Death," *Los Angeles Times,* June 11, 2005.

114   **10 to 20 percent of cases:** Mark L. Graber, Robert M. Wachter, and Christine K. Cassel, "Bringing Diagnosis into the Quality and Safety Equations," *JAMA* 308, no. 12 (2012): 1211–1212; Eta S. Berner and Mark L. Graber, "Overconfidence as a Cause of Diagnostic Error in Medicine," *American Journal of Medicine* 121, no. 5A (2008): S2–S23.

114   **forty thousand and eighty thousand preventable deaths:** Lucian L. Leape, Donald M. Berwick, and David Bates, "Counting Deaths from Medical Errors [Letter Reply]," *JAMA* 288, no. 19 (2002): 2405.

114   **A 2014 study found that one in five breast cancers:** Gina Kolata, "Vast Study Casts Doubts on Value of Mammograms," *New York Times,* February 11, 2014; Anthony B. Miller et al., "Twenty Five Year Follow-Up for Breast Cancer Incidence and Mortality of the Canadian National Breast Screening Study," *BMJ,* February 11, 2014. Also see Denise Grady, "Breast Biopsies Leave Room For Doubt, Study Finds," *New York Times,* March 17, 2015.

114   **pathologists identifying tissue samples:** Stephen S. Raab et al., "Clinical Impact and Frequency of Anatomic Pathology Errors in Cancer Diagnoses," *Cancer* 104, no. 10 (2005): 2205–2213; Cohen, *The Empowered Patient.*

114   **radiologists judging chest X-rays:** E. James Potchen, "Measuring Observer Performance in Chest Radiology: Some Experiences," *Journal of the American College of Radiology* 3, no. 6 (2006): 423–432; Jerome Groopman, *How Doctors Think* (New York: Houghton Mifflin, 2007).

114   **In the 1980s, researchers:** Lee Goldman et al., "The Value of the Autopsy in Three Medical Eras," *New England Journal of Medicine* 305 (1983): 1000–1005; Atul Gawande, *Complications: A Surgeon's Notes on an Imperfect Science* (New York: Metropolitan Books, 2002), 197.

115   **Wilhelm Kirch and Christine Schafii:** Wilhelm Kirch and Christine Schafii, "Misdiagnosis at a University Hospital in 4 Medical Eras," *Medicine* 75, no. 1 (1996): 29–40.

115   **to diagnose appendicitis:** Shannon Brownlee, *Why Too Much Medicine Is Making Us Sicker and Poorer* (New York: Bloomsbury USA, 2007), 151; David Flum et al., "Misdiagnosis of Appendicitis and the Use of Diagnostic Imaging," *Journal of American College of Surgeons* 201, no. 6 (2005): 933–939.

115 **and the challenge now is:** Atul Gawande, *The Checklist Manifesto: How to Get Things Right* (New York: Picador, 2009).

115 **"always appraised in rigorous studies":** C. David Naylor, "Grey Zones of Clinical Practice: Some Limits to Evidence-Based Medicine," *Lancet* 345 (1995): 840–842.

116 **"The core predicament of medicine":** Gawande, *Complications*, 228.

116 **Vera Luther and Sonia Crandall pointed out:** Vera P. Luther and Sonia J. Crandall, "Ambiguity and Uncertainty: Neglected Elements of Medical Education Curricula," *Academic Medicine* 86, no. 7 (2011): 799–800.

116 **theorist Donald Schön:** Donald Schön, "Knowing-in-Action: The New Scholarship Requires a New Epistemology" *Change* 27, no. 6 (1995): 26–34.

116 **a 2011 book on overdiagnosis:** H. Gilbert Welch, Lisa M. Schwartz, and Steven Woloshin, *Overdiagnosed: Making People Sick in the Pursuit of Health* (Boston: Beacon Press, 2011).

117 **ninety-eight thousand Americans die each:** Linda T. Kohn, Janet M. Corrigan, and Molla S. Donaldson, eds., *To Err Is Human: Building a Safer Health System* (Washington, DC: National Academy Press, 2000).

118 **The patient empowerment movement:** Cohen, *The Empowered Patient*; Jan Hoffman, "Awash in Information, Patients Face a Lonely, Uncertain Road," *New York Times*, August 14, 2005; Gawande, *Complications*. Also see Robert M. Anderson and Martha M. Funnell, "Patient Empowerment: Myths and Misconceptions," *Patient Education and Counseling* 79, no. 3 (2010): 277–282; Peter J. Schulz and Kent Nakamoto, "Health Literacy and Patient Empowerment in Health Communication: The Importance of Separating Conjoined Twins," *Patient Education and Counseling* 90 (2013): 4–11.

118 **By 2005, according to one poll:** Hoffman, "Awash in Information."

118 **how ambiguity can undermine:** For scales measuring patients' aversion to ambiguity, see Paul K. J. Han et al., "Aversion to Ambiguity Regarding Medical Tests and Treatments: Measurement, Prevalence, and Relationship to Sociodemographic Factors," *Journal of Health Communication: International Perspectives* 14, no. 6 (2009): 556–572. The study includes statements for which the participants had to rate their agreement or disagreement. For example, "Conflicting expert opinions

would lower my trust in the experts," "Conflicting expert opinions about a medical test would make me upset," and "I would avoid making a decision about a medical test or treatment if experts had conflicting opinions about it." On the doctor side, see Jason Hancock et al., "Medical Student and Junior Doctors' Tolerance of Ambiguity: Development of a New Scale," *Advances in Health Sciences Education*, May 20, 2014. For background on how patient and doctor attitudes toward uncertainty interact, see David B. Portnoy et al., "Physicians' Attitudes About Communicating and Managing Scientific Uncertainty Differ by Perceived Ambiguity Aversion of Their Patients," *Health Expectations* 16, no. 4 (2013): 362–372. For background on suggestions of incorporating measures of ambiguity tolerance into medical education, see Gail Geller, "Tolerance for Ambiguity: An Ethics-Based Criterion for Medical Student Selection," *Academic Medicine* 88, no. 5 (2013): 581–584. Also see Luther and Crandall, "Ambiguity and Uncertainty"; John Lally and Peter Cantillon, "Uncertainty and Ambiguity and Their Association with Psychological Distress in Medical Students," *Academic Psychiatry* 38, no. 3 (2014): 339–344; Greta B. Raglan et al., "Need to Know: The Need for Cognitive Closure Impacts the Clinical Practice of Obstetrician/Gynecologists," *BMC Medical Informatics and Decision Making*, December 24, 2014.

118 **About two-thirds of primary care:** David B. Seaburn et al., "Physician Responses to Ambiguous Patient Symptoms," *Journal of General Internal Medicine* 20, no. 6 (2005): 525–530. Also see Loïc Berger, Han Bleichrodt, and Louis Eeckhoudt, "Treatment Decisions Under Ambiguity," *Journal of Health Economics* 32 (2013): 559–569.

120 **Lisa Sanders confirmed:** Lisa Sanders, *Every Patient Tells a Story: Medical Mysteries and the Art of Diagnosis* (New York: Broadway Books, 2009), 230.

120 **In 2011, the *New York Times*:** Gina Kolata, "Sports Medicine Said to Overuse M.R.I.'s," *New York Times*, October 28, 2011; John Helyar, "Dr. James Andrews Still Works on the Cutting Edge," *ESPN.com*, September 17, 2007; Sam Farmer, "Dr. Andrews Says Brady Getting Better," *Los Angeles Times*, October 24, 2008.

121 **Patients are practically drowning in diagnostic tests:** Rebecca Smith-Bindman et al., "Use of Diagnostic Imaging Studies and Associated Radiation Exposure for Patients Enrolled in Large Integrated

Health Care Systems," *JAMA* 307, no. 22 (2012): 2400–2409. Additional background came from John Horgan, "How Can We Curb the Medical-Testing Epidemic?" *Scientific American*, November 7, 2011; Denise Dador, "Doctor Says Medical Profession 'Over-Tests' Patients," *ABC News*, July 18, 2012; Jesse M. Pines and Zachary F. Meisel, "Why Doctors Order Too Many Tests (It's Not Just to Avoid Lawsuits)," *Time*, February 25, 2011; "Diagnostic Tests: Another Frontier for Less Is More," editorial, *Archives of Internal Medicine* 171, no. 7 (2011): 619; Deborah Grady, "Why Physicians Order Tests," *JAMA Internal Medicine* 173, no. 17 (2013): 1383; Deborah Grady, "The 'Top 5' Health Care Activities for Which Less Is More," *Archives of Internal Medicine* 171, no. 5 (2011): 1390; "Less Is More: How Less Health Care Can Result in Better Health," editorial, *Archives of Internal Medicine* 170, no. 9 (2010): 749–750.

121 **"for every scan that helps"**: Brownlee, *Too Much Medicine*, 149.

121 **Sah speculated that ambiguous**: Sunita Sah, Pierre Elias, and Dan Ariely, "Investigation Momentum: The Relentless Pursuit to Resolve Uncertainty," *JAMA Internal Medicine* 173, no. 10 (2013): 932–933. For bringing this study to my attention, I'm indebted to David DiSalvo, "How Uncertainty Overpowers Evidence in Matters of Health: Study Shows That Many Invasive Procedures Are Fueled by Uncertainty, Not Facts," *Psychology Today*, May 12, 2013.

123 **In one case, a man in his fifties**: Meredith A. Niess, "Preoperative Chest X-rays: A Teachable Moment," *JAMA Internal Medicine* 174, no. 1 (2014): 12. Also see Matthew C. Becker, John M. Galla, and Steven E. Nissen, "Left Main Trunk Coronary Artery Dissection as a Consequence of Inaccurate Coronary Computer Tomographic Angiography," *Archives of Internal Medicine* 171, no. 7 (2011): 698–701.

124 **Medical professionals are aware**: Jerome Greenberg and Jonas B. Green, "Over-testing: Why More Is Not Better," *American Journal of Medicine* 127, no. 5 (2014): 362–363; Ray Moynihan, Jenny Doust, and David Henry, "Preventing Overtesting: How to Stop Harming the Healthy," *BMJ* 344 (2012): 1–6; Tanner J. Caverly et al., "Too Much Medicine Happens Too Often: The Teachable Moment and a Call for Manuscripts from Clinical Trials," *JAMA Internal Medicine* 174, no. 1 (2014): 8–9.

124 **Roughly $200 billion**: Donald M. Berwick and Andrew D. Hack-

barth, "Eliminating Waste in US Health Care," *JAMA* 307, no. 14 (2012): 1514. Their estimate is for 2011.

124   **In a 2014 survey:** PerryUndem Research/Communication, "Unnecessary Tests and Procedures in the Health Care System: The Problem, the Causes, and the Solutions," results from a national survey of physicians conducted for the ABIM Foundation, May 1, 2014.

124   **in 2010 *JAMA Internal Medicine*:** At that time, they were *Archives of Internal Medicine*: Rita F. Redberg, "Less Is More," *Archives of Internal Medicine* 170, no. 7 (2010): 584.

124   **diagnostic testing as one critical problem area:** Rita Redberg, Mitchell Katz, and Deborah Grady, "Diagnostic Tests: Another Frontier for Less Is More, or Why Talking to Your Patient Is a Safe and Effective Method of Reassurance," *Archives of Internal Medicine* 171, no. 7 (2011): 619. Also see Deborah Grady and Rita Redberg, "Less Is More: How Less Health Care Can Result in Better Health," *Archives of Internal Medicine* 170, no. 9 (2010): 749–750; Good Stewardship Working Group, "The 'Top 5' Lists in Primary Care: Meeting the Responsibility of Professionalism," *Archives of Internal Medicine* 171, no. 15 (2011): 1385–1390. Shubha V. Srinivas, "Application of 'Less Is More' to Low Back Pain," *Archives of Internal Medicine* 172, no. 13 (2013): 1016–1020.

125   **In Minnesota, for example:** Lauran Neergaard, "Overtreated: More Medical Care Isn't Always Better," *Boston Globe*, June 7, 2010.

125   **the dangers of certain drugs:** Richard A. Friedman, "A Call for Caution on Antipsychotic Drugs," *New York Times*, September 24, 2012.

126   **a campaign called Choosing Wisely:** Bruce Japsen, "Doctors Call Out 90 More Unnecessary Medical Tests, Procedures," *Forbes*, February 21, 2013; Chris Crawford, "Two Years Down the Road, Choosing Wisely Still Picking Up Steam," *American Academy of Family Physicians*, May 14, 2014.

126   **the Canadian Medical Association launched:** Jessica McDiarmid, "Canadian Doctors to Tackle Unnecessary Medical Tests," *The Star*, August 22, 2013.

126   **one study of resident doctors:** Lauren Block et al., "In the Wake of the 2003 and 2011 Duty Hours Regulations, How Do Internal Medicine Interns Spend Their Time?" *Journal of General Internal Medicine* 28, no. 8 (2013): 1042–1047; J.R. Hampton, "Relative Contributions of

History-Taking, Physical Examination, and Laboratory Investigation to Diagnosis and Management of Medical Outpatients," *The British Medical Journal* 2, no. 5969 (1975): 486–489. These studies are referenced in Leana Wen, "Don't Just Do Something, Stand There!" *The Huffington Post*, August 22, 2013; Leana Wen, "When More Medicine Isn't Better," *The Huffington Post*, August 11, 2013.

126 **as cure-alls, especially in the "developing" world:** Thanks go to Annie Murphy Paul, "Technology Is Not a 'Magic Cure-All' for Education," *Brilliant Blog*, May 4, 2012, www.anniemurphypaul .com/2012/05/technology-is-not-a-magic-cure-all-for-education; Julián P. Cristia et al., "Technology and Child Development: Evidence from the One Laptop per Child Program," Working Paper IDB-WP 304, Inter-American Development Bank, Washington, DC, February 2012. On MOOCs, see Tamar Lewin, "After Setbacks, Online Courses are Rethought," *New York Times*, December 10, 2013. For online courses, see "The Trouble With Online College," editorial, *New York Times*, February 18, 2013. I've made the mistake of putting too much faith in technological solutions myself. See Jamie Zimmerman and Jamie Holmes, "The M-Banking Revolution: Why Cell Phones Will Do More for the Developing World Than Laptops Ever Could," *Foreign Policy*, August 27, 2010. As we'll touch on later in the book, the use of cell phones for money *transfers* has been wildly successful, but the use of cell phones for *saving* money has yet to really pan out. Curious as to why, I recently asked Ignacio Mas (interview with author, July 15, 2013), an independent consultant and senior fellow at the Fletcher School at Tufts University. Mas explained that one false assumption is that cell phone savings accounts fill a completely unmet need. In reality, the "poor" have many tools for informal savings. These tools operate effectively and are almost impossible to replicate digitally. Mas says: "The number one challenge of digital finance is that digital makes everything so goddamn explicit. In contrast, think about how a farmer uses a cow, for example, as a savings instrument. You can't liquidate immediately, since there's a waiting period involved in selling a cow. There's an indivisibility. You can't sell bits of a living cow. There's a transaction cost. There's also a social barrier, a visibility. Everybody in the village knows if you sold a cow, and you

may not want everybody to know that you're having financial troubles. So there's all these frictions; none of them are explicit but everybody understands them. How do you project those sorts of frictions onto an electronic account? It will all appear entirely arbitrary. You would have to tell people, 'Well, for this account, you can only liquidate with forty-eight-hour notice, and you can only sell five-hundred-dollar lots, and we're going to tell all your neighbors that you cashed out.' It's this explicitness about digital banking which is so awkward." In short, mobile banking doesn't try to fill an unmet need. It's trying to replace existing informal savings techniques, which are nuanced, useful, and hard to replicate.

127 **(despite the car warning lights analogy I borrowed earlier):** And despite other language I've adopted in this book in reference to our "mental machinery."

127 **we've finally discovered a window:** Malcolm Gladwell touched on this point some years ago: "pictures promise to clarify but often confuse." Malcolm Gladwell, "The Picture Problem: Mammography, Air Power, and the Limits of Looking," *New Yorker*, December 13, 2004.

127 *Neurolaw* **applies brain imaging:** The statistics on neuroscientific evidence in court came from Nita Farahany, email to author, July 11, 2014. James Fallon and I originally spoke in 2011. He confirmed via email on July 11, 2014, that the quote about neuroimaging not being "ready for prime time" still reflects his current views. I've also drawn on Jeffrey Rosen, "The Brain on the Stand," *New York Times Magazine*, March 11, 2007; Eric Bailey, "Defense Probing Brain to Explain Yosemite Killings," *Los Angeles Times*, June 15, 2000; Amanda C. Pustilnik, "Violence on the Brain: A Critique of Neuroscience in Criminal Law," *Harvard Law School Faculty Scholarship Series* 14 (2008); Richard E. Redding, "The Brain-Disordered Defendant: Neuroscience and Legal Insanity in the Twenty-First Century," *American University Law Review* 56, no. 1 (2006): 51–127.

129 **Brown prescribed a three-week course:** In other contexts, as Choosing Wisely emphasizes, it's important to avoid antibiotics overuse. See Choosing Wisely, "Antibiotics: When You Need Them and When You Don't," published in collaboration with *Consumer Reports Health*, February 2014.

· CHAPTER SIX

130   **John Fairchild, the dimpled-chin:** The story of *WWD* and the midi
was drawn from "Midi vs. Mini: The Battle of the Hemline," *Newsweek*,
March 16, 1970; "The Great Hemline Hassle: Onward and Downward
with Hemlines," *Life*, March 13, 1970; Julie Byrne, "Clothes Purr at
Full Throttle," *Los Angeles Times*, August 16, 1970; "Fashion: Up, Up &
Away," *Time*, December 1, 1967; Claire McCormack, "The Miniskirt:
Top 10 British Invasion," *Time*, January 18, 2011; "Fashion: Anyone
She Wants to Be," *Time*, June 23, 1967; "Business: Fashion Show in
the Office," *Time*, August 2, 1968; "Fashion: Next, the Maxiskirt?"
Time, May 12, 1967; "Modern Living: The French Line," *Time*, Feb-
ruary 9, 1970; Meryl Gordon, "Fashion's Most Angry Fella," *Vanity
Fair*, September 2012; "Modern Living: The Long Way Out," *Time*,
October 26, 1970; "Fashion: Hold That Mini Line!" *Time*, August 8,
1969; "Modern Living: Claude and the Long Look," *Time*, March 9,
1970; "Modern Living: Compulsory Midi," *Time*, June 29, 1970; An-
astasia Toufexis, "Living: A Rousing No to Mini-pulation," *Time*,
April 25, 1988; "Press: Stalking the Elusive Hemline," *Time*, March
31, 1980; "Modern Living: The Midi's Compensations," *Time*, June
8, 1970; "The Press: Out on a Limb with the Midi," *Time*, September
14, 1970; "Nation: Women on the March," *Time*, September 7, 1970;
"Modern Living: All in the Jeans," *Time*, January 11, 1971; "People:
May 17, 1968," *Time*, May 17, 1968; "Nation: Midis Verboten," *Time*,
September 28, 1970; Edward Gold et al., *Fashion, Retailing and a By-
gone Era: Inside* Women's Wear Daily (Washington, DC: Beard Books,
2005); Eugenia Sheppard, "Midi May Be Flight from Reality," *Hartford Courant*, May 25, 1970; Isadore Barmash, "Long-Skirt Fiasco Lin-
gers On," *New York Times*, May 13, 1973; Marylin Bender, "This Year
Even the Shoe Designers Are Confused," *New York Times*, February
23, 1970; Nan Ickeringill, "Oh the Times They Are A-Changing: Daring Now Means Mid-Calf," *New York Times*, February 23, 1968; Marylou Luther, "A Letdown for Miniskirts? How the Midi Poll Sees It,"
Los Angeles Times, February 9, 1970; Eugenia Sheppard, "Gloria Goes
All Out for the Midi," *Hartford Courant*, December 23, 1969; Isadore
Barmash, "Designers' Sales Go Up as Hem Lines Fall," *New York*

Times, June 1, 1970; Alison Adburgham, "Femme Chic and Tough Chick," *Guardian* (Manchester), August 4, 1970; United Press International, "Funeral for the Midi," *Washington Post,* October 28, 1970; Marian Christy, "Skirts the Issue in Lengthy Debate," *Boston Globe,* April 12, 1970; Nancy L. Ross, "The Midi Fad," *Washington Post,* March 19, 1970; Eleanor Page, "The Great Hemline Hassle," *Chicago Tribune,* July 2, 1970; Gertrude Wilson, "Midi Can't Make It," *New York Amsterdam,* September 5, 1970; Marylou Luther, "Pantsuit Voted Tops for Fall," *Los Angeles Times,* September 13, 1970; "Midi Length Is Dead, Oxford Industries' Chief Tells Holders," *Wall Street Journal,* October 1, 1970; "Putting It All Together," *Newsday,* September 29, 1970; David McLean, "Heard on the Street," *Wall Street Journal,* December 7, 1970; Marian Christy, "Designers Insist the Midi is Here to Stay," *Boston Globe,* November 8, 1970; Marian Christy, "Farewell to Frivolity: The Midi Is Here," *Boston Globe,* May 5, 1970; Ellen Zack, "Prices Are Up, Selection Down As Inflation Hits Clothing Stores," *Boston Globe,* September 1, 1974; Marilyn Goldstein, "Won't Anybody Buy a Midi?" *Newsday,* October 12, 1970; Margaret Crimmins, "Buyers . . . : Seven Inches of Leg and a Foot," *Washington Post,* September 27, 1970; Art Buchwald, "Report from the Front," *Boston Globe,* September 15, 1970; "Modern Living: Line of Most Resistance," *Time,* March 23, 1970. Note that "midi lengths" include midi coats.

134 **Daniel Ellsberg's famous thought experiment:** Daniel Ellsberg, "Risk, Ambiguity, and the Savage Axioms," *Quarterly Journal of Economics* 75, no. 4 (1961): 643–669. For evidence that trust involves ambiguous, not risky evidence, see Anne Corcos, François Pannequin, and Sacha Bourgeois-Gironde, "Is Trust an Ambiguous Rather Than a Risky Decision?" *Economics Bulletin* 32, no. 3 (2012): 2255–2266.

135 **monkeys also prefer known odds:** Benjamin Y. Hayden, Sarah R. Heilbronner, and Michael L. Platt, "Ambiguity Aversion in Rhesus Macaques," *Frontiers in Neuroscience* 4, no. 166 (2010).

135 **chimpanzees and bonobos, too:** Alexandra G. Rosati and Brian Hare, "Chimpanzees and Bonobos Distinguish Between Risk and Ambiguity," *Biology Letters* 7, no. 1 (2011): 15–18.

135 **even with *partial* ambiguity:** Ifat Levy et al., "Neural Representation of Subjective Value Under Risk and Ambiguity," *Journal of Neurophysiology* 103, no. 2 (2010): 1036–1047; Levy and several others conducted

a fascinating study suggesting that adolescents may actually be less risk-tolerant than adults. The adolescent tolerance of ambiguity, the study found, compels teens to test the unknown. See Agnieszka Tymula et al., "Adolescents' Risk-Taking Behavior Is Driven by Tolerance to Ambiguity," *Proceedings of the National Academy of Sciences* 109, no. 42 (2012): 17135–17140.

135 **Evidence from brain science:** Ming Hsu et al., "Neural Systems Responding to Degrees of Uncertainty in Human Decision-Making," *Science* 310, no. 5754 (2005): 1680–1683; Ifat Levy, "Ambiguous Decisions in the Human Brain," in *Comparative Decision Making*, ed. Thomas R. Zentall and Philip H. Crowley (Oxford: Oxford University Press, 2013); Ming Hsu and Lusha Zhu, "Ambiguous Decisions in the Human Brain," in *Comparative Decision Making*.

136 **Michael Raynor, a business writer:** Michael E. Raynor, *The Strategy Paradox: Why Committing to Success Leads to Failure (and What to Do About It)* (New York: Random House, 2007).

136 **Completely unanticipated events:** Raynor, ibid.; Paul J. H. Schoemaker, *Profiting from Uncertainty: Strategies for Succeeding No Matter What the Future Brings* (New York: Free Press, 2002).

137 **Cisco once wrote off:** James Surowiecki, "Cisco-Holics Anonymous," *New Yorker*, May 21, 2001; "Cisco: Behind the Hype," *Bloomberg Businessweek*, January 20, 2002. Other details on the financial impacts of inventory problems come from Blair Speedy, "Retailers Puncture Post-Poll Optimism," *Australian* (Sydney), October 25, 2013; Jim Dwyer, "A Clothing Clearance Where More Than Just the Prices Have Been Slashed," *New York Times*, January 5, 2010; Sue Mitchell, "TWE Slumps as Wine Dumped," *Australian Financial Review*, July 16, 2013; Justin Grant, "New Elmo Doll's Not So Special—Analyst," *Reuters Blog*, December 18, 2007; Alex Veiga, "Mattel Posts 6 Pct. Rise in 3Q Profit," *Fox News*, October 6, 2006; Trefis Team, "Abercrombie & Fitch's Tough Run with Inventory Management," *Trefis.com*, June 25, 2013. For background on Abercrombie & Fitch versus fast fashion, see Reuters, "Teens Aren't Shopping at Abercrombie, American Eagle and Aeropostale Anymore," *New York Daily News*, August 23, 2013; Reuters, "Abercrombie & Fitch Sales Decline for Seventh Straight Quarter," *Huffington Post*, November 21, 2013; Ben Levisohn, "Can Anything Save Abercrombie & Fitch?" *Barron's*, November 6, 2013.

The company advertising toy destruction is called Security Engineered Machinery.

138   **known as the bullwhip effect:** Hau L. Lee, V. Padmanabhan, and Seungjin Whang, "The Bullwhip Effect in Supply Chains," *MIT Sloan Management Review*, April 15, 1997. Injazz J. Chen, YeonYeob Lee, and Anthony Paulraj, "Does a Purchasing Manager's Need for Cognitive Closure (NFCC) Affect Decision-Making Uncertainty and Supply Chain Performance?" *International Journal of Production Research*, April 22, 2014, looked directly at purchasing managers' decisions and the need for closure. It concluded that "when confronting uncertainty, high NFCC purchasing managers are more likely to employ and master decision rules that mitigate uncertainty and improve chances of success."

138   **In 1997, Stanford's:** Lee, Padmanabhan, and Whang, "Bullwhip Effect in Supply Chains."

139   **a business professor at De La Salle University:** Aida L. Velasco, "The View from Taft: Brand Piracy," *BusinessWorld*, April 14, 2011.

139   **In 2012, researchers examining over four thousand US companies:** Robert L. Bray and Haim Mendelson, "Information Transmission and the Bullwhip Effect: An Empirical Investigation," *Management Science* 58, no. 5 (2012): 860–875. Robert Bray, interview with author, March 18, 2015. Bray emphasized that the bullwhip effect has multiple causes. Buffers can be caused by what Lee, Padmanabhan, and Whang call rationing and shortage gaming, as buyers anticipate supply shortages. Demand forecast updating is also a key cause.

142   **the supermarket chain Piggly Wiggly:** Mike Freeman, *Piggly Wiggly: The Rise & Fall of a Memphis Maverick* (London: History Press, 2011); "Business & Finance: Piggly Wiggly Man," *Time*, February 25, 1929.

143   **Taiichi Ohno visited America:** The background on Toyota comes from Taiichi Ohno, *Toyota Production System: Beyond Large-Scale Production* (Portland, OR: Productivity Press, 1988), 23; Taiichi Ohno with Setsuo Mito, *Just-In-Time for Today and Tomorrow*, trans. Joseph P. Schmelzeis Jr. (Cambridge, MA: Productivity Press, 1988); David Magee, *How Toyota Became #1: Leadership Lessons from the World's Greatest Car Company* (New York: Portfolio, 2007); Adam S. Maiga and Fred

A. Jacobs, "JIT Performance Effects: A Research Note," *Advances in Accounting (incorporating Advances in International Accounting)* 25 (2009): 183–189; James P. Womack, Daniel T. Jones, and Daniel Roos, *The Machine That Changed the World* (New York: Free Press, 2007).

143 **Ohno would later contrast:** Taiichi Ohno, *Taiichi Ohno's Workplace Management: Special 100th Birthday Edition* (New York: McGraw-Hill, 2013).

143 **Tofu aficionados, like P&G's distributors:** As implied in Lee, Padmanabhan, and Whang, "Bullwhip Effect in Supply Chains," stockpiling can reduce uncertainty. Of course, confident predictions of future demand—high or low—serve the same function.

143 **purchases, in fact, can serve to reduce:** If you haven't yet read the following book, it's a must-buy: Sendhil Mullainathan and Eldar Shafir, *Scarcity: Why Having Too Little Means So Much* (New York: Times Books, 2013).

144 **higher insurance premiums:** Laure Cabantous, "Ambiguity Aversion in the Field of Insurance: Insurers' Attitude to Imprecise and Conflicting Probability and Conflicting Probability Estimates," *Theory and Decision* 62 (2997): 219–240. For other areas of decision making affected by ambiguity aversion, see Levy, "Ambiguous Decisions in the Human Brain"; Colin Camerer and Martin Weber, "Recent Developments in Modeling Preferences: Uncertainty and Ambiguity," *Journal of Risk and Uncertainty* 5 (1992): 325–370.

144 **In the early 1990s:** Enrique Badía, *Zara and Her Sisters: The Story of the World's Largest Clothing Retailer* (New York: Palgrave Macmillan, 2008), 83; Pankaj Ghemawat and José Luis Neuno, "ZARA: Fast Fashion," Case 9-703-497, Harvard Business School, Boston, December 2006.

145 **Amancio Ortega Gaona:** Details on Ortega, Inditex, Zara, and fast fashion were drawn from a variety of sources, primarily Covadonga O'Shea, *The Man from Zara: The Story of the Genius Behind the Inditex Group* (London: LIT Publishing, 2008); Badía, *Zara and Her Sisters;* John R. Wells and Galen Danskin, "Inditex: 2012," Case 9-713-539, Harvard Business School, Boston, March 2014; Tobias Buck, "Fashion: A Better Business Model," *Financial Times,* June 18, 2014; Suzy Hansen, "How Zara Grew into the World's Largest Retailer," *New York Times,*

November 8, 2012; Vivienne Walt, "Meet Amancio Ortega: The Third-Richest Man in the World," *Fortune,* January 8, 2012; Donald Sull and Stefano Turconi, "Fast Fashion Lessons," *Business Strategy Review* 19, no. 2 (2008): 4–11. Additional details came from Mark Tungate, *Fashion Brands: Branding Style from Armani to Zara* (Philadelphia: Kogan Page, 2008), 49–53; Nebahat Tokatli, "Global Sourcing: Insights from the Global Clothing Industry—the Case of Zara, a Fast Fashion Retailer," *Journal of Economic Geography* 8, no. 1 (2007): 21–38; Carita Vitzthum, "Just-in-Time Fashion: Spanish Retailer Zara Makes Low-Cost Lines in Weeks by Running Its Own Show," *Wall Street Journal,* May 18, 2001; Alexandra Jacobs, "Where Have I Seen You Before? At Zara, in Midtown, It's All a Tribute," *New York Times,* March 27, 2012; Cecilie Rohwedded and Keith Johnson, "Zara Stores' Fast Fashion to Get Even Faster: Inditex Tries to Shave Minutes in Logistics as Rivals Catch Up," *Wall Street Journal Europe,* February 20, 2008; Marilyn Alva, "Foreign Apparel Chains Invade U.S. with Fast Fashion," *Investor's Business Daily,* January 21, 2011; Nelson M. Fraiman et al., "Zara," Jerome Chazen Case Series no. 080204, Columbia Business School, New York, 2008; Seth Stevenson, "Polka Dots Are In? Polka Dots It Is!" *Slate,* June 21, 2012; Andrew McAfee, Vincent Dessain, and Anders Sjöman, "Zara: IT for Fast Fashion," Case 9-604-081, Harvard Business School, Boston, September 2007; James Surowiecki, "The Most Devastating Retailer in the World," *New Yorker,* September 18, 2000; "Fashion Forward: Zara, Spain's Most Successful Brand, Is Trying to Go Global," *Economist,* May 24, 2012; Kasra Ferdows, Michael A. Lewis, and Jose A. D. Machuca, "Rapid-Fire Fulfillment," in *Harvard Business Review on Managing Supply Chains* (Boston: Harvard Business Review Press, 2011); Stephanie O. Crofton and Luis G. Dopico, "Zara-Inditex and the Growth of Fast Fashion," *Essays in Economic & Business History* 25 (2007): 41–53; Carmen Lopez and Ying Fan, "Internationalization of the Spanish Fashion Brand Zara," *Journal of Fashion Marketing and Management* 13, no. 2 (2009): 279–296; Graham Keeley, "Zara Overtakes Gap to Become World's Largest Clothing Retailer," *Guardian* (Manchester), August 11, 2008; Julie Cruz and Vinicy Chan, "Esprit Gets Instant Value with Zara Fast-Fashion Leader," *Bloomberg,* August 8, 2012.

145   **at the age of twelve:** Walt, "Meet Amancio Ortega," says that Ortega

was thirteen when he quit school. Other sources say fourteen. Badía, *Zara and Her Sisters*, reports that he was "barely eleven." Ortega himself reports his age at the time as twelve: O'Shea, *The Man from Zara*, 35.

147 **New York City's Fifth Avenue:** This transformation has been going on for at least a decade. See "The New Face of Fifth: Populist Movement Hits Luxe Street of Retailers," *WWD*, August 19, 2004; Julie Satow, "Discount Stores Crop Up in Manhattan's Elite Neighborhoods," *New York Times*, October 13, 2010. For information on the downside of fast fashion, see Elizabeth L. Cline, *Over-Dressed: The Shockingly High Cost of Cheap Fashion* (New York: Portfolio/Penguin, 2012); Amy Merrick, "Are Clothing Companies Moving Fast Enough to Fix Factory Problems?" *New Yorker*, September 13, 2014. For Hollister, see Joann Lublin and Sara Germano, "Abercrombie Plans to Remake Hollister Stores," *Wall Street Journal*, March 6, 2014.

148 **If a retailer can halve:** See George Stalk Jr. and Thomas M. Hout, *Competing Against Time: How Time-Based Competition Is Reshaping Global Markets* (New York: Simon & Schuster, 1990).

151 **a CEO's capacity to tolerate ambiguity:** Again, this is a related but distinct concept from the need for closure. See Mats Westerberg, Jagdip Singh, and Einar Häckner, "Does the CEO Matter? An Empirical Study of Small Swedish Firms Operating in Turbulent Environments," *Scandinavian Journal of Management* 13, no. 3 (1997): 251–270; Hai Yap Teoh and See Liang Foo, "Moderating Effects of Tolerance for Ambiguity and Risk-Taking Propensity on the Role Conflict-Perceived Performance Relationship: Evidence from Singaporean Entrepreneurs," *Journal of Business Venturing* 12 (1997): 67–81; Adrian Furnham and Joseph Marks, "Tolerance of Ambiguity: A Review of the Recent Literature"; Jeff Sandefer, "The One Key Trait for Successful Entrepreneurs: A Tolerance for Ambiguity," *Forbes*, May 17, 2012.

152 **In May 2013, the midi:** Liz Jones, "Midi Skirts Aren't Just for Supermodels with Legs Like Flamingoes and They'll be Autumn's Biggest Trend," *Daily Mail Online*, May 19, 2013; Rebecca Edge, "ASOS Midi Dress with Full Skirt and Belt—A Must Have!" *Female First*, December 21, 2013; Bianca London, "Rise of the Midi! Sales of Victoria Beckham and Nicole Scherzinger's Favourite Dress Style Shoot Up as Hemlines Come Down," *Mail Online*, December 2, 2013.

CHAPTER SEVEN

157 **2004 was supposed to be a banner year:** This chapter owes a particular debt to Francesca Gino and Gary Pisano, "Why Leaders Don't Learn from Success," *Harvard Business Review*, April 2011. Also see Francesca Gino and Gary Pisano, "Ducati Corse: The Making of a Grand Prix Motorcycle," Case 9-605-090, Harvard Business School, Boston, June 2005. Additional background on MotoGP and Ducati's 2004 season that appears here and later in the chapter is from Alastair Moffitt, "Rossi Set for New Adventure," *Birmingham Evening Mail*, April 12, 2004; Australian Associated Press, "Ducati's Bayliss Keen to Step on the Gas," *Hobart Mercury*, April 15, 2004; Rick Broadbent, "Hodgson Is Revving Up for Heat of New Battle," *Times* (London), April 16, 2004; Reuters, "Rossi to Yam It Up," *Herald Sun* (Melbourne, Australia), April 17, 2004; Gary James, "Motorcycle: Rossi Stuns Rivals by Going Fastest on Yamaha Debut," *Independent* (London), April 17, 2004; "No Luck for Hodgson in South Africa," *Isle of Man Examiner*, April 18, 2004; Rick Broadbent, "Another Bike, Another Victory for Tearful Magician Rossi," *Times* (London), April 19, 2004; Bob Jennings, "Rossi the Greatest Yet, Says Gardner," *Sydney Morning Herald*, April 20, 2004; James Stanford, "Ducati Struggles," *Herald Sun* (Melbourne, Australia), April 30, 2004; AAP, "Bayliss Revved to Make up for Lost Time," *Hobart Mercury*, May 13, 2004; Steve Hardcastle, "Rossi Roars to Victory at Home," *Independent* (London), June 7, 2004; Bob Jennings, "Rossi Overwhelmed by Six-Lap Dash," *Sydney Morning Herald*, June 8, 2004; Dave Fern, "Just What the Doc Ordered," *Daily Star* (London), June 14, 2004; Rick Broadbent, "Rossi Victory Is Just What the Doctor Ordered," *Times* (London), June 14, 2004; James Stanford, "X-Rays Clear Sore Troy," *Herald Sun* (Melbourne, Australia), June 15, 2004; Robert Grant, "Bruised Bayliss Tests New Weapon," *Advertiser*, June 16, 2004; James Stanford, "Aussie Vows to Troy Harder," *Herald Sun* (Melbourne, Australia), July 20, 2004; Mike Nicks, "Rossi Hopes New Engine Will Keep Him Ahead of Pack," *Independent* (London), July 22, 2004; Gary James, "Rossi Defines the Modern Era in Chess at 300ft Per Second," *Independent* (London), July 24, 2004; James Stanford, "No Joy in the Battle for Troy," *Herald Sun*

(Melbourne, Australia), August 27, 2004; Robert Grant, "Ducati Move Could Force Bayliss Out," *Daily Telegraph* (Sydney, Australia), September 4, 2004; Robert Grant, "Bayliss Fed Up as Poor Run Continues," *Daily Telegraph* (Sydney, Australia), September 6, 2004; Dan Oakes and Michael Lynch, "Italian Ace Revs Up as Fourth World Title Awaits," *Sun Herald* (Melbourne, Australia), October 17, 2004; Dan Oakes and Michael Lynch, "How a Maestro Beat the Odds," *Sunday Age* (Melbourne, Australia), October 17, 2004; Robert Grant, "Rossi Rated Unbeatable by Bayliss," *Sun Herald* (Melbourne, Australia), October 17, 2004; Bob Jennings, "Two-Wheeled Warriors Now Fighting for Rides," *Sydney Morning Herald*, October 19, 2004; "Bayliss Dumped by Ducati," *Canberra Times*, October 12, 2004; Rick Broadbent, "Hodgson Looking Forward to End of Grim Season," *Times* (London), October 16, 2004. General background also came from Tom Rostance, "MotoGP vs F1: Two Wheels Good, Four Wheels Better?" *BBC Sport*, April 4, 2012; Matt Carroll, "Back-Seat Rider: MotoGP Riders Hurtle Round the Asphalt at Speeds of Up to 200 mph," *Independent* (London), July 6, 2003; *Faster*, directed by Mark Neale (2003; Los Angeles: Docurama, 2004), DVD; *Faster and Faster*, directed by Mark Neale (2004; New York: Spark Productions, 2013), iTunes.

159   **it improved steadily over the 2005 and 2006 seasons:** In all three categories: rider, team, and manufacturer. See www.motogp.com for precise numbers.

159   **in 2007, its rider won:** Warwick Green, "Power and the Passion," *Sunday Age* (Melbourne, Australia), October 14, 2007.

159   **Rossi was threatening to quit Yamaha:** Robert Grant, "Rossi: If I Can't Beat Him . . . ," *Herald Sun* (Melbourne, Australia), November 14, 2007.

159   **as a victory of ideas:** *The Age of 27: The MotoGP Career of Casey Stoner*, directed by Sergi Sendra Vives (2012; Madrid: Dorna Sports, 2013), iTunes.

160   **Ducati's entrance into MotoGP:** Gino and Pisano, "Why Leaders Don't Learn from Success"; Gino and Pisano, "Ducati Corse: The Making of a Grand Prix Motorcycle." Additional background on Ducati's 2003 season that appears here and later in the chapter was drawn from MATP (Mirror Australian Telegraph Publications), "Rampant

Rossi Is Doohan Fine," *Daily Telegraph* (Sydney, Australia), June 14, 2003; Guy Hand, "Bayliss in Battle to Regain Lost Confidence," *Courier Mail* (Brisbane), June 13, 2003; Reuters, "Rossi Holds Off Rivals as Aussies Bomb Out," *Hobart Mercury*, June 10, 2003; Rick Broadbent, "Rossi Digs Deep to Repel Rivals," *Times* (London), June 9, 2003; Tim Roberts, "Capirossi Breaks Own Record," *Independent* (London), June 7, 2003; Rick Broadbent, "Rossi Has Goal of Being Fastest in Italy," *Times* (London), June 7, 2003; MATP, "Bayliss 'Hometown Hero,' in Italy," *Daily Telegraph* (Sydney, Australia), June 5, 2003; AAP, "Play Time for Hot Bayliss," *Hobart Mercury*, May 22, 2003; Del Jones, "Motorcycles: Regal Rossi Reigns in Spain," *Sports Argus*, May 17, 2003; MATP, "Troy's Ducati Gets Closer," *Daily Telegraph* (Sydney, Australia), May 13, 2003; Robert Grant, "Bayliss Snatches No. 2 Spot on Grid for Spanish GP," *Advertiser*, May 12, 2003; AAP, "Stunning Bayliss on Track to Glory," *Hobart Mercury*, May 8, 2003; MATP, "Mystery Ride for 'Rookie' Bayliss," *Daily Telegraph* (Sydney, Australia), April 26, 2003; Simnikiwe Xabanisa, "Dynamic New Ducatis on a High for Africa's MotoGP," *Sunday Times* (London), April 20, 2003; "Rossi Takes Win in Japan Opener," *Morning Star* (London), April 7, 2003; MATP, "Bayliss Takes Aim at History," *Daily Telegraph* (Sydney, Australia), April 5, 2003; Hamish Cooper, "Ducati's Hot Challenge," *Hobart Mercury*, April 5, 2003; Alastair Himmer, "Melandri Breaks Leg in Crash," *Independent* (London), April 5, 2003; Rick Broadbent, "Bitter Biaggi Adds Fuel to Feud with Rossi," *Times* (London), April 5, 2003; Rick Broadbent, "Capirossi Eager to Prove His Point," *Times* (London), April 4, 2003; Michael Lynch, "McCoy, Bayliss Lead Local Charge for MotoGP Season," *The Age*, April 3, 2003; Peter McKay, "Pray for a Close Grand Prix but Don't Put Money on It," *Sun Herald* (Melbourne, Australia), March 23, 2003; Bob Jennings, "Confident Bayliss Ready to Rumble," *Sydney Morning Herald*, August 19, 2003; AAP, "Bayliss on Pace to Break GP Drought," *Newcastle Herald*, August 16, 2003; Gary James, "Rossi Responds to Keep Ducati Duo at Bay," *Independent* (London), July 12, 2003; Gary James, "Capirossi Dream Team Ready to Challenge the Champion," *Independent* (London), July 12, 2003; "Too Fast Fears for Valentino," *Lincolnshire Echo*, July 12, 2003; David Booth, "MotoGP Puts the 'Must See' Back in Speed TV," *National Post*

(Toronto), June 27, 2003; "Capirossi Breaks Japan's GP Hold," *Morning Star* (London), June 16, 2003; MATP, "Troy Blasts Them Away," *Daily Telegraph* (Sydney, Australia), October 18, 2003; Robert Grant, "Bayliss Raring to Go After Crash," *Courier Mail* (Brisbane), October 25, 2003.

162 **eighteen times a year:** sixteen times in 2003 and 2004, eighteen times in 2014.

162 **"Innovation drags you into the realm":** Gary Pisano, interview with author, October 31, 2014. Notice that Pisano intends the term *ambiguity* to mean "uncertainty about odds."

162 **In some scientific fields:** Amy C. Edmondson, "Strategies for Learning from Failure," *Harvard Business Review*, April 2011.

162 **new food products flop:** "How to Prevent a New Product from Becoming a Museum Piece," *New Legal Review*, June 12, 2014. Some dispute the Inez Blackburn statistics. See, for instance, John Stanton, "Market View, New Product Success Rate Higher Than Most Believe," March 27, 2014, www.foodprocessing.com/articles/2014/new-product-success-rate-higher-than-most-believe. Hat tip to John Geoghegan, "Embracing Failure," *Huffington Post*, October 2, 2013.

162 **"failures are more common":** Rita Gunther McGrath, "Failing by Design," *Harvard Business Review*, April 2011.

162 **in the S&P 500 index:** "Fail Often, Fail Well," *Economist*, April 14, 2011.

163 **"long-term health":** Tony Wagner, *Creating Innovators: The Making of Young People Who Will Change the World* (New York: Scribner, 2012).

163 **only innovators and entrepreneurs will be safe:** Thomas Friedman and Michael Mandelbaum, *That Used to Be Us: How America Fell Behind in the World It Invented and How We Can Come Back* (New York: Farrar, Straus and Giroux, 2011).

163 **the way most golfers practice:** See, for example, Bill Pennington, "At the Range, Drive Less and Practice More," *New York Times Golf Blog*, April 26, 2010.

163 **some years ago, a sports psychologist:** Bob Christina, telephone interview with author, September 20, 2012, and interview in person with author, March 4, 2013. Additional background was drawn from Debra J. Rose, ed., *A Multilevel Approach to the Study of Motor Control*

and Learning (Boston: Allyn and Bacon, 1997), 161–165; Bob Christina, Eric Alpenfels, and Nabori Santiago, "Transfer of Driving Performance as a Function of Two Practice Methods," in *Science and Golf V: Proceedings of the World Scientific Congress of Golf,* ed. Debbie Crews and Rafer Lutz (Mesa, AZ: Energy in Motion, 2008), 293–300; Robert W. Christina and Robert A. Bjork, "Optimizing Long-Term Retention and Transfer," in *In the Mind's Eye: Enhancing Human Performance,* ed. Daniel Druckman and Robert A. Bjork (Washington, DC: National Academy Press, 1991), 23–56; Robert W. Christina and Eric Alpenfels, "Why Does Traditional Training Fail to Optimize Playing Performance?" in *Science and Golf IV: Proceedings of the World Scientific Congress of Golf,* ed. Eric Thain (New York: Routledge, 2002), 231–245; Robert W. Christina and John B. Shea, "More on Assessing the Retention of Motor Learning Based on Restricted Information," *Research Quarterly for Exercise and Sport* 64, no. 2 (1993): 217–222.

164   **he called** *transfer practice:* For background on transfer learning, see Sharan B. Merriam and Brendan Leahy, "Learning Transfer: A Review of the Research in Adult Education and Training," *PAACE Journal of Lifelong Learning* 14 (2005): 1–24.

165   **Creativity expert Ken Robinson:** Ken Robinson, "Changing Paradigms: How We Implement Sustainable Change in Education," speech, RSA Edge, London, June 16, 2008.

165   **Another education-reform guru:** Sugata Mitra, "Build a School in the Cloud," speech, TED2013, Long Beach, CA, February 26, 2013.

165   **the standard form of teaching:** Craig Lambert, "Twilight of the Lecture," *Harvard Magazine,* March–April 2011.

165   **ten seconds had usually elapsed:** Young Hye Cho et al., "Analysis of Questioning Technique During Classes in Medical Education," *BMC Medical Education* 12, no. 39 (2012): 1–7; Robert J. Stahl, "Using 'Think-Time' and 'Wait-Time' Skillfully in the Classroom," ERIC Publications (Washington, DC: Office of Educational Research and Improvement, 1994); Kenneth Tobin, "The Role of Wait Time in Higher Cognitive Level Learning," *Review of Educational Research* 57, no. 1 (1987): 69–95.

166   **stunning ratio of teacher-to-student:** Donald Clark, "Don't Lecture Me," keynote speech, Association for Learning Technology Conference: "Into Something Rich and Strange: Making Sense of the Sea

Change," Nottingham, England, September 7, 2010; Guy Claxton, *What's the Point of School? Rediscovering the Heart of Education* (London: Oneworld, 2008); James T. Dillon, *The Practice of Questioning* (London: Routledge, 1990).

166 **the downside of the traditional technique:** Donald A. Bligh, *What's the Use of Lectures?* (London: University Teaching Methods Unit, 1971).

166 **since in the Middle Ages, a lecture meant:** Lambert, "Twilight of the Lecture." The lecture isn't likely to disappear so much as evolve beyond its traditional form. See Norm Friesen, "The Lecture as a Transmedial Pedagogical Form: A Historical Analysis," *Educational Researcher* 40, no. 3 (2011): 95–102.

166 **"The problem is not with the lecture":** Dominik Lukeš, "Putting Lectures in Their Place with Cautious Optimism," *Tech Czech*, January 22, 2012.

166 **Did you learn it because:** Clark, "Don't Lecture Me."

166 **Claire Cook, a cognitive scientist:** Claire Cook, interview with author, July 13, 2013. Cook now works in the private sector. For some of her work on ambiguity and learning, see Claire Cook, Noah D. Goodman, and Laura E. Schulz, "Where Science Starts: Spontaneous Experiments in Preschoolers' Exploratory Play," *Cognition* 120, no. 3 (2011): 341–349.

167 **Jim Lang of Assumption College:** James M. Lang, interview with author, February 28, 2013. I also drew on James M. Lang, "The Benefits of Making It Harder to Learn," *Chronicle of Higher Education*, June 3, 2012.

167 **Lang offered just enough guidance:** Also see Jack McShea, "The Inverted Classroom," *HG2S Training Blog*, November 14, 2009; Maureen J. Lage, Glenn J. Platt, and Michael Treglia, "Inverting the Classroom: A Gateway to Creating an Inclusive Learning Environment," *Journal of Economic Education* 31, no. 1 (2000): 30–43; Jack McShea, "At a Loss for Words: The Future of the Lecture Might Be in Less Talk," *HG2S Training Blog*, July 15, 2011; Jack McShea, "Shut Up and Teach—or— Why Science Says the Lecture Is a Bad Idea," *HG2S Training Blog*, January 25, 2012; Holly Epstein Ojalvo and Shannon Doyne, "Five Ways to Flip Your Classroom with the 'New York Times'," *New York Times*, December 8, 2011.

168 **Manu Kapur, a researcher:** Manu Kapur and Katerine Bielaczyc,

"Designing for Productive Failure," *Journal of the Learning Sciences* 21 (2012): 45–83; Manu Kapur and Nikol Rummel, "Productive Failure in Learning From Generation and Invention Activities," *Instructional Science* 40, no. 4 (2012): 645–650. Thanks go to Annie Murphy Paul, "Why Floundering Is Good," *Time*, April 25, 2012.

168 **their "quality of failure"**: Edward Burger, "Teaching to Fail," *Inside Higher Ed*, August 21, 2012; Stephen Spencer Davis, "Star Math Teacher Applies the Power of Failure, Squared," *Globe and Mail* (Toronto), August 31, 2012.

169 **move beyond standard grading**: Anne Sobel, "How Failure in the Classroom Is More Instructive Than Success," *Chronicle of Higher Education*, May 5, 2014. Sobel also points to Angela Duckworth's research on "grit," which is a similar construct to willpower. I've come to think that the emphasis on grit, like that on willpower, is misplaced. See, for instance, Alfie Kohn's criticisms in Valerie Strauss, "Ten Concerns About the 'Let's Teach Them Grit' Fad," *Washington Post*, April 8, 2014. As Kohn points out, this framing puts improper focus on teaching kids to "be able to resist temptation [and] put off doing what they enjoy in order to grind through whatever they've been told to do—and keep at it for as long as it takes." Persistence is obviously important, but I'm not convinced that persistence derives from the ability to delay pleasure. On the contrary, people who achieve great things persist because of their passion for what they do and because they admire and respect people who have achieved great things in the past. They *love* what they do. In research emphasizing willpower, this problem is usually handled by underscoring that to succeed, people also need to have a goal in addition to self control. See Pamela Druckerman, "Learning How to Exert Self-Control," *New York Times*, September 12, 2014. Again, this framing really downplays the importance of one form of pleasure (pursuing and achieving a goal) as a key reason people resist distracting temptations. Also see Carol Sansone and Dustin B. Thoman, "Interest as the Missing Motivator in Self-Regulation," *European Psychologist* 10, no. 3 (2005): 175–186.

169 **a section on embracing confusion**: Eric Mazur, letter to the author, March 25, 2013. Thanks go to Eric Mazur for his time. The quote is from Mazur's spring 2011 syllabus for his class Physics 11b. Also see Eric Mazur, "Farewell, Lecture?" *Science* 323 (2009): 50–51.

169 **"With kids, you can clearly see the tension":** Piotr Winkielman, interview with author, November 1, 2012; Marieke de Vries et al., "Happiness Cools the Warm Glow of Familiarity: Psychophysiological Evidence That Mood Modulates the Familiarity-Affect Link," *Psychological Science* 21, no. 3 (2010): 321–328.

170 **a confusing idea into an interesting one:** For more on the relationship between confusion and interest, see Paul J. Silvia, "Confusion and Interest: The Role of Knowledge Emotions in Aesthetic Experience," *Psychology of Aesthetics, Creativity, and the Arts* 4, no. 2 (2010): 75–80; Todd B. Kashdan and Paul J. Silvia, "Curiosity and Interest: The Benefits of Thriving on Novelty and Challenge," in *Oxford Handbook of Positive Psychology*, ed. Shane J. Lopez and C. R. Snyder (New York: Oxford University Press, 2011); Paul J. Silvia, *Exploring the Psychology of Interest* (New York: Oxford University Press, 2006); Paul J. Silvia, "Interest: The Curious Emotion," *Current Directions in Psychological Science* 17, no. 1 (2008): 57–60. Paul J. Silvia, interview with author, July 2, 2013, described interest and confusion as "strangely, strangely close." He later clarified the point: "I think they are close because they both get sparked by new things. When people don't feel able to 'get' the complicated or unusual thing, they feel confused. When facing really unusual things, people can shift between interest and confusion as their sense of how well they can grasp or understand the things changes—confusing things can suddenly become interesting when a spark of insight allows people to 'get it.'"

170 **"People come alive when the world breaks down":** Sidney K. D'Mello, interview with author, November 2, 2012. Also see Sidney K. D'Mello and Arthur C. Graesser, "Confusion," in *International Handbook of Emotions in Education*, ed. Reinhard Pekrun and Lisa Linnenbrink-Garcia (New York: Routledge, 2014), 289–310; Sidney K. D'Mello et al., "Confusion Can Be Beneficial for Learning," *Learning and Instruction* 29 (2014): 153–170. For drawing the work of D'Mello to my attention, I'm indebted to Annie Murphy Paul, "What Do Emotions Have to Do with Learning?" *MindShift*, July 6, 2012. For more background on learning emotions, see Paul A. Schutz and Reinhard Pekrun, "Introduction to Emotion in Education," in *Emotion in Education*, ed. Paul A. Schutz and Reinhard Pekrun (Waltham, MA: Academic Press, 2007), 3–4.

170   **series of experiments investigating:** Christopher G. Myers, Bradley R. Staats, and Francesca Gino, " 'My Bad!' How Internal Attribution and Ambiguity of Responsibility Affect Learning from Failure," Working Paper 14-104, Harvard Business School, Boston, April 18, 2014.

172   **a 40 percent chance:** Christopher Myers, email to author, September 23, 2014.

172   **performed slightly worse:** Myers, Staats, and Gino characterize the tendency to err after succeeding at another task as a "marginally significant negative effect." The study's sample size was small, and $p < .10$, but I've included their findings because they mirror what Sim Sitkin, Gino, and Pisano found in other research.

173   **"Companies often do debriefs":** Gary Pisano, interview with author, October 31, 2014.

174   **"There are very few cases where":** Christopher Myers, interview with author, September 23, 2014.

174   **the *hedonic bias*:** Lawrence A. Pervin and Oliver P. John, eds., *Handbook of Personality: Theory and Research*, 2nd ed. (New York: Guilford Press, 1999), 607.

174   **Sim Sitkin published a now-classic analysis:** Sim B. Sitkin, "Learning Through Failure: The Strategy of Small Losses," in *Organizational Learning*, ed. Michael D. Cohen and Lee S. Sproull (Thousand Oaks, CA: Sage, 1995), 549.

175   **"have a really successful first project":** *The Pixar Story*, directed by Leslie Iwerks (2007; Burbank, CA: Walt Disney Pictures, 2008), iTunes.

176   **fourteen straight number one box-office:** Scott Bowles, " 'Monsters' Outruns Zombies, Superman at the Box Office," *USA Today*, June 23, 2013.

176   **learned that employees would rather:** Ed Catmull, "How Pixar Fosters Collective Creativity," *Harvard Business Review*, September 2008; Gino and Pisano, "Why Leaders Don't Learn from Success."

176   **what he dubbed "the Hidden":** Ed Catmull, with Amy Wallace, *Creativity, Inc.: Overcoming the Unseen Forces That Stand in the Way of True Inspiration* (New York: Random House, 2014), 170–174.

176   **"Any company that had four hits":** *The Pixar Story*, directed by Leslie Iwerks.

177 **The greatest asset of the scientific tradition:** Imre Lakatos and Alan Musgrave, eds., *Criticism and the Growth of Knowledge* (London: Cambridge University Press, 1970).

177 **"is the engine of science":** Tamsin Edwards, "There Is Some Uncertainty in Climate Science—and That's a Good Thing," *Vice News*, September 24, 2014.

177 **The editors of *Nature*:** "How Not to Respond to the X-Files," *Nature* 394, no. 6696 (1998): 815.

178 **"no safeguard to rest on":** John Stuart Mill, *On Liberty*, ed. David Spitz (New York: W. W. Norton, 1975), 21–22.

CHAPTER EIGHT

179 **Before basic mobile phones took off:** I've written about these topics before. Some content here overlaps with Jamie Holmes, "Why Texting Is the Most Important Information Service in the World," *Atlantic*, August 2, 2011. Also see Jamie Zimmerman and Jamie Holmes, "The M-Banking Revolution: Why Cell Phones Will Do More for the Developing World Than Laptops Ever Could," *Foreign Policy*, August 27, 2010. The Filipino origin story is in Paul van der Boor, Pedro Oliveira, and Francisco M. Veloso, "Users as Innovators in Developing Countries: The Global Sources of Innovation and Diffusion in Mobile Banking Services," *Research Policy* 43, no. 9 (2014): 1594-1607. For more on M-PESA, see "Is It a Phone, Is It a Bank?" *Economist*, March 30, 2013.

180 **Researchers in Botswana, Ghana, and Uganda:** Simon Batchelor, "Changing the Financial Landscape of Africa: An Unusual Story of Evidence-Informed Innovation, International Policy Influence and Private Sector Engagement," *IDS Bulletin* 43, no. 5 (2012): 84–90.

180 **the ratio of M-PESA agents to banks:** Chad Bray and Reuben Kyama, "Tap to Pay (Not So Much in the U.S.)," *New York Times (Dealbook)*, April 1, 2014.

180 **As of 2013, M-PESA:** "Why Does Kenya Lead the World in Mobile Money?" *Economist*, May 27, 2013.

180 **The floodgates were open:** See, for instance, Sokari Ekine, ed., *SMS Uprising: Mobile Activism in Africa* (Cape Town: Pambazuka Press, 2010). Not all mobile money services use SMS technology.

180 **In May 2011, Coca-Cola's:** Tomi Ahonen, "What's Happenin' in

Mobile Marketing?" *Communities Dominate Brands* (blog for the book of the same name), with Alan Moore, May 6, 2011.

180 **SMS was in use by 5.78 billion:** Karl Whitfield, "17 Incredible Facts About Mobile Messaging That You Should Know," *Portio Research* (blog), August 9, 2013; Trevor Knoblich, "5 Reasons SMS Is Here to Stay," *Idea Lab* (blog), PBS, January 14, 2013.

181 **In the Philippines:** Emmanuel C. Lallana "SMS, Business, and Government in the Philippines," 2006; Tony Dwi Susanto and Robert Goodwin, "Factors Influencing Citizen Adoption of SMS-Based E-Government Services," *Electronic Journal of e-Government* 8, no. 1 (2010): 55–71. For the programs in other countries, see Tony Dwi Susanto and Robert Goodwin, "User Acceptance of SMS-Based E-Government Services: Differences Between Adopters and Non-Adopters," *Government Information Quarterly* 30 (2013): 486–497. For flood warnings, see Saysoth Keoduangsine, Robert Goodwin, and Paul Gardner-Stephen, "A Study of an SMS-Based Flood Warning System for Flood Risk Areas in Laos," *International Journal of Future Computer and Communication* 3, no. 3 (2014): 182–186. For the mobile payment vending pumps, see Ekine, *SMS Uprising*. The crop insurance program in Kenya is Kilimo Salama.

181 **Carnegie Mellon University researchers:** van der Boor, Oliveira, and Veloso, "Users as Innovators in Developing Countries."

182 **how groundbreaking inventions are usually hatched:** Anthony J. McCaffrey, Innovation Relies on the Obscure: A Key to Overcoming the Classic Problem of Functional Fixedness," *Psychological Science* 23, no. 3 (2012): 215–218. McCaffrey's work is further discussed later in this chapter.

182 **Before the telegraph took off:** Background on Bell, Gray, and the telegraph was drawn from David A. Hounshell, "Elisha Gray and the Telephone: On the Disadvantages of Being an Expert," *Technology and Culture* 16, no. 2 (1975): 133–161; W. Bernard Carlson, "Entrepreneurship in the Early Development of the Telephone: How Did William Orton and Gardiner Hubbard Conceptualize This New Technology?" *Business and Economic History* 23, no. 2 (1994): 161–192; Paul Starr, *The Creation of the Media: Political Origins of Modern Communications* (New York: Basic Books, 2004); Stephen B. Adams and Orville R. Butler,

Manufacturing the Future: A History of Western Electric (New York: Cambridge University Press, 1999); Michael E. Gorman and W. Bernard Carlson, "Interpretation Invention as a Cognitive Process: The Case of Alexander Graham Bell, Thomas Edison, and the Telephone," *Science, Technology, & Human Values* 15, no. 2 (1990): 131–164; Tom Standage, *The Victorian Internet: The Remarkable Story of the Telegraph and the Nineteenth Century's On-Line Pioneers* (New York: Bloomsbury USA, 2009); Robert V. Bruce, *Bell: Alexander Graham Bell and the Conquest of Solitude* (Ithaca, NY: Cornell University Press, 1990); Tim Wu, *The Master Switch: The Rise and Fall of Information Empires* (New York: Knopf, 2010); George B. Prescott, *History, Theory, and Practice of the Electric Telegraph* (Boston: Ticknor and Fields, 1860); Ithiel de Sola Pool, ed., *The Social Impact of the Telephone* (Cambridge, MA: MIT Press, 1977). Ithiel de Sola Pool et al., "Foresight and Hindsight: The Case of the Telephone," in *The Social Impact of the Telephone*, 146, compares Gray's mistake to another that Edison made: "Daniel Boorstin argues that Thomas Edison committed the same fallacy with the phonograph: he invented it as a repeater because he believed that few people would be able to afford their own telephone. His notion was that offices (such as telegraph offices) would use it to record spoken messages that would be transmitted by phone to a recorder at another office where the addressee could hear it. Partly as a result of this misperception, it took Edison fifteen years to realize the entertainment potential of the phonograph." The reference is Daniel Boorstin, *The Americans: The Democratic Experience* (New York: Random House, 1937), 145.

186 **In 1766, a London cartographer:** Margaret Drabble, *The Pattern in the Carpet: A Personal History with Jigsaws* (New York: Houghton Mifflin Harcourt, 2009), 111; Anne D. Williams, *The Jigsaw Puzzle: Piecing Together a History* (New York: Berkley Books, 2004), 111.

187 **Art students face a similar hurdle:** For visuals of "canonic representations of cups and saucers," see Robert L. Solso, *The Psychology of Art and the Evolution of the Conscious Brain* (Cambridge, MA: MIT Press, 2003), 241.

188 **Henri Matisse once said:** Gertrude Stein, *Picasso* (Mineola, NY: Dover, 1984), 17.

188   **Friedrich Nietzsche observed:** Friedrich Nietzsche, *Beyond Good and Evil: Prelude to a Philosophy of the Future*, trans. Walter Kaufmann (New York: Vintage Books, 2010).

188   **psychologists at the University of California:** Eleanor Rosch et al., "Basic Objects in Natural Categories," *Cognitive Psychology* 8 (1976): 382.

188   **"effectively pulling them toward the prototype":** Patricia K. Kuhl, "Human Adults and Human Infants Show a 'Perceptual Magnet Effect' for the Prototypes of Speech Categories, Monkeys Do Not," *Perception & Psychophysics* 50, no. 2 (1991): 93–107.

189   **he called *functional fixedness*:** Karl Duncker, *On Problem-Solving*, trans. Lynne S. Lees (Westport, CT: Greenwood Press, 1971), 86–88.

189   **three logic puzzles:** For these, I'm indebted to McCaffrey, "Innovation Relies on the Obscure."

191   **Starting in 2005, and building:** Background on McCaffrey and his research came from Anthony J. McCaffrey and Lee Spector, "Behind Every Innovative Solution Lies an Obscure Feature," *Knowledge Management & E-Learning: An International Journal* 4, no. 2 (2012): 146–156; Anthony J. McCaffrey and Lee Spector, "How the Obscure Features Hypothesis Leads to Innovation Assistant Software," *Proceedings of the Second International Conference on Computational Creativity* (2011): 120–122; Anthony J. McCaffrey, *The Obscure Features Hypothesis for Innovation: One Key to Improving Performance in Insight Problems* (Ann Arbor, MI: Proquest, UMI Dissertations Publishing, 2012); Oliver Burkeman, "This Column Will Change Your Life: Creative Thinking," *Guardian* (New York), January 11, 2013; McCaffrey, "Innovation Relies on the Obscure"; Anthony J. McCaffrey, "Feeling Stumped? Innovation Software Can Help," *HBR Blog Network*, March 18, 2013; Anthony J. McCaffrey, "Why We Can't See What's Right in Front of Us," *HBR Blog Network*, May 10, 2012; Amy Mayer, "Rethinking Labels Boosts Creativity," *Scientific American*, July 23, 2012, Jack Challoner, ed., *1001 Inventions That Changed the World* (Hauppauge, NY: Barron's Educational Series, 2009); Anthony J. McCaffrey, interviews with author, beginning May 28, 2013.

193   **the iceberg that sank the *Titanic*:** "Bergs of Giant Size: Hydrographic Office Says 'Titanic' May Have Struck One Rising 400 Feet and Half Mile Long," *Boston Daily Globe*, April 18, 1912; "Bodies of

Titanic Victims Are at Bottom of the Sea and Are There to Remain," *Atlantic Constitution*, April 18, 1912. No one is sure of the exact size of the iceberg, if it was indeed a single iceberg. The shape of the iceberg also has some bearing on McCaffrey's point. See, for instance, "Says Titanic Hit 'Growler': Term Applied by Mariners to Iceberg All but Submerged," *New York Tribune*, April 16, 1912.

194   **"What makes puzzles puzzling?":** Anthony J. McCaffrey, interview with author, August 28, 2013.

196   **a candle company, Pilgrim Candle:** Thanks go to Joseph Shibley, the president of Pilgrim Candle, for confirmation (Joseph Shibley, interview with author, October 10, 2014).

199   **On April 1, 1880, Alexander Bell:** Bruce, *Bell*, 333–339. The problem was that beams of light were unstable transmitters. Fiber-optic communications, which first saw global success in the 1980s, are descendants of Bell and Tainter's breakthrough. See Stewart E. Miller, "Lightwaves and Telecommunication: Pulses of Light Transmitted Through Glass Fibers Are Lowering Costs, Increasing Speed and Capacity, and Stimulating New Uses of Telecommunications Systems," *American Scientist* 72, no. 1 (1984): 66–71.

199   **As his son-in-law, David Fairchild:** Seth Shulman, *The Telephone Gambit: Chasing Alexander Graham Bell's Secret* (New York, W. W. Norton, 2008), 19.

200   **"The capacity to be puzzled":** The sentences leading up to the quote are also informative: "Children still have the capacity to be puzzled. Their whole effort is one of attempting to orient themselves in a new world, to grasp the ever-new things which they learn to experience. They are puzzled, surprised, capable of wondering, and that is what makes their reaction a creative one. But once they are through the process of education, most people lose the capacity of wondering, of being surprised. They feel they ought to know everything, and hence that it is a sign of ignorance to be surprised at or puzzled by anything. The world loses its characteristic of being full of wonder and is taken for granted. The capacity to be puzzled is indeed the premise of all creation, be it in art or in science." Erich Fromm, "The Creative Attitude," in *Creativity and Its Cultivation: Addresses Presented at the Interdisciplinary Symposia on Creativity*, ed. Harold H. Anderson (New York: Harper & Brothers, 1959), 48.

200 **In his biography of Edison, Paul Israel:** Paul Israel, *Edison: A Life of Invention* (New York: John Wily & Sons, 1998), 67.

201 **"genre crossing":** John Gardner, *The Art of Fiction: Notes on Craft for Young Writers* (New York: Vintage Books, 1991), 19. For insight into how a particular narrative structure might be exported, see the description of the format of *Blue's Clues* in Malcolm Gladwell, *The Tipping Point: How Little Things Can Make a Big Difference* (Boston: Little, Brown, 2000).

202 **In Brazil, a mechanic:** Tina Rosenberg, "Innovations in Light," *New York Times*, February 2, 2012. For Haiti, see Jamie M. Zimmerman and Kristy Bohling, *Helping Ti Manman Cheri in Haiti: Offering Mobile Money-Based Government-to-Person Payments in Haiti* (Washington, DC: Bankable Frontier Associates, CGAP and UKAID, July 2013).

203 **Concern Worldwide, an international humanitarian:** I've written about this before in my role as a policy analyst at the New America Foundation. In the Kerio Valley pilot, groups of ten beneficiaries were given both a cell phone and a solar charger. See Concern Worldwide, "Cash Transfers by Phone in Kenya: Using Mobile Phones, Concern Distributed Cash to Over 3,000 People in the Kerio Valley, Kenya," video and report, accessed March 4, 2015, www.concern.net/where-we-work/africa/kenya/cash-transfers-by-phone-in-kenya. For the Nairobi transfers, see Cathy Majtenyi, "Technology Makes Cash Transfers Safer in Kenya," *Voice of America*, October 19, 2011.

CHAPTER NINE

204 **Jerusalem is a metropolis:** The opening here is a tribute to Amos Elon, *Jerusalem: City of Mirrors* (Boston: Little, Brown, 1989), 173. Amos was a family friend. I first met him when I was eleven, and I grew up admiring him and his writing. He is missed. Danae Elon, the filmmaker profiled later in this chapter, is his daughter.

204 **Take a right off Yaakov Patt:** Some details are from my June 11, 2013, visit.

204 **high-rises seem conspicuously absent:** *High-rises* is obviously a relative term. Thanks go to Sari Kronish, Maya Frankforter, and the Bimkom organization for helping me understand building rights and land reserves in Beit Safafa and Jerusalem in general. In parts of Beit Safafa,

it is possible to build a residential structure up to six stories tall. See www.bimkom.org for details.

205 **work crews had begun constructing:** See "New Jerusalem Highway Threatens Arabs' Homes," *Al Jazeera*, March 11, 2013; Joel Greenberg, "In Jerusalem, Road Project Takes Political Turn As It Cuts Through Arab Neighborhood," *Washington Post*, April 20, 2013.

205 **the Supreme Court upheld Israel's:** Daniel K. Eisenbud, "Beit Safafa Residents Angry Over Highway Set to Divide Village," *Jerusalem Post*, January 27, 2014.

205 **Hand in Hand:** For background, I'm indebted to Debra Kamin, "In Some Israeli Schools, It's Arabic in First Period and Hebrew in Second," *Atlantic*, April 25, 2013; Kenneth Bandler, "Bilingual Education Strengthens Jewish-Arab Relations," *Jerusalem Post*, June 25, 2012; Jodi Rudoren and Isabel Kershner, "After Attacks, Israeli Schools Confront Hate," *New York Times*, August 27, 2012.

206 **Studying the effects of bilingualism:** See Anatoliy V. Kharkhurin, *Multilingualism and Creativity* (Buffalo, NY: Multilingual Matters, 2012); Mark Leikin, "The Effects of Bilingualism on Creativity: Developmental and Educational Perspectives," *International Journal of Bilingualism* 17, no. 4 (2013): 431–447; Lina Ricciardelli, "Bilingualism and Cognitive Development in Relation to Threshold Theory," *Journal of Psycholinguistic Research* 21, no. 4 (1992): 301–315.

206 **One literature review:** Lina A. Ricciardelli, "Creativity and Bilingualism," *Journal of Creative Behavior* 26, no. 4 (1992): 242–254.

206 **Dean Simonton, a psychologist at the University of California:** Some of the background on creativity and multiculturalism comes from Dean Keith Simonton, email exchange, July 9, 2013; Dean Keith Simonton, "Foreign Influence and National Achievement," *Journal of Personality and Social Psychology* 72, no. 1 (1997): 86–94; Dean Keith Simonton, *Greatness: Who Makes History and Why* (New York: Guilford Press, 1994); Dean Keith Simonton, "Sociocultural Context of Individual Creativity: A Transhistorical Time-Series Analysis," *Journal of Personality and Social Psychology* 32, no. 6 (1975): 1119–1133; William W. Maddux, Hajo Adam, and Adam Galinsky, "When in Rome . . . Learn Why the Romans Do What They Do: How Multicultural Learning Experiences Facilitate Creativity," *Personality and Social Psychology Bul-*

letin 36, no. 6 (2010): 731–741. Also see Peter Merrotsy, "Tolerance of Ambiguity: A Trait of the Creative Personality?" *Creativity Research Journal* 25, no. 2 (2013): 232–237. The Damian and Simonton quotes come from Rodica Ioana Damian and Dean Keith Simonton, "Diversifying Experiences in the Development of Genius and Their Impact on Creative Cognition," in *The Wiley Handbook of Genius*, ed. Dean Keith Simonton (Chichester, UK: John Wiley & Sons, 2014), 376; Simone M. Ritter, "Diversifying Experiences Enhance Cognitive Flexibility," *Journal of Experimental Social Psychology* 48, no. 4 (2012): 961–964.

207 **One well-known study:** Mildred George Goertzel, Victor Goertzel, and Ted George Goertzel, *300 Eminent Personalities: A Psychosocial Analysis of the Famous* (San Francisco: Jossey-Bass, 1978). Also see Victor Goertzel and Mildred G. Goertzel, *Cradles of Eminence: A Provocative Study of the Childhoods of over 400 Famous Twentieth-Century Men and Women* (Boston: Little, Brown, 1962).

207 **distinguished US mathematicians:** Damian and Simonton, "Diversifying Experiences in the Development of Genius," 380. The percentage of US patents figure also comes from this source and page.

207 **In 2009, an experiment showed that simply:** William W. Maddux and Adam D. Galinsky, "Cultural Borders and Mental Barriers: The Relationship Between Living Abroad and Creativity," *Journal of Personality and Social Psychology* 95, no. 5 (2009): 1047–1061.

208 **has emphasized throughout his entire career:** Jerome Bruner, *Acts of Meaning* (Cambridge, MA: Harvard University Press, 1990), 34; Jerome Bruner, interview with author, February 11, 2013.

208 **It can be partly defined as a set of instructions:** Fascinating work has been done on the various cultural attitudes toward ambiguity. To be sure, American culture in particular is known to prefer directness, while various other cultures tend to favor ambiguity. Yet even a preference for ambiguity, ultimately, can function as a rule that disambiguates and deselects. A preference for ambiguity may actually represent a form of closure, in the same way one might decide not to decide. See Arie W. Kruglanski, *The Psychology of Closed Mindedness* (New York: Psychology Press, 2004), 8.

208 **purely at the level of brain function:** Ellen Bialystok, interview with

author, April 13, 2012; Ellen Bialystok, *Bilingualism in Development: Language, Literacy, & Cognition* (Cambridge, UK: Cambridge University Press, 2001); Ellen Bialystok, "Reshaping the Mind: The Benefits of Bilingualism," *Canadian Journal of Experimental Psychology* 65, no. 4 (2011): 229–235; Ellen Bialystok and Xiaoji Feng, "Language Proficiency and Executive Control in Proactive Interference: Evidence from Monolingual and Bilingual Children and Adults," *Brain & Language* 109, no. 2–3 (2009): 93–100; Ellen Bialystok, "Metalinguistic Aspects of Bilingual Processing," *Annual Review of Applied Linguistics* 21 (2001): 169–182; Ellen Bialystok, "Levels of Bilingualism and Levels of Linguistic Awareness," *Developmental Psychology* 24, no. 4 (1988): 560–567; Ellen Bialystok, Fergus I. M. Craik, and Gigi Luk, "Bilingualism: Consequences for Mind and Brain," *Trends in Cognitive Science* 16, no. 4 (2012): 240–250; Ellen Bialystok and Michelle M. Martin, "Attention and Inhibition in Bilingual Children: Evidence from the Dimensional Change Card Sort Task," *Developmental Science* 7, no. 3 (2004): 325–329; Albert Costa et al., "On the Bilingual Advantage in Conflict Processing: Now You See It, Now You Don't," *Cognition* 113, no. 2 (2009): 135–149; Karen Emmorey et al., "The Source of Enhanced Cognitive Control in Bilinguals: Evidence from Bimodal Bilinguals," *Psychological Science* 19, no. 12 (2008): 1201–1206; Núria Sebastián-Gallés, "A Bilingual Advantage in Visual Language Discrimination in Infancy," *Psychological Science* 23, no. 8 (2012): 994–999; Ellen Bialystok, "Bilingualism: The Good, the Bad, and the Indifferent," *Bilingualism: Language and Cognition* 12, no. 1 (2009): 3–11; Ellen Bialystok and Mythili Viswanathan, "Components of Executive Control with Advantages for Bilingual Children in Two Cultures," *Cognition* 112, no. 3 (2009): 494–500.

209 **perform better at the Stroop test:** Ellen Bialystok, Gigi Luk, and Fergus Craik, "Cognitive Control and Lexical Access in Younger and Older Bilinguals," *Journal of Experimental Psychology: Learning, Memory, and Cognition* 34, no. 4 (2008): 859–873. Malgorzata Kossowska et al., "Individual Differences in Epistemic Motivation and Brain Conflict Monitoring Activity," found that individuals with a high need for closure performed worse on the Stroop test. For some background on the Stroop test's various uses, see Colin M. MacLeod, "Half a Century of Research on the Stroop Effect: An Integrative Review," *Psychologi-*

cal Bulletin 109, no. 2 (1991): 163–203. The original referred to here is Experiment 2 in J. Ridley Stroop, "Studies of Interference in Serial Verbal Reactions," *Journal of Experimental Psychology* 18, no. 6 (1935): 634–662.

209 **Stroop's test would look something:** This was adapted from Wayne Chase, *How Music Really Works: The Essential Handbook for Songwriters, Performers, and Music Students*, 2nd edition (Vancouver, Canada: Roedy Black Publishing, 2006).

210 **During the Cold War, the CIA:** Roy F. Baumeister and John Tierney, *Willpower: Rediscovering the Greatest Human Strength* (New York: Penguin, 2011), 29.

210 **even seven-month-old babies:** Ágnes Melinda Kovács and Jacques Mehler, "Cognitive Gains in 7-Month-Old Bilingual Infants," *Proceedings of the National Academy of Sciences* 106, no. 16 (2009): 6556–6560. I'm also indebted to Yudhijit Bhattacharjee, "Why Bilinguals Are Smarter," *New York Times*, March 17, 2012.

211 **to symptoms of Alzheimer's disease:** Tamar Gollan, "Degree of Bilingualism Predicts Age of Diagnosis of Alzheimer's Disease in Low-Education but Not in Highly Educated Hispanics," *Neuropsychologia* 49, no. 14 (2011): 3826–3830. Also see Fergus I. M. Craik, Ellen Bialystok, and Morris Freedman, "Delaying the Onset of Alzheimer Disease: Bilingualism as a Form of Cognitive Reserve," *Neurology* 75, no. 19 (2010): 1726–1729.

211 **as the European Commission reported:** Bernhard Hommel et al., "Bilingualism and Creativity: Benefits in Convergence Come with Losses in Divergent Thinking," *Frontiers in Psychology* 2, no. 273 (2011): 1–5; European Commission, *Study on the Contribution of Multilingualism to Creativity* (Brussels: Directorate General Education and Culture, July 16, 2009), annex 2, compendium part 2 (Inventory).

211 **In 2005, Bialystok and Dana Shapero:** Study 2 in Ellen Bialystok and Dana Shapero, "Ambiguous Benefits: The Effect of Bilingualism on Reversing Ambiguous Figures," *Developmental Science* 8, no. 6 (2005): 595–604.

212 **the researcher Sandra Ben-Zeev:** Sandra Ben-Zeev, "The Influence of Bilingualism on Cognitive Strategy and Cognitive Development," *Child Development* 48, no. 3 (1977): 1009–1018.

212   **Jean Piaget once devised:** Ellen Bialystok, "Metalinguistic Dimensions of Bilingual Language Proficiency," in *Language Processing in Bilingual Children*, ed. Ellen Bialystok (Cambridge, UK: Cambridge University Press, 1991), 136.

212   **a clever little exercise:** Dean Keith Simonton, "Bilingualism and Creativity," in *An Introduction to Bilingualism: Principles and Processes*, ed. Jeanette Altarriba and Roberto R. Heredia (New York: Lawrence Erlbaum, 2008).

212   **In a car, my dictionary tells me:** Faye Carney, ed., *French-English English-French Dictionary*, unabridged ed. (Paris: Larousse-Bordas, 1998).

213   **In Welsh, the word for "school":** Colin Baker, *Foundations of Bilingual Education and Bilingualism*, 5th ed. (Buffalo, NY: Multilingual Matters, 2011), 149.

213   **Yaffa Shira Grossberg, has taught for twenty-one years:** Yaffa Shira Grossberg, interview with author, June 11, 2013.

214   **Across from Jerusalem's Yad Vashem Holocaust:** Danae Elon, interview with author, Jerusalem, June 11, 2013. Additional background is from Alissa Simon, review of *Partly Private*, documentary film by Danae Elon, *Variety*, May 10, 2009; Dave Itzkoff, "Tribeca Film Festival Names Prizewinner," *New York Times*, May 1, 2009; and the following reviews of Danae Elon, *Another Road Home* (2004), documentary film: Steven Rea, "A Jew's Search for Her Former Arab Caregiver," *Philadelphia Inquirer*, June 10, 2005; Gary Arnold, "Elon's 'Road Home' a Union of Divides," *Washington Times*, May 19, 2005; Ann Hornaday, "An Israeli Woman's Search for Peace," *Washington Post*, May 13, 2005; Anemona Hartocollis, "From Jerusalem to Paterson," *New York Times*, April 24, 2005; Ronnie Scheib, "Another Road Home," *Variety*, June 7–13, 2004; Jeannette Catsoulis, "The Personal and Political Mix on a Journey to the Past," *New York Times*, April 29, 2005. Also see A. O. Scott, "A Chaotic Galaxy of Films, Unknowns and Noble Goals," *New York Times*, April 30, 2004; Michael Liss, "Danae Elon: The Heeb Interview," *Heeb Magazine*, April 29, 2009.

218   **Months before my visit:** See Hand in Hand, "Hand in Hand Students Attacked on Public Bus," *E-Newsletter*, winter 2013; Shuli Dichter, "We Are All the Other," *Jewish Week*, February 26, 2013.

219   **a price-tag crime:** Sally Abrams, "Traveling 'Hand in Hand' Toward a Better Future," *MinnPost*, February 29, 2012.

219   **Superland, a local amusement park:** See, for instance, Ilan Lior, "Separate but Equal? Superland Amusement Park to Reconsider Arab-Jewish Segregation Policy," *Haaretz*, May 30, 2013.

219   **a fire burned down part:** "Jerusalem Bilingual Hebrew-Arabic School Ablaze in Suspected Hate Crime," *Jerusalem Post*, November 29, 2014.

219   **psychologists Arne Roets and Alain Van Hiel:** Arne Roets and Alain Van Hiel, "Allport's Prejudiced Personality Today: Need for Closure as the Motivated Cognitive Basis of Prejudice," *Current Directions in Psychological Science* 20, no. 6 (2011): 349–354; Gordon W. Allport, *The Nature of Prejudice, 25th Anniversary Edition* (New York: Basic Books, 1979). Also see Michael R. Smith and Randall A. Gordon, "Personal Need for Structure and Attitudes Toward Homosexuality," *Journal of Social Psychology* 138, no. 1 (1998): 83–87; Melody Manchi Chao, Zhi-Xue Zhang, and Chi-yui Chiu, "Adherence to Perceived Norms Across Cultural Boundaries: The Role of Need for Cognitive Closure and Ingroup Identification," *Group Processes & Intergroup Relations* 13, no. 1 (2009): 69–89. The same basic idea can also be found in Mark Rubin, Stefania Paolini, and Richard J. Crisp, "A Processing Fluency Explanation of Bias Against Migrants," *Journal of Experimental Social Psychology* 46, no. 1 (2010): 21–28; Bertram Gawronski et al., "Cognitive Consistency in Prejudice-Related Belief Systems," in *Cognitive Consistency: A Fundamental Principle in Social Cognition*, ed. Bertram Gawronski and Fritz Strack (New York: Guilford Press, 2012). Of course, if we keep going back in time, such as Jack Block and Jeanne Block, "An Investigation of the Relationship Between Intolerance of Ambiguity and Ethnocentrism," *Journal of Personality* 19, no. 3 (1951): 303–311, we soon reach Frenkel-Brunswik.

220   **"is seen in its least attractive form":** Robert Buckhout, "Eyewitness Testimony," *Scientific American* 231, no. 6 (1974): 23–31.

221   **"two contradictory ideas":** The full quote apparently first appeared online in 2012 and reads as follows (www.brainbuffet.com/news/contradiction): "In art, and maybe just in general, the idea is to be able to be really comfortable with contradictory ideas. In other words, wisdom might be, seem to be, two contradictory ideas both expressed at

their highest level and just let to sit in the same cage sort of, vibrating. So, I think as a writer, I'm really never sure of what I really believe." In an email to me on July 13, 2014, George Saunders graciously confirmed that this was indeed something he recalled saying, likely in an interview.

221 **William Empson showed:** William Empson, *Seven Types of Ambiguity* (London: Chatto and Windus, 1949).

222 **"This alienation . . . is often reflected in another":** John Gardner, *On Moral Fiction* (New York: Basic Books, 1978), 180.

222 **"travel is fatal to prejudice":** Mark Twain, *The Innocents Abroad, or The New Pilgrim's Progress* (Hartford, CT: American Publishing Co., 1869), 650. Of course, travel without immersion won't do the trick. See Brent Crane, "For a More Creative Brain, Travel," *Atlantic*, March 31, 2015.

222 **And it's why reading fiction:** Maja Djikic, Keith Oatley, and Mihnea C. Moldoveanu, "Opening the Closed Mind: The Effect of Exposure to Literature on the Need for Closure," *Creativity Research Journal* 25, no. 2 (2013); Maja Djikic and Keith Oatley, "The Art in Fiction: From Indirect Communications to Changes of the Self," *Psychology of Aesthetics, Creativity, and the Arts* 8, no. 4 (2014): 498–505; Liz Bury, "Reading Literary Fiction Improves Empathy, Study Finds," *Guardian* (Manchester), October 8, 2013; Alison Floor, "Reading Fiction 'Improves Empathy,' Study Finds," *Guardian* (Manchester), September 7, 2011; Annie Murphy Paul, "Your Brain on Fiction," *New York Times*, March 17, 2012. Also relevant to the effects of fiction is the finding that the study of cases in business schools can improve students' tolerance of ambiguity: Kevin C. Banning, "The Effect of the Case Method on Tolerance for Ambiguity," *Journal of Management Education* 27, no. 5 (2003): 556–567.

223 **positive intergroup experiences:** Roets and Van Hiel, "Allport's Prejudiced Personality Today," 352; Kristof Dhont and Alain Van Hiel, "Direct Contact and Authoritarianism as Moderators Between Extended Contact and Reduced Prejudice," *Group Processes & Intergroup Relations* 14, no. 2 (2011): 224–237; Gunnar Lemmer and Ulrich Wagner, "Can We Really Reduce Ethnic Prejudice Outside the Lab? A Meta-Analysis of Direct and Indirect Contact Interventions," *Euro-*

pean Journal of Social Psychology, in press. Also see Carmit T. Tadmore et al., "Multicultural Experiences Reduce Intergroup Bias Through Epistemic Unfreezing," *Journal of Personality and Social Psychology* 103, no. 5 (2012): 750–772; Arnd Florack et al. "How Initial Cross-Group Friendships Prepare for Intercultural Communication: The Importance of Anxiety Reduction and Self-Confidence in Communication," *International Journal of Intercultural Relations* 43 (2014): 278–288. Martine Powers, "Does Riding the Commuter Rail Change Attitudes on Immigration?" *Boston Globe,* February 25, 2014, which addresses a study reported in Ryan D. Enos, "Causal Effect of Intergroup Contact on Exclusion Attitudes," *Proceedings of the National Academy of Sciences* 111, no. 10 (2014): 3699–3704. Gordon Hodson, "Do Ideologically Intolerant People Benefit from Intergroup Contact?" *Current Directions in Psychological Science* 20, no. 3 (2011): 154–159; Zvi Bekerman, Ayala Habib, and Nader Shhadi, "Jewish-Palestinian Integrated Education in Israel and Its Potential Influence on National and/or Ethnic Identities and Intergroup Relations," *Journal of Ethnic and Migration Studies* 37, no. 3 (2011): 389–405.

223   **he calls the fifth reaction to anomalies** *assembly*: Travis Proulx and Michael Inzlicht, "The Five 'A's of Meaning Maintenance: Finding Meaning in the Theories of Sense-Making," *Psychological Inquiry* 23, no. 4 (2012): 317–335.

223   **took parents of another bilingual program to court:** "Taking to Court Jewish and Arab Parents Who Just Want Their Kids Educated Together," editorial, *Haaretz,* March 10, 2013; or Kashti, "Co-Existence or a Crime? Jewish-Arab Education Earns Parents a Court Date," *Haaretz,* March 12, 2013.

223   **There is no civil marriage:** Ariel David, "Who Would You Be Allowed to Marry in Israel Today?" *Haaretz,* June 3, 2014.

EPILOGUE

224   **A team of psychologists:** Jordi Quoidbach, Daniel T. Gilbert, and Timothy D. Wilson, "The End of History Illusion," *Science* 339 (2013): 96–98. This study first came to my attention thanks to John Tierney, "Why You Won't Be the Person You Expect to Be," *New York Times,* January 3, 2013.

225 **"The most interesting finding":** Jordi Quoidbach, interview with author, July 11, 2013.

225 **Quoidbach's heading was a nod to Francis:** Francis Fukuyama, "The End of History?" *National Interest* 16 (summer 1989): 3–18; Francis Fukuyama, *The End of History and the Last Man* (New York: Free Press, 1992). With bias, I'd recommend a review of Fukuyama's book that I recalled and reread: Stephen Holmes, "The Scowl of Minerva," review of *The End of History and the Last Man*, by Francis Fukuyama, *New Republic*, March 12, 1992.

225 **even the author moved on:** Steve Kettmann, "Fukuyama Rethinks End of History," *Wired*, April 15, 2002.

228 **Four thousand people began to walk:** The background on Chekhov's death comes from Donald Rayfield, *Chekhov: A Life* (New York: Harper Collins, 1997), 595–599; Earnest J. Simmons, *Chekhov: A Biography* (Chicago: University of Chicago Press, 1962). I've also drawn from Maxim Gorky, Alexander Kuprin, and I. A. Bunin, *Reminiscences of Anton Chekhov*, trans. S. S. Koteliansky and Leonard Woolf (New York: B.W. Huebsch, 1921). Some of the material here overlaps with sections of a previous column I wrote; see Jamie Holmes, "President Obama and Remembering Chekhov," *Huffington Post*, January 28, 2010. Also, Rayfield writes that Chekhov awoke at 2 a.m.; Simmons that he awoke at 12:30 a.m.

229 **"peasant blood flowing in [his] veins":** See Richard Pevear, introduction to *The Complete Short Novels*, by Anton Chekhov, trans. Richard Pevear and Larissa Volokhonsky (New York: Vintage Classics, 2004).

229 **"The people I am afraid of are the ones who":** Anton Chekhov, *Letters of Anton Chekhov*, trans. Michael Henry Heim in collaboration with Simon Karlinsky (London: Bodley Head: 1973), 109, cited in Richard Pevear, introduction to *Stories by Anton Chekhov*, by Anton Chekhov, trans. Richard Pevear and Larissa Volokhonsky (New York: Random House, 2009).

230 **"It is time for writers to admit":** Francine Prose, *Reading Like a Writer: A Guide for People Who Love Books and for Those Who Want to Write Them* (New York: Harper Collins, 2006). A slightly different translation appears in Anton Chekhov, *Letters of Anton Chekhov to His*

Family and Friends, trans. Constance Garnett (New York: Macmillan, 1920), 89. Another is in Chekhov, *Letters of Anton Chekhov*, 104.

230   **"he is very gifted":** Cited in Pevear, introduction to *Stories by Anton Chekhov*.

231   **"The Betrothed":** Anton Chekhov, *The Schoolmaster and Other Stories*, trans. Constance Garnett (New York: J. J. Little & Ives, 1921), 47–75.

232   **"solve such problems as God":** Anton Chekhov, *Selected Stories*, trans. Ann Dunnigan (New York: Signet Classic, 2003).

232   **Virginia Woolf noted how:** Virginia Woolf, *The Essays of Virginia Woolf, vol. 2, 1912–1918*, ed. Andrew McNeillie (New York: Harcourt Brace Jovanovich, 1986), 245.

232   **"we authors do most of our lying":** Paul Engle, "Salt Crystals, Spider Webs, and Words," *Saturday Review*, March 16, 1964.

232   **Days before beginning it, Chekhov wrote:** Simmons, *Chekhov: A Biography*, 140–141.

233   **A young boy of nine, Egor:** One of the men is Egor's uncle. Chekhov, *The Complete Short Novels*.

INDEX

About the Author

JAMIE HOLMES IS a Future Tense Fellow at New America and a former research coordinator at Harvard University in the Department of Economics. He holds an MIA from Columbia's School of International and Public Affairs, and his writing has appeared in *The New Yorker*, the *New York Times*, *Slate*, *Politico*, the *Christian Science Monitor*, the *New Republic*, the *Atlantic*, *Foreign Policy*, and the *Daily Beast*.